200

P9-DBY-082

Land
of Plenty

Land
of Plenty

Oklahomans in the Cotton Fields of Arizona,
1933–1942

Marsha L. Weisiger

University of
Oklahoma Press
Norman and London

This book is published with the generous assistance of The McCasland Foundation, Duncan, Oklahoma.

Library of Congress Cataloging-in-Publication Data

Weisiger, M. L. (Marsha L.)
    Land of plenty : Oklahomans in the cotton fields of Arizona, 1933–1942 / Marsha L. Weisiger.
      p.   cm.
    Includes bibliographical references and index.
    ISBN 0–8061–2696–5
    1. Migrant agricultural laborers—Arizona—History—20th century.
2. Migrant agricultural laborers—Oklahoma—History—20th century.
3. Cotton picking—Arizona—History—20th century.   4. Migration, Internal—United States—History—20th century—Case studies.
I. Title.
HD1527.A6W45   1995   94–36880
331.5′44′09791—dc20   CIP

Text design is by Cathy Carney Imboden. The typeface is Berkeley Old′ Style Medium.

1 2 3 4 5 6 7 8 9 10

In memory of
my mother and father,
Rose Marie Weisiger and
John Marshall Weisiger,
and my friend
Betti Arnold Albrecht

Contents

Illustrations

Photographs

Preface

Writing this book involved a somewhat personal odyssey. In the fall of 1973 my husband and I moved from Oklahoma to Arizona, journeying westward along Interstate 40 with all our belongings crammed into a small U-Haul trailer. Without knowing it, we followed a historic trail blazed by fellow Oklahomans, if not by our families, who had stayed firmly rooted during the Great Depression. During my early years in Arizona when my twang was more pronounced, small incidents signaled that Oklahomans had once been a disparaged people in my adopted state. But like many from Oklahoma, I imputed those uncomfortable moments to some lingering influence of John Steinbeck's *The Grapes of Wrath,* never realizing the factual basis of his book. Not until I undertook this research did the real meaning of those incidents become clear.

Other experiences in Arizona began to crystalize. Living near the barrio of Guadalupe, a Hispanic and Yaqui community, I sometimes saw along the irrigation canals the shacks of agricultural workers from Mexico or glimpsed the Immigration Service vans filled with deportees. I did not know then the historical connection between those workers and the migrants from my native state. In joining those two fragments of history, I hope not only to provide coherence to the story of the Oklahoma migrants in Arizona but also to bring my experiences full circle.

This interpretation of the history of the rural Oklahomans who migrated westward during the Great Depression focuses on those who found their way to the cotton fields of central Arizona. The Oklahoma migrants were not unique in their poverty during the Depression, nor were they the only agricultural workers exploited. They were, however, among the most visible during the period and came to signify the plight of the poor, the dispossessed, the homeless. Before Edward R. Murrow coined the phrase "Harvest of Shame," the migrant workers from Oklahoma came to represent the wretched lives of agricultural laborers everywhere.

My reasons for writing about the Oklahoma migrants in Arizona are many. By placing their story within the larger context of the history of agricultural labor in Arizona, I show that socioeconomic class rather than race lay at the root of the exploitation of agricultural workers. Rarely are we presented with such an opportunity to untwine the tendrils of class and race to understand better the dynamics of these two social divisions. Furthermore, I explain the geographical origins of the Oklahoma migrants, joining the chorus begun by Carey McWilliams, Donald Worster, Douglas Hurt, Sheila Manes, James Gregory, and others in an effort to debunk once and for all the myth that the migrants fled the Dust Bowl. Most important, I explore more fully the environmental, economic, social, and political milieu that gave rise to the rural migration from Oklahoma and the role played by the Arizona cotton industry in attracting Oklahomans westward.

Finally, I offer a case study that permits comparison with the migrants' experience in California. In some ways my story reinforces the conclusions of those historians who have examined the migration to California, and in other ways it points to the multiplicity of the migration experience. Walter Stein, in his fine study *California and the Dust Bowl Migration,* explored the underlying causes of the anti-"Okie" hysteria in the Golden State. The absence of a similar hysteria in Arizona, where migrants stayed in fewer numbers and wielded little perceived political power, supports his analysis of the political dynamics of that powerful outburst of prejudice. My study also shows that the cultural similarities of the migrants and their employers in Arizona helped them find acceptance in the larger community. Those similarities diluted the development of the distinctive Okie subculture found by James Gregory in *American Exodus: The Dust Bowl Migration and Okie Culture in California.* Indeed, the Oklahomans who made their home in Arizona found a community whose social and religious values mirrored their own.

I am indebted to many people for their assistance and encouragement in the creation of this book. My deepest gratitude goes to my mentor, Paul W. Glad, who guided me throughout my research and believed the work important. His help in honing my writing gave my words a more acute edge than they would otherwise have had. I also thank him for his patience, for allowing me to take the time to create the study that I envisioned, and for his encouragement to publish it. He had far more faith in me than I had in myself. William W. Savage, Jr., freely shared his insights and provided needed criticism, guidance, and encouragement. He gave crucial direction to my research at an early stage. His wise counsel and friendship will long be remembered. Richard Lowitt gave me a broader perspective of the West in the New Deal era. He also provided me the invaluable opportunity to audition my interpretation of events before the annual meeting of the Western History Association. David W. Levy, William T. Hagan, and Paul A. Gilje made important contributions to my understanding of history and critical thinking. Special thanks goes to Norman Crockett, who inspired me to study history in the first place.

Particular appreciation is due several institutions and the people who staff them. The National Archives; the Library of Congress; the Arizona State Department of Library, Archives, and Public Records; the Casa Grande Valley Historical Society; Interlibrary Loan Services and Government Documents at the Bizzell Library, University of Oklahoma; the Bancroft Library and the Government Documents Division of the general library at the University of California, Berkeley; the California Odyssey Project Collection at California State University, Bakersfield; and the Arizona Collection and the Arizona Historical Foundation at the Hayden Library, Arizona State University, all provided materials and assistance indispensable to my research. I am especially indebted to Carolyn Mahin, Cindi Wolff, Maria Hernandez, Cindy Myers, Laura Stone, Barbara Mitchell, and Andrea Sevetson, who all provided invaluable assistance. I also thank the Maricopa County Farm Bureau and the Arizona Cotton Growers' Association for providing access to their records.

This book could not have been written without the financial support of a number of organizations. Research grants from the University of Oklahoma Graduate College and Graduate Student Senate made possible my visit to the National Archives and the Library of Congress. The Oklahoma Foundation for the Humanities, the Arizona Humanities Council, and the National Endowment for the Humanities provided financial support to examine manuscript collections in Bakersfield and Berkeley and to conduct interviews in Arizona. The Oklahoma Historical Society made it possible to present a portion of my research to the Western History Association and to conduct research in Arizona.

I want to thank the people from the cotton towns of central Arizona who enriched my understanding of the Oklahoma migrant experience. Ewell Bennett, Jarrell Bowlan, Sam Cambron, T. L. Cambron, Flora Davis, W. D. Durant, Naomi Durant, Vivian Estes, J. D. Estes, Lee Faver, Ned Gladden, Mo Harris, K. K. Henness, Lucille Henry, Edward Hooper, Dennis Kirkland, Donel Leatherbury, Betty McGrath, A. L. Mercer, Dewey Phares, Ann Stephens, and Kenneth Taber opened the doors of their homes and allowed me to pry into their past. Each provided insight and helped to shape my perspective.

A number of colleagues deserve credit for important assistance at various stages of my work. Jack Wardlow, Suzanne Schrems, Nigel Sellars, Melvena Heisch, Susan Allen, Katja May, and Frank Parman provided seeds of information that proved fruitful and prevented embarrassing errors. Michael Duchemin of the Arizona Historical Society critiqued one chapter and generously shared his research into the early agricultural history of the Salt River Valley. Bruce J. Dinges and Nancy Bell Rollings, with the *Journal of Arizona History,* suggested a number of revisions that improved the manuscript considerably. Portions of Chapters 4 and 5 appeared in a somewhat revised form in that journal, which has kindly granted permission to reprint those words. Vicki Gardner and Barbara Million transcribed oral history tapes, and Barbara graciously stayed up late to help me with the clerical chores.

Friends helped me in many ways. My research would have been more difficult financially and a lot less enjoyable had it not been for my family of friends in Arizona. In particular, John and Peggy Dole, John and Jan Hays, Dennis and Kelly Dean Price, Frances Lechner, and Regina Morgan shared their homes, allowed me to intrude in their lives, and listened as I talked endlessly about my work. They gave me more than I can ever repay. The generous hospitality of Katja May and Qingmin Hu in Berkeley will always be remembered. Sarah Weisiger-Mulhollan and Kelly Mulhollan provided more insight and inspiration than they know.

Finally, I thank Timothy Cockrum, who encouraged me every step of the way.

MARSHA L. WEISIGER

Madison, Wisconsin

Land
of Plenty

Chapter One

Prologue

Five thousand transient families, lured to Arizona by advertisements for cotton pickers, are facing starvation and 'living like hogs.'"[1] A delegation of cotton pickers assembled in the office of Arizona governor Rawghlie C. Stanford in mid-March 1938 leveled this charge. Outside, at least one hundred migrant farm workers gathered on the statehouse lawn to publicize their plight. The governor listened sympathetically as the men described the destitution of families hailing from Oklahoma, Texas, Arkansas, and Missouri. They had been drawn to the cotton fields ringing Phoenix by newspaper advertisements and handbills distributed ostensibly by agencies associated with the U. S. Employment Service. With the cotton harvest over, the migrant families found themselves stranded without food or money, most of them living in tents, dirt-floor shacks, or hovels made of cardboard or cast-off bits of tin.

These migrant farm workers, who moved westward by the thousands during the latter half of the Great Depression, came to personify that era. Through the medium of photography, particularly the work of Dorothea Lange, America knew their faces. The careworn countenance and haunting eyes of a migrant mother, her children clinging to her, became the icon of the poor and outcast.[2] But the most influential images came from the typewriter of an emerging novelist, John Steinbeck. With *The Grapes of Wrath,* Steinbeck focused the eyes of the nation on the exodus from America's heartland. As with photographs, Steinbeck's words exposed essential truths, but his lens also distorted. Like most of his contemporaries, he assumed that the flow of migrants was destined for California, since the course of events ultimately deposited them there. Moreover, he accused the Associated Farmers of California of enticing uprooted farmers westward with an inflated demand for agricultural labor.[3]

Steinbeck helped stimulate two congressional investigations—one exploring the causes of the migration, the other exposing the exploitation of agricultural workers.[4] But little evidence surfaced to prove his charge that California's agribusinessmen had conspired to lure migrant workers from the depressed "drought states." Certainly Californians welcomed and exploited the surplus labor force that streamed into their fertile valleys. And in isolated incidents labor contractors and individual growers distributed circulars and placed newspaper advertisements in the western cotton belt. But the La Follette Civil Liberties Committee, which subpoenaed the files of the Associated Farmers in its Senate investigation of unfair labor practices, found no evidence of collusion in California. Drawing cheap agricultural labor westward, the committee found, was the province of Arizona's cotton industry.

The 1937–38 harvest stands out in the history of the cotton industry in Arizona. Since 1933, the Farm Labor Service, an agency funded by the ginners and growers of the Salt River and Casa Grande valleys of central Arizona, had recruited cotton pickers from Oklahoma, Texas, Arkansas, and Missouri. Each year, as the cotton harvest ended, growers prodded the migrants across the border into California to follow the ripening crops. But 1938 was different. Floods in California's Central Valley prevented migrants from moving out of Arizona at the end of the harvest and revealed the poverty intrinsic to labor surpluses, low wages, and substandard housing.

The story of the migrant cotton pickers from the south-central states represents a dark chapter in the saga of agricultural labor in Arizona. But it is not unique. What distinguishes this episode is ethnicity. Traditionally, Arizona's cotton growers had relied on workers from Mexico, who came and went with the seasons. The Depression changed all that. Immigration laws restricting the use of imported labor forced the cotton industry to depend on recruits from the western cotton belt. Happily for Arizona's growers, this turn of events coincided with a massive expulsion of tenant farmers and sharecroppers, largely white native-born families, from Oklahoma and surrounding states. Thousands responded to the cotton industry's extensive efforts to attract a sizable labor force, a campaign mounted with federal and state support, in an effort to keep wages low and discourage unionization.

A related distinction of this episode was the federal government's efforts to ameliorate labor conditions during the Depression era. The obvious poverty of many migrants and their origins in the agricultural heartland seemed to some contemporary observers, including administrators in the Farm Security Administration, to signal the end of the American agrarian ideal. Industrial agriculture would be the wave of the future. To address the social problems attendant to this transformation of the agricultural order and render it more humane, the New Deal erected an economic infrastructure of housing and financial support in California, Arizona, and other western states. Administrators intended the program to be a model to be emulated by the industry it served. In Arizona, it became a subsidy to the cotton growers, relieving many of the responsibility to provide for the welfare of their workers. Labor practices remained virtually unchanged.

This study focuses on the migration of rural Oklahomans to Arizona in the years between the Agricultural Adjustment Act of 1933 and America's entry into World War II and on their experiences as Arizona's new agricultural underclass. Oklahomans constituted only a portion of the migrants who streamed into the cotton fields of central Arizona during this period, but they formed a majority. During the 1937–38 harvest, for example, more than one-half of the cotton pickers came from Oklahoma. Oklahomans made up the largest segment of the agricultural migrants in California as well. The concentration on this part of the migrant population, therefore, seems appropriate. As for the focus on Arizona, numerous historians have trained their lenses on the epic migration from the south-central region to California where most westward migrants ultimately settled. But few have recognized the important role played in that drama by the Arizona cotton industry, thereby distorting our understanding of the scene.[5] I hope to correct that myopia.

Chapter Two

Exodus

The Depression decade witnessed the migration of thousands of impoverished families from Oklahoma to California and Arizona. Pushed off the land by a combination of environmental forces and changes in the agricultural economy and drawn by mythic fields of plenty, tenant farmers and their weary families pulled up stakes and left Oklahoma's cotton belt. Forming a fragmentary procession of jalopies, they trekked along U.S. Highway 66 and Highway 70 across half a continent, their rattletraps laden with boxes of clothing and dishes, jars of home-canned food, quilts, featherbeds, mattresses, tarpaulins, wash tubs, kerosene stoves, the Singer sewing machine, a favorite rocking chair—all their worldly possessions.[1] It was an epic migration comparable to those that had peopled the West in population waves since the 1840s. Oklahomans abandoned

America's last farming frontier, a frontier that had failed them, and made their way across the desert to a land with promise.[2]

These migrants have come to symbolize Depression-era Oklahoma in the national imagination. John Steinbeck called them the Joads. The national press depicted them as victims, "drought refugees." Californians and Arizonans commonly referred to them as Okies, although many Arizonans knew them simply as migrant cotton pickers. None of these portrayals, however, captured the complexities of each family's decision to move west, a decision grounded less in despair than hope.

"Over the Concrete Ribbons of Highway Come the Refugees"

The Oklahomans who streamed to the agricultural valleys of Arizona and California participated in a mass exodus. During the second half of the Depression decade alone, nearly 309,000 Oklahomans moved out of the state in search of new opportunities. Most of those migrants went to states contiguous to Oklahoma. For many, the move was essentially a return home to family. One of every two people living in Oklahoma in 1930 had been born elsewhere, principally in Arkansas, Missouri, Texas, and Kansas. For others, the states nearby offered a familiar landscape and economies to which they were accustomed; political boundaries proved mere artificial constructs. Nearly 69,000 Oklahomans moved to Texas between 1935 and 1940, and more than 52,000 went to Kansas, Arkansas, or Missouri (see Table 1). The oil fields, mining districts, and agricultural lands of eastern Illinois also attracted large numbers of Oklahomans, nearly 14,000 in all.[3]

Others headed west. California and Arizona drew more than one-third of the migrants, a disproportionate share,

Table 1. Outmigration of Oklahomans, 1935–1940

Region of Residence in 1940	Number of Migrants
New England	432
Middle Atlantic	2,602
East North Central	20,039
West North Central	38,994
South Atlantic	4,939
East South Central	4,319
West South Central	89,334
Mountain	43,610
Pacific	104,569
Total Outmigration	308,838

Major Recipient States	Number of Migrants
California	94,659
Texas	68,794
Kansas	22,147
Arizona	17,371
Arkansas	16,877
Illinois	13,721
Missouri	13,055
New Mexico	11,436
Colorado	9,198
Oregon	5,369

Source: Donald J. Bogue, Henry S. Shryock, Jr., and Siegfried A. Hoermann, Subregional Migration, table 1.

considering the distance of those states from Oklahoma. It required relatively little determination to move across the border to Texas. On the other hand, the decision to journey more than one thousand miles to Arizona or almost fourteen hundred miles to California took pluck. Nevertheless, in the

latter years of the thirties nearly 95,000 Oklahomans moved
to California, making it the most popular terminus. Another
17,000 settled in Arizona.[4]

This westward migratory stream followed two major
courses. One flowed from Tulsa, Muskogee, Oklahoma City,
and other Oklahoma towns to the metropolitan centers of Arizona and California, principally Los Angeles, the San Francisco Bay area, San Diego, and Phoenix.[5] Classified advertisements in Oklahoma City newspapers attested to this current:
"Married man, family of 4, will drive car to Calif. for transportation or share expenses." "Nearly new Ford leaving for
Phoenix Thursday. Take 3, share exp."[6] The second stream,
more significant socially and politically, surged from Oklahoma's distressed rural areas, across Texas and New Mexico,
into the rich alluvial valleys of the Salt, Gila, San Joaquin, and
Sacramento rivers. A smaller tributary meandered across
Texas, New Mexico, Arizona, California, and back again.

Contrary to popular notion, the rural migrants were not fleeing the Dust Bowl region. The black blizzards of dust that peri-
odically rolled across the Oklahoma panhandle between 1935
and 1938 coincided with the period of massive migration from
the state, so journalists linked the two phenomena as cause
and effect. "After the drifting dust clouds drift the people,"
wrote economist Paul Taylor in *Survey Graphic*. "Over the
concrete ribbons of highway . . . come the refugees." Taylor
went on to explain the complex origins of the migration, but
other writers simply borrowed his imagery and persisted in
referring to the migrants as Dust Bowl refugees.[7] Oklahoma
folksinger Woody Guthrie also mistakenly helped perpetu-
ate the myth with such songs as "Dust Bowl Refugee" and
"Talkin' Dust Bowl Blues." Yet less than 5 percent of those
who left for Arizona and California (including those from
urban areas) began their journey in the westernmost part of
Oklahoma known as the Dust Bowl (see Map 1).[8]

Map 1. Oklahoma Cotton Belt and Dust Bowl. (Drawn by Bill Nelson.)

While not a center of westward outmigration, the Oklahoma Dust Bowl did experience a significant loss of population. A region that had been bonanza wheat country in the late 1920s lay desolate, victim of drought and plow. Many farm families packed up and left. By the end of the "dirty thirties," the population of the state's five Dust Bowl counties had dropped by 25 percent as more than 12,000 residents left to find their fortunes elsewhere. Hardest hit were Cimarron and Texas counties, where nearly a third of the people quit the land. Many of those who moved from the region left the state. Nearly 5,500 people (about one in six) living in the panhandle in 1935, the year the dusters became an almost daily occurrence, no longer lived in Oklahoma five years later. Most landed in Texas or California, where about 1,000 Dust Bowl migrants settled, primarily in the Los Angeles area and to a far lesser extent, the San Joaquin and Imperial valleys. But the vast majority of the residents of the windblown region held on tenaciously to the land.[9]

Land-tenure patterns, federal aid, and plain stubbornness tied people to the wind-eroded soil. Dust Bowl farmers generally owned their land, making it difficult just to walk away. About 65 percent held title to their farms, and many of those enumerated as tenants were simply renting land from their parents until they could purchase farms of their own. Federal programs helped to tide those farmers over until the prayed-for rains began to fall in 1938. With jobs, loans, and cash payments for reducing crops and conserving soil, agencies like the Works Progress Administration, the Federal Emergency Relief Administration, the Agricultural Adjustment Administration, the Farm Credit Administration, the Resettlement Administration, and later the Farm Security Administration made survival in the Dust Bowl possible. Other programs, such as the Civilian Conservation Corps, the Soil Conservation Service, and the Shelterbelt Project, brought erosion control and with it hope.[10]

But perhaps as much as anything, old-fashioned determination kept people from leaving the Dust Bowl. Darrel Coble, who as a small boy appeared with his father and brother in Arthur Rothstein's memorable photograph *Fleeing a Dust Storm,* recalled that his family stayed "just 'cause this country's home." Although the Cobles had relatives in California who offered to pay the family's way west, the elder Coble refused to leave his farm. Like Coble, most Dust Bowl farmers would not surrender. Relatively few westward migrants were dusted out of that region.[11]

Most Oklahomans who migrated to the agricultural valleys of the West had made their homes in the cotton belt, an area roughly encompassing the southern and eastern two-thirds of the state (see Map 1). In particular, they migrated from that part of the cotton belt known as the Central Cross Timbers, an area of rolling hills formerly wooded with thick stands of post oak and blackjack oak, and from the prairies and sandstone hills of eastern Oklahoma, also wooded with oak. More than 26 percent of the migrants left the central part of the cotton belt, and another 20 percent quit the eastern cotton region. Many families moved from the extensive cotton farms that spread across the subhumid plain of the southwestern part of the state, roughly west of the ninety-eighth meridian. About 19 percent of the migrants hailed from that region, especially Beckham, Caddo, and Grady counties.[12]

The exodus did not begin in earnest until the middle of the Depression. In fact, in the early thirties, the farm population swelled in the cotton counties east of the ninety-seventh meridian as farmers sought refuge from the Dust Bowl and the drought-stricken western tier and impoverished towns-people moved back to the land with hopes of self-sufficiency. After 1935, however, the cotton belt experienced dramatic losses of farm population, particularly along a broad swath extending diagonally from the northeast to the southwest, paralleling U.S. Highway 66. People in areas like LeFlore County, which had grown by nearly 10 percent in the early thirties, watched almost a third of their neighbors leave their farms by the end of the decade. The exodus accelerated after 1935 in the central and southwestern sections as well. McClain County lost only about 5 percent of its farm population in the early years of the Depression, but by 1940 more than one in three had moved off their farms. In Kiowa County, 18 percent fewer people worked the red soil at middecade; five years later, 44 percent had gone. Of thirty-eight counties in that diagonal swath through the cotton belt, twenty-one experienced an estimated net loss of 30 percent or more of the farm population, and the figure rose to more than 40 percent along the western tier. Another twelve counties lost at least a fifth of their farmers seeking survival and opportunity.[13]

"Move or Starve"

"Move or starve" were the words Thomas L. Derryberry of Pittsburg County chose to describe his options in eastern Oklahoma.[14] Like Derryberry, the rural Oklahomans who joined the migratory stream were mostly tenant farmers, farm laborers, and sharecroppers, who faced destitution if they stayed and perceived a chance to make a new start if they left. Often portrayed as perpetual losers, the migrants possessed an indomitable instinct to survive and a willingness to pursue opportunity elsewhere. Thomas Higgenbottom watched his chickens, mule, and cow die of starvation before he decided to pack up and head west, resolving, "I will never see anything else that I have got starve to death."[15] Marvin Montgomery, living on a farm near Stigler, admitted, "I might have drug by like some of the rest of them, and sort of lived." Instead he decided to move to California, where he had a son

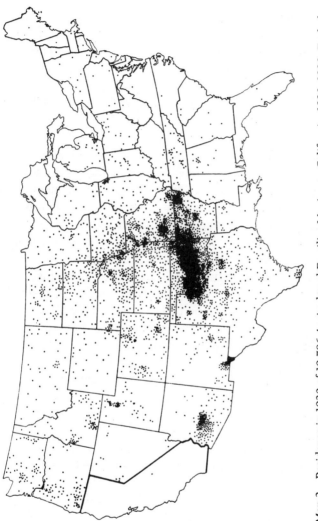

Map 2. Residence in 1930 of 19,786 Agricultural Families Moving to California, 1930–1939. Each dot represents five families. (From Tolan Committee, *Interstate Migration*, Pt. 6, *San Francisco Hearings*, 2282.)

and a married daughter. "I wanted to change countries to see if I couldn't find something better."[16] Similarly, Ruth Criswell and her husband left their farm in the southwestern part of the state because "there was nothing to look forward to in Oklahoma. There was nothing to work towards." Tired of merely existing from day to day, her husband "wanted to see if he could find a place where there was a better chance for his children."[17]

Until relatively recently, however, the root causes of the exodus have been widely misinterpreted, largely because the migrants felt reluctant to admit failure as farmers or to criticize federal programs while dependent on government largess. When WPA researchers and congressional investigators asked migrants why they left Oklahoma, many simply replied, "Drought." This response fit neatly with the preconception that the migrants were refugees from the Dust Bowl, but it told only part of the story. Drought, mechanized farming, and erosion all helped to push people off the land, yet they were not the principal catalysts. "Lack of work," another recurring explanation provided by the migrants, came closer to the truth. Tenant farmers and sharecroppers had been sacrificed in an effort to eliminate the system of farm tenancy from cotton agriculture and modernize the agricultural economy, an effort the New Deal's farm policies helped accomplish.[18]

Tenant farming, lineal descendant of the plantation system, had persisted as the bedrock of Oklahoma's cotton culture since the 1870s when landless cotton farmers from the Reconstruction South migrated into Indian Territory to work leased Indian land. Even after the federal government lifted restrictions against the sale of Indian lands, tenant farming prevailed. The ranks of the tenantry swelled as Indians and freedmen sold their allotments or lost them to swindlers and as poor whites who had bought land relinquished their farms to creditors. Many lost their farms and equipment to foreclosure after a precipitous drop in cotton prices at the end of World War I brought on an agricultural depression that continued through the 1930s. By 1935, Oklahoma had the highest rate of tenancy in the nation—among white farmers, that is. More than 60 percent of the state's white farmers rented their land as tenants, and the percentage was even higher in the cotton belt. In 1930, about 75 percent of Oklahoma's cotton farmers were tenants, compared with a rate of just over 50 percent on other types of farms. And on the poorer cotton soils of eastern Oklahoma, more than 80 percent of farmers rented on shares.[19]

The farm-leasing system entwined the fortunes of the landlord with his tenant. Most of the state's tenants rented on shares, paying the landlord one-fourth of the cotton crop and one-third of any other crops. Under this system the owner furnished the land and the buildings, and the renter provided his own equipment, workstock, seed, and so forth. A relatively small percentage of tenants paid rent solely in cash, and an even smaller portion were sharecroppers, working as employees to earn half of the crop. The customary practice of tying the value of the rent to crop yields rendered tenants ever more vulnerable as the decade wore on and landlords began to disentangle themselves from an increasingly unprofitable labor system.[20]

Most tenant families led meager lives, largely circumscribed by their landlords. "When it rains they go out of doors to keep dry," a rural activist quipped in 1937.[21] A typical tenant farmstead consisted of a small unpainted wooden house, a well, an outhouse, and a few outbuildings for equipment and animals. Not all families lived in mean circumstances. In southwestern Oklahoma, many tenants lived in sound clapboard houses, much like those of their neighbors who owned their farms. But in the southeastern

A typical tenant farmstead consisted of a small, unpainted wooden house, a well, an outhouse, and a few outbuildings for equipment and animals. (Photograph by Russell Lee, June 1939, courtesy of the Library of Congress.)

part of the state, landlords provided their tenants with
wretched quarters. Many tenant families lived in board-and-
batten houses without interior walls, and their roofs often
leaked.[22]

Dennis Kirkland's home in southern Choctaw County
typified these dwellings. He, his parents, six brothers and
sisters, and an uncle lived in a two-bedroom house in which
the living room doubled as a third sleeping room. The board-
and-batten house was so poorly constructed, "you could
throw a cat through the cracks in it," Kirkland recalled.
"We'd take newspaper and paper inside the house to try to
keep some of the wind out."[23] Terry Clipper remembered his
home in eastern Oklahoma: "We didn't have wallpaper on the
walls. We had newspapers and my mother would mix . . .
flour and water and make a paste and we'd paste these papers
on the house. Our house was [built of] about three-quarter
inch plank boards, and that's as thick as the walls were. . . .
When it rained in the summertime the roof would leak and
we'd have to set pans on the floor to catch the water. You
could get in the attic and look up through there and . . . see
daylight."[24]

Such impoverished living conditions, perpetuated by the
dependence on landlords inherent in the farm-leasing system, were endemic throughout much of the Oklahoma cotton belt; nonetheless, tenant farming afforded a degree of
self-sufficiency. Many tenant families kept food on the table
by growing corn for meal; tending vegetable gardens and
fruit trees; keeping milk cows, pigs, and chickens; fishing;
and hunting quail, rabbits, and squirrels. The fare was simple
and somewhat monotonous, but it sustained cash-poor families through the hardest of times. Indeed, once the Depression hit, tenant farmers and their families often ate better
than their town-dwelling counterparts. That is, until drought
struck.[25]

Drought made the tenants' hold on the land crumble away in the middle years of the Depression. Although not nearly as hard hit as the Dust Bowl, Oklahoma's cotton belt suffered periodic drought and blowing dust during the mid-1930s. On the eve of the decade, dry hot weather had begun to stunt the plants and reduce yields in some southwestern counties. By 1934, the drought became severe and general, spreading eastward into the normally humid sections of the cotton belt. That year no rain fell—not a sprinkle—for nearly seventy days during the prime growing season from mid-June to the third week of August, and farmers in some sections saw little rain after the crop was planted in April.[26]

High temperatures and hot winds withered the fields. A farmer in Beckham County, bordering the Texas panhandle, reported in August that "the country is taking on [a] desert-like appearance." The desiccated lands extended as far east as LeFlore County on the Arkansas boundary. One farm woman called the drought the worst she had seen in her twenty years in the area. "Two months of prolonged drouth with scorching winds and torrid heat of sun has parched the fields," she wrote. "Timber is dying. Older settlers never saw anything like it."[27]

In some areas the crop was so poor that the harvest seemed hardly worthwhile. According to reports from McIntosh County, some farmers did not bother with a second picking before turning their livestock into the fields. Indeed the 1934 cotton crop was nearly a complete failure. The average yield in Beckham County dropped to 53 pounds of lint per acre, down from 207 pounds the year before. In neighboring Kiowa County the yield per acre plummeted from 254 pounds in 1933 to 25 pounds. A farmer in southwestern Oklahoma recalled, "I picked six bales of cotton off of 80 acres. There's people down three miles from me on higher ground—I was right down in the river bottom—that didn't pick a sack in the field. There was nothing to pick."

Farther east, McIntosh and LeFlore counties averaged only 76 and 71 pounds of lint per acre, respectively. Two years later, in 1936, drought again consumed the crop.[28] Many farmers could not withstand such repeated losses. As one woman whose family headed west explained, "The drought come and burned it up. We'd have gone back to Oklahoma from Arizona, but there wasn't anything to go to."[29]

Drought compounded the effects of erosion and soil exhaustion already spreading like a cancer across the land. Farmers in the cotton belt had mined the fertility of the soil, seriously depleting its productivity after only twenty to fifty years of extensive agriculture. Between 1905 and 1930, the average yield dropped 43 percent, from 235 to 135 pounds of lint per acre. Erosion became most severe in the eastern sections of the cotton belt where the rocky terrain restricted the availability of arable land. Overpopulation of the area by poor farmers from the South in the last decades of the nineteenth century forced many families onto sloping and wooded tracts already low in humus and nitrogen and even onto stony soils with limited agricultural utility. Small farms soon dotted the landscape, denuded of its natural forest cover and lined with rows of cotton following the slope of the land.

By placing these marginal lands under the plow without conforming to the natural contours of the terrain or building terraces to help increase the absorption of rainwater, farmers unwittingly accelerated sheet erosion throughout the region and washed away the topsoil. "Many farms, especially on the sloping lands, are severely eroded and have a run-down, neglected appearance," observed a soil expert studying Pittsburg County. Gullies scarred the land, rendering much of it untillable. Thousands of acres lay abandoned.[30] The pattern was repeated across the undulating fields of the Central Cross Timbers as farmers plowed up the native grasses. And on the flatlands of the southwestern cotton region, where sheet erosion posed less threat, the harrowed soil in some areas drifted readily in high winds, nearly exposing the sandstone bedrock.[31]

The tenant-farming system promoted abuse of the land. Landlords typically required their tenants to maximize income by growing cotton to the virtual exclusion of other crops. Tenants did grow corn and other feed and food crops to provide for their families and livestock, but landlords expected payment in cotton. Most farmers planted their cotton on the same ground year after year, thereby exhausting the soil. The system coupled cotton monoculture with a short-term perspective. Because leases commonly extended for only one year at a time, tenants felt little motivation to terrace the land or replenish the nutrients in the soil. Those who did improve their farms often risked punishment in the form of higher rent. Landlords with more desirable farms could demand a cash payment, a "bonus" or "privilege rent," in addition to the standard share agreement. And so the wasteland spread, pushing farmers from one marginal tract to another.[32]

On the southwestern plain the growing popularity of mechanized farming compounded the effects of drought and erosion. Between 1930 and 1940, the number of tractors in Oklahoma increased by 75 percent, with one tractor for every four farms. These were concentrated in the western part of the state where the level topography seemed ready-made for tractor farming. With tractors, owners could plow, list, plant, and cultivate the cotton crop in a fraction of the time it took using mule teams and consequently could manage larger acreages themselves. The tractor thereby made it possible to release year-round tenants and rely on seasonal wage labor for chopping and picking. Concomitantly, by the 1930s, wheat farming, including harvesting, had become highly mechanized, creating a gradual shift from cotton to wheat.

The average farmer could handle twice the acreage of wheat as cotton with about the same amount of his own labor and only a small amount of hired help. This movement toward wheat farming helped stimulate consolidation of land. The seven most mechanized counties in the southwestern cotton belt experienced a general expansion in the size of farms between 1935 and 1940 as farmers absorbed smaller neighboring tracts into their holdings or evicted their tenants. One family lived where two had lived before.[33]

In the eastern cotton belt, relatively few farmers owned tractors, largely because hilly terrain and small farm size made them impractical. Farmers continued to plow with teams of mules or horses. Machinery, however, did displace some tenants on fertile bottomlands, which proved most suitable for mechanization. Wheeler Mayo, editor of the *Sequoyah County Times,* reported that absentee owners had introduced tractor farming on the most desirable farmlands along the river bottoms and terraces. One tractor could replace many tenants. According to Otis G. Nation, an organizer for the Oklahoma Tenant Farmers Union, one landowner in Creek County bought three tractors and evicted thirty-one of his tenants and croppers. Thus tenants who had farmed the choicest lands found themselves looking for new places on poorer, less productive soils. But not until after World War II did mechanization result in mass displacement from the eastern cotton belt.[34]

And yet, during the Depression landowners throughout Oklahoma's cotton belt began phasing out tenant farming in favor of seasonal wage labor. Agronomists advised landowners to modernize the agricultural economy and conserve the soil by eliminating the tenantry. The federal government unwittingly exacerbated this trend with the Agricultural Adjustment Act (AAA) of 1933, a New Deal program to raise the price of cotton lint by voluntarily reducing production.

Drought, erosion, and mechanization all played roles in the elimination of the tenantry, but the AAA provided the financial backing. Low crop yields resulting from drought and erosion meant that tenant farms no longer brought profit to the landowner. Increasingly the cash value of the landlord's share of the crop did not cover the taxes on the land. When the crop reduction program made it more profitable to rent acreage to the government than to tenant farmers, landowners reduced the state's cotton acreage by nearly 30 percent.[35] Farmers therefore gradually moved down the tenure ladder, from cash or share tenant to sharecropper to wage laborer, each step less secure than the last.

The crop-reduction payments helped stimulate the mechanization of farms in the southwestern part of the cotton belt, further reducing the need for tenants. Although the AAA payments were to be shared with the tenant, based on his rental arrangement and his share of the crop, many owners instead used the check to buy a tractor. "And with each tractor purchased," observed the *Farmer-Stockman,* "one or more croppers must hit the section line."[36] One landlord in southwestern Oklahoma admitted, "I let 'em all go. . . . In '34 I had I reckon four renters and I didn't make anything. I bought tractors on the money the government give me and got shet o' my renters. You'll find it everywhere all over the country thataway."[37]

The AAA prohibited landowners from evicting tenants, but that provision naively overlooked the reality of tenancy in Oklahoma. Oral contracts, the most common tenant agreements in Oklahoma, could be made for only one year at a time, according to state statute. At the end of the year, a tenant family could be treated as trespassers and ousted upon three days' notice unless the farmer secured a new lease.[38] Those allowed to stay could not count on receiving their share of the crop-reduction check. One farmer in Creek

County reported, "Some land owners are having their renters sign contracts so they will not receive any of the benefits from the government. Happy days may be here again but not for the renter; his troubles are just begun."[39] Landlords who chose to evict their tenants or keep their checks had little fear of penalty since complaints were handled by local committees of landowners. In any event, each year more than half of the tenantry shifted from farm to farm as they sought more productive land or a fairer deal. The landlords merely had to sit back and wait. In 1935, for example, almost 55 percent of Oklahoma's tenants had lived on their farms for one year or less.[40] This state of affairs caused one eyewitness to observe that the tenants "break loose like the tumbleweed every year and go rolling across the prairie until they lodge for a year against a barbwire fence, only to break loose next year and go tumbling on again."[41]

After 1933, the tumbleweeds that rolled across the prairie found it increasingly difficult to find another place to lodge. Between 1930 and 1935, the competition for tenancies in the central and eastern sections of the cotton belt increased dramatically with the influx of drought-stricken farmers from the western part of the state and unemployed urban dwellers and oil-field workers seeking survival on farms. In the western part of the cotton belt, one in seven tenant farms disappeared during the first half of the decade. Farmers in Greer, Tillman, and Washita counties were especially hard hit. Thousands across the cotton belt found themselves landless. Dispatches from the countryside printed in the *Farmer-Stockman* spoke of a tenantry set adrift. Nora Boyd of Johnston County reported that "lots of moving is going on with no vacant farms left."[42] A farmer in Jackson County echoed her words: "The demands for housing are in excess of the supply. The outgoing tenant can't vacate for the incoming tenant because no vacant tenaments [sic] are available."[43]

These problems intensified after 1934 when the Bankhead
Act made acreage reduction mandatory and established state
quotas. The U.S. Supreme Court temporarily suspended the
AAA when it held portions of the act unconstitutional in
January 1936, but cotton cultivation in Oklahoma continued
to drop under the subsequent Soil Conservation and Domestic Allotment Act and the Agricultural Adjustment Act of
1938. Over the course of the New Deal agriculture program,
Oklahoma's cotton acreage fell from more than 4 million
acres in 1933 to about 1.7 million acres in 1941, thereby
reducing the need for tenant farmers. By the end of the
decade, one in four tenant farms in the cotton belt were
gone.[44]

For those pushed off the land, the prospects looked bleak.
Tenants who could not get work often found no relief.
Corruption, patronage, and ineptitude characterized Oklahoma's administration of New Deal programs, so that federal
relief funds frequently did not reach those in need. Compounding the problem, as late as 1940, more than 60,000
men and women in the state who had been certified for WPA
employment still awaited assignment to nonexistent jobs.
Private welfare agencies considered able-bodied men inelig-
ible for assistance.[45]

As the decade progressed, increasing numbers of homeless
families congregated in the squatters' camps of Tulsa and
Oklahoma City. During the early years of the Depression,
these singularly squalid camps, home to hundreds of former
tenant farmers and sharecroppers, began to proliferate in the
capital along the North Canadian River and along Reno
Avenue and Commerce. Elm Grove, a so-called transient
camp established by the city, typified these enclaves. In 1933
it was home to approximately 350 families, about half former
tenant farmers or sharecroppers. The camp was located next
to a junkyard along the banks of the North Canadian and

consisted of shacks made of scraps of wood, cardboard, tin, canvas, and other castoffs. By 1935, the city had eliminated garbage collection out of fear that clean camps would attract more homeless people to the county. Open toilets went uncleaned, and only one water pump served some 2,000 residents.[46] After Helen Gahagan Douglas, an activist for the migrants in California and later a congresswoman from Los Angeles County, visited Elm Grove and the May Avenue camp in June 1940, she reported, "I really have never seen anything in California to equal the degradation of the camps outside of Oklahoma City."[47]

The image of tenants as shiftless and incompetent drones who preferred to live in squalor was widespread among Oklahoma's leadership, as it was throughout the South.[48] A *Tulsa Tribune* editorial describing Oklahoma's tenant population as largely a "subnormal peasant type" typified this view.[49] Such attitudes, combined with the overwhelming desire to modernize the state's agricultural economy, served as rationales for looking the other way as a displaced tenantry migrated to urban areas to join the ranks of the unemployed or left the state in search of opportunities elsewhere.

Oklahoma governor Leon C. Phillips dismissed them as floatsam and jetsam, but few tenants drifted away easily. Some tried to stand their ground, to fight dislocation. In 1935 Odis L. Sweeden, a Cherokee from Muskogee, organized the Oklahoma branch of the Southern Tenant Farmers Union (STFU), an organization based in Arkansas, later Tennessee, to represent the interests of sharecroppers and tenant farmers. Within a year nearly eighty locals were reportedly active in the state, primarily in Muskogee, McIntosh, Creek, and Wagoner counties. Sweeden sought to shape the organization along the lines of an industrial trade union and advocated written five-year contracts for tenant farmers and sharecroppers, collective bargaining, the extension of industrial labor

As the Depression decade progressed, increasing numbers of homeless families congregated in squatters' camps in Tulsa and Oklahoma City. These squalid "Hoovervilles"—nicknamed after President Herbert Hoover, whom many blamed for the Depression—became home to hundreds of former tenant farmers and sharecroppers. (Photograph by Russell Lee, July 1939, courtesy of the Library of Congress.)

Hoovervilles lined the North Canadian River in Oklahoma City. The May Avenue camp extended under the May Avenue bridge, which provided shade. (Photograph by Russell Lee, July 1939, courtesy of the Library of Congress.)

laws to protect agricultural workers, and continued development of large-scale cooperative farms under the New Deal's
agricultural program. With Sweeden's leadership, the Oklahoma STFU achieved a measure of success. He helped per-
suade Governor E. W. Marland to call a statewide conference
on farm tenancy, which led to the passage of a state tenancy
act in 1937 and the establishment of an Oklahoma Farm
Landlord and Tenant Relationship Department within the
Agricultural Extension Service. And in the summer of 1938,
nearly 3,500 people attended a Landlord-Tenant Day conference in Stillwater.

With these achievements, the farm tenancy movement
reached its climax. In February 1939 the state legislature
repealed the Farm Landlord and Tenant Relationship Act four
months before it was scheduled to expire. By that time, the
Oklahoma STFU had waned. A host of problems sapped the
strength of the national and the Oklahoma organizations,
including infighting, inadequate finances, mismanagement
of funds, and a schism brought on by an ill-fated eighteen-
month federation between the STFU and the United Cannery,
Agricultural, Packing and Allied Workers of America, an
affiliate of the Congress of Industrial Organizations. Moreover, pressures on tenants had become so intense and migration from the state so extensive that the entire membership of
some STFU locals reportedly moved to California. They
found they could not wrest power from landowners. Their
best option, it seemed, was to move on.[50]

The decision to move west did not always come easily.
Most farm families struggled along for some time in Oklahoma before they loaded up the truck and headed for what they
hoped would be a new beginning. First, Oklahoma was
home, and ties to the state were often strong despite frequent
moves from farm to farm. The majority of the westward
migrants from Oklahoma, particularly the rural regions, had

lived in the same county for at least twenty years. Second, and just as important if not more, the move took money—not a lot, perhaps, in today's terms or even by middle-class standards of the time, but most of those who found themselves landless and homeless had never earned much cash. Many first had to scrape together the money to purchase a used truck or automobile for the trip. Charles Price had to sell all of his farm equipment and the family's household goods to buy his first automobile, a used Graham Dodge, leaving him with thirty or forty dollars in cash for the journey westward.

The typical migrant tenant farmer left home with only forty or fifty dollars to his name. To be sure, those with kinfolk living in California or Arizona left with some sense of security; relatives could help them find jobs perhaps, or at least provide food and shelter until they found work.[51] For many others, the westward journey meant uncertainty. But confronted with the certainty of continued hardship at home, displacement by landlords, and little federal or state relief, what did tenant families have to lose? The West, they had heard, was good cotton country. It sounded something like home, only better.

But as the migrants faced westward, a farmland that in many ways resembled the preindustrial plantation South receded into the background. Before them, in the cotton fields of California and Arizona, loomed one of the most capitalized industrial agricultural systems the world had known.

Chapter Three

Factories in
the Fields

Almost from its beginnings corporate organization colored the landscape of central Arizona's farming regions, particularly that of its cotton industry. The irrigated agricultural region encompassed the Salt River Valley, including the area known as the Buckeye Valley between the Hassayampa and Agua Fria rivers, and the Casa Grande Valley, composed of the overlapping floodplains of the Gila and Santa Cruz rivers.[1] There the cotton growers created a tightly-knit integrated enterprise best described as industrial agriculture. This system grew out of the organized irrigation efforts required for desert agriculture, the early leadership role played by mature vertically-integrated, outside corporations, and the coalescence of the industry in its infancy into a series of cooperative associations.

Arizona's "factories in the fields" depended on a cheap, exploitable labor force. Moving from Mexico to Puerto Rico

to the western cotton belt, growers cast the seeds of opportunity across ever-widening expanses in an effort to cultivate
a perennial crop of workers whose numbers would grow and
decay in harmony with the seasons.[2]

"We Are Empire Builders"

Agriculture in the arid Salt River Valley had its origins in the
development of extensive irrigation projects financed by
joint-stock companies. The initial Phoenix settlement was
founded in 1867 by the Swilling Irrigating and Canal Company, the first such enterprise to operate in the valley. Swilling's
company, organized with the financial backing of a group of
businessmen in the Arizona mining town of Wickenburg,
preempted land west of the Papago Buttes near the present
boundary of Phoenix and Tempe and filed a water right and a
right-of-way claim for an irrigation ditch. To raise capital for
construction of the canal, the company sold quarter sections
of land at public auction, and each purchaser received a share
of company stock.

Swilling's enterprise established a model for corporate
canal development emulated throughout the Salt River Valley, most significantly by the Arizona Canal Company and
the Arizona Improvement Company. Together, these two
corporations transformed the distribution of water in the
valley. First the Arizona Canal Company consolidated the
irrigation system on the north side of the Salt River by
acquiring majority stock in three older canal companies and
physically linking those relatively primitive ditches to the
new, more sophisticated, and extensive Arizona Canal. Then,
in 1887, the major shareholders of the Arizona Canal incorporated the Arizona Improvement Company as a parent real
estate investment corporation, which they capitalized through
the sale of stocks and bonds to investors, chiefly in the Los
Angeles area, San Francisco, and Chicago.

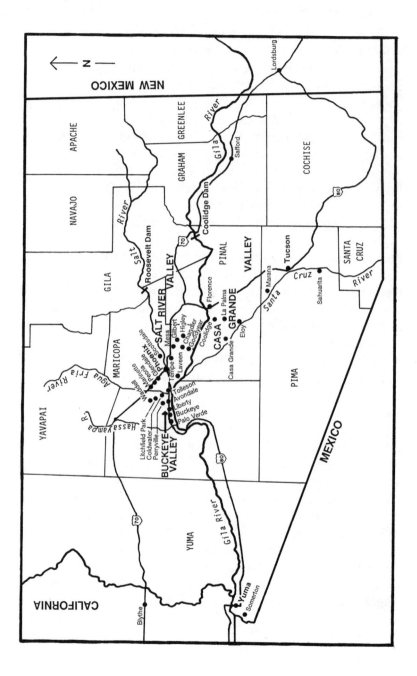

The company proceeded to establish a virtual monopoly over the valley north of the Salt River by purchasing lands vested with early water rights. Under the doctrine of *prior appropriation*—"first in time, first in right"—those lands irrigated at an early date received priority for water during times of scarcity. Ownership of those early water rights made it possible for the Arizona Improvement Company to control the development of desert land by selling and leasing access to water. The company then embarked on a national campaign to promote the potential of the Salt River Valley for commercial agriculture, particularly for high-value crops like citrus, in an effort to attract investors and settlers.[3]

Despite the success of the Arizona Improvement Company in drawing farmers and citrus growers to the valley, seasonal water shortages and periodic flooding continued to retard agricultural development. Then in 1911, the obstacles posed by an arid environment seemed overcome as former president Theodore Roosevelt dedicated the dam named in his honor. Roosevelt Dam became the cornerstone of the vast Salt River Project, a multipurpose program to provide irrigation and hydroelectricity to the valley. Agricultural leaders took pride in landing the first major reclamation project developed under the National Reclamation Act of 1902, commonly known as the Newlands Act.

Financing for the project came from a federal reclamation loan secured by the Salt River Valley Water Users' Association, whose membership eventually comprised nearly all the agricultural landowners within the project boundaries, east of the Agua Fria River and west of the Eastern Canal. To finance the project, members of the water users' association mortgaged their land to the organization as collateral for the loan. The development of the Salt River Project thereby assembled not only a sprawling labyrinth of canals and

On facing page: Map 3. Arizona Cotton Towns. (Drawn by Susan Kahre-Stradford, based on WPA, *Migratory Cotton Pickers in Arizona*, xiv.)

laterals but a network of men who governed the valley with influence that extended far beyond the fields.[4]

Similarly, the San Carlos Irrigation Project, inaugurated by the completion of Coolidge Dam, stimulated agricultural development in the Casa Grande Valley. After the project began operation in late 1928, cropland in Pinal County increased by more than 75 percent, from less than 75,000 acres to nearly 132,000 acres a decade later. Here, as in the valley to the north, growers in the San Carlos Irrigation and Drainage District created a cohesive, interdependent agricultural community.[5]

In securing these large-scale reclamation projects, the agriculturalists solidified their hegemony over the valleys of central Arizona. C. S. Brown, a Mesa cotton farmer, perhaps best captured the sense of historical achievement felt by those who lobbied long and hard to transform the flood-plains of the Salt and Gila rivers into an agricultural oasis. Referring to the Salt River and San Carlos projects and the growth they betokened, he boasted, "We are empire builders in the West."[6]

Cotton first became king of that empire in the Salt River Valley. The valley's genesis had been agricultural, but large-scale cotton production in Arizona began with World War I. During the war years, the valley became an important producer of Pima cotton, an American-Egyptian extra-long-staple variety vital for the manufacture of pneumatic truck tires and airplane fabrics. When submarine warfare cut off the supply of long-staple lint from Egypt and the boll weevil ruined the Sea Island crop, Goodyear Tire and Rubber Company, based in Akron, Ohio, turned to the Arizona desert where American-Egyptian varieties had been grown experimentally since 1901. Southwest Cotton Company, Goodyear's subsidiary, developed farms at Litchfield Ranch and Marinette Ranch, both northwest of Phoenix, and at Goodyear Ranch, southeast of Phoenix near Chandler, and established gins in Glendale, Phoenix, Tolleson, Tempe, Mesa, and Chandler.[7]

After Goodyear demonstrated the profitability of growing the long-staple fiber, cotton fever swept through the valley. The Firestone, Fisk, and Dunlop tire companies also turned to the valley for cotton, further stimulating the development of farms. Farmers switched from diversified crops and dairy herds to cotton monoculture. By the time the market collapsed in late 1920, growers had planted nearly three-fourths of the valley's irrigated land in Pima cotton. That year the price of long-staple cotton plummeted from a high of $1.35 per pound to 28¢, the result of a market glutted by foreign cotton in a year of lower peacetime demand.

The cotton depression was severe but brief. Three years later, more than half of the agricultural fields again bloomed white. But this time the cultivation of upland varieties, principally Acala, overshadowed Pima cotton, in part because the short-staple plants yielded more lint per acre and were easier and thus cheaper to harvest. In Phoenix, the manufacture of by-products, cottonseed oil and cottonseed meal, developed into an important subsidiary industry in the 1920s and 1930s. Cotton production concentrated in the Salt River Valley, or Maricopa County, where growers produced about 60 percent of the state's crop. Growers in the Casa Grande Valley, Pinal County, cultivated another 20 percent of the total, and the balance was distributed in the vicinity of Tucson, Yuma, and Safford.[8]

By 1930, the cotton industry had developed into an important commercial enterprise. Granted, most agricultural operations in Maricopa and Pinal counties fit the profile of the family farm. In 1930, 90 percent of the farms in Maricopa County and 83 percent of those in Pinal County measured less than 175 acres. And yet, some farmers increased their domain considerably by leasing additional land. Fred Faver, one of the most important growers in the Buckeye area, leased three farms in addition to his own land, totaling about 1,400 acres. Indeed, although relatively few in number, large-scale operations overshadowed the smaller farms and garnered an increasingly disproportionate share of land. Clarence O. Vosburgh, perhaps the most prominent grower in the Buckeye Valley, cultivated some 3,500 acres. In fact, about 20 percent of the harvested cropland in Maricopa County and 16 percent in Pinal County lay in holdings of at least 1,000 acres in 1929. A decade later, nearly two hundred large-scale operations controlled 25 percent of the cropland in Maricopa County and more than 35 percent of Pinal County.

Cotton growers in particular favored larger holdings. In 1929 fewer than 3 percent of the growers produced more than 25 percent of the state's income from cotton. Moreover, many growers owned far more extensive holdings than those planted with crops. In 1930, more than half of central Arizona's irrigated fields were in holdings of 1,000 acres or more, despite the 160-acre limitation imposed by the Newlands Act. Spreads of at least 5,000 acres accounted for nearly one-third of the farm acreage in the Salt River Valley. And this concentration became even more pronounced in the Casa Grande Valley where nearly two-thirds of the farmland lay in such broad expanses. Much of this land, however, sat idle, held primarily for speculative purposes.

Farms may have been large, but they generally remained family businesses. Local residents who oversaw their own operations owned most of central Arizona's farms, although many owners lived in town and trusted the day-to-day supervision to managers. But absentee ownership was fairly sizable in the Casa Grande Valley. Out-of-state growers operated several large-scale farms on lands leased from the state at a nominal charge of less than one dollar per acre.

Indeed, the owners of nearly 30 percent of the farms in the area lived out of state, principally in California. Even so, corporate ownership of farmland remained the exception. By 1939, fifteen corporations owned only 7 percent of the farmland in the Casa Grande Valley.[9]

Nevertheless, a corporate structure overlay the cotton industry. In 1929 the J. G. Boswell Company, headquartered in Los Angeles, joined the Southwest Cotton Company in the Buckeye Valley. At that time its holdings included six gins, a cottonseed mill, and 3,000 acres planted in cotton. In 1936 Boswell leased from Southwest Cotton Company the town of Marinette, complete with 8,000 acres of cotton fields, a gin, a store, a post office, and farm labor camps. Most significant, however, was the Western Cotton Products Company, a Houston-based subsidiary of Anderson, Clayton and Company, one of the largest cotton merchants in the world. The company expanded its operations into Arizona and California in the late 1920s. As the single largest gin operator in Maricopa and Pinal counties, Western Cotton Products exerted considerable influence over cotton agriculture and fashioned a highly integrated industry. Of twelve gins in the Casa Grande Valley, Western Cotton Products owned nine (another two belonged to J. G. Boswell Company), and it operated gins in Avondale, Buckeye, Palo Verde, Chandler, and Gilbert. The company ginned 45 percent of the state's 1937–38 harvest. It then processed the cottonseed in its oil mills, and its parent company merchandised the lint. In addition, the company functioned as banker. It financed the production of crops, more than a third of the state's cotton acreage in 1937, and in some cases provided loans for the purchase of farms by tenants. Corporate interests thereby dominated the industry.[10]

Indeed the cotton growers, although ostensibly independent producers, created a corporate structure among themselves. While in its infancy, the industry thereby developed into an interdependent organism. In 1912 and 1913 the cotton growers of Mesa, Tempe, and Chandler formed producers' cooperatives. These groups joined forces in 1914, forming the Salt River Valley Egyptian Cotton Growers' Association, later the Arizona Pimacotton Growers' Association and the Arizona Cotton Growers' Association. The growers' associations oversaw marketing, promoted varietal purity, and lobbied for protective legislation; the local cooperatives continued to operate gins and arrange financing for members. In the early 1920s, the Arizona Pimacotton Growers' Association held a one-quarter interest in the Mutual Oil and Cotton Company, which operated ginning facilities in Phoenix, Chandler, Tempe, Glendale, and Peoria, and it founded the *Associated Arizona Producer,* the official publication of the cotton growers. Other states, of course, had formed growers' cooperatives in the early decades of the twentieth century. The Oklahoma Cotton Growers' Association, founded in 1920, provided marketing and warehousing services to its members and lobbied in their collective interest. In Arizona, however, the cotton growers' association became far more integral to the cotton industry of Maricopa and Pinal counties. It functioned as the principal labor recruiter and annually established the prevailing harvest wage.[11]

"An Elastic Supply of Labor"

A large force of seasonal harvesters proved indispensable to the industrial character of Arizona's cotton agriculture. Relatively few residents would willingly toil for the wages offered during the brief four-month season, so growers soon came to depend on migrant labor imported from Mexico and the western cotton belt of the United States. When the cotton industry experienced its first expansion during World War I, growers supplied the acute demand for labor with contract workers, or *braceros,* from Mexico, primarily the state of Sonora. In 1917 the commissioner general of immigration temporarily suspended restrictions on alien contract labor in response to wartime shortages in agriculture and other industries.

To coordinate recruitment efforts, the cotton growers' association employed as its agent Rafael Estrada, a Mexican American with light sandy hair and a ruddy complexion. Estrada's brother Pedro operated a store in Tempe that delivered groceries and other provisions to the labor camps. Each season Rafael Estrada and his labor scouts went to Mexico and border towns where they would load recruits onto chartered trains, which carried the braceros to the Salt River Valley. At the end of the harvest, the trains shipped the cotton pickers home. Between 1918 and 1920, the growers' association brought approximately 35,000 Mexicans across the border into Arizona. Thousands more crossed illegally.[12]

With the seasonal importation and repatriation of Mexican workers, Arizona's cotton farmers quickly grew habituated to exploitative labor practices. An official of the Arizona Cotton Growers' Association boasted that "the cotton growers of the Salt River Valley maintained as perfectly an elastic supply of labor as the world has ever seen and *maintained an even low level of prices for wages throughout its territory* [sic]."[13] The association made every effort to keep not just wages but all labor costs low. The workers repaid the costs of transportation from Mexico, guaranteed by a 25¢-per-day deduction from wages. And growers kept housing costs to a minimum despite the Ninth Proviso to the Immigration Act of 1917, which stipulated that housing and sanitation would meet standards established by the secretary of labor. Living in large labor camps, the braceros slept in tents with dirt floors and used water from irrigation ditches for drinking, cooking, and bathing.

In the summer of 1920, an investigation by the Mexican consul in Phoenix, Eduardo C. Gonzáles, revealed the extent to which Arizona's cotton growers exploited Mexican workers. In one example, a family had been charged $72 for transportation and meals from Sinaloa to Tempe. To cover this cost, the growers' association deducted $9 from a weekly income of $18. The association then placed the balance on a credit account at a local store to cover the cost of food, which proved inadequate for the family's sustenance. When workers complained about their living conditions, low or unpaid wages, or the exorbitant prices of goods in company-owned commissaries, representatives of the association responded with threats of jail or deportation and the importation of new recruits. Efforts to form labor unions met with swift reprisals.[14]

A crisis arose in the wake of the 1921 crash of the cotton market, foreshadowing the events of 1937–38. When prices for Pima cotton plunged from $1.25 to 25¢ per pound, many overextended farmers went bankrupt, and banks and businesses across the valley failed as the effects of the crash rippled through the economy. The Arizona Cotton Growers' Association suspended wage payments to Mexican workers and reneged on its contract to repatriate the braceros at harvest end. Thousands of Mexican nationals found themselves penniless, stranded in the agricultural valleys. The situation attracted the attention of the Mexican government, which demanded action. Eduardo Ruiz, special envoy from the Republic of Mexico, and Gonzalo Córdoba, the Mexican consul at Phoenix, maintained that the cotton growers' association bore responsibility for the workers and should be compelled to fulfill their obligations. Their report to Governor Thomas E. Campbell documented the circumstances of more than 160 workers and their families stranded in the Salt River Valley with money owed to them in amounts ranging from $2 to more than $400. In numerous cases, the braceros had been promised wages far higher than they were offered once they arrived. Worse yet, many of those stranded had been brought to the valley near the end of the harvest with a promise of six months' employment by the firm Manning and Gonzales, an unscrupulous labor contractor that received a $4 fee for each bracero whether or not the person found work.[15]

In a typical example, Enrique Lopez had been sent to work on the West Avondale Ranch by the Arizona Cotton Growers' Association and still had $31.60 coming to him. "He informs us," wrote Ruiz and Córdoba, "that this is all the money that he has in this world and at this time is entirely without funds and is unable to secure payment for the amount. He wishes to be transported to the Mexican border."[16] Another unfortunate was Alejandra Ramirez, a widow with two children who had picked cotton for the Chandler Improvement Company and lived in a company-owned labor camp. Early in February 1921 a man from the company ordered Señora Ramirez and at least seventy-five other unemployed Mexican laborers to evacuate their tents, and his men then proceeded to take down the canvas shelters before Rameriz could remove her belongings. Ruiz and Córdoba found her crying over her situation. She "begged us to get her transportation at least to the Mexico line."[17] When Simon Gonzales demanded that he be returned to Mexico, labor agent Rafael Estrada replied that his company "was not giving bums any tickets to the Mexican border."[18]

No action was taken by the growers' association to alleviate the desperate situation until local political pressure compelled it to keep its promises. On February 5, in an agreement signed by Ruiz, acting as the official emissary of President Alvaro Obregón of Mexico, and W. H. Knox, representing the association, the cotton growers' organization committed to financing the repatriation of all those contract workers who lacked funds to return home. Knox also agreed that the association would pay the Mexican workers the wages owed by insolvent growers. As weeks went by, however, the association ignored this agreement. Individual growers maintained that the organization, not they, bore responsibility for the welfare of the braceros. As soon as it became clear that the agricultural community would not assist the farm workers, the Phoenix Central Labor Union, headquarters for the Arizona Federation of Labor, set up a soup kitchen, which attracted as many as one thousand Mexicans a day. Many of the destitute headed home on foot, and others returned home at the expense of the Mexican government or that of Maricopa County. Finally, in response to pressure from all levels of government, including the Mexican consul, U.S. Secretary of Labor William B. Wilson, Governor Campbell, a handful of state legislators, the Maricopa County Board of Supervisors, and the city governments of Glendale, Phoenix, and Tempe, the growers' association repatriated more than twenty thousand workers.[19]

A similar scenario took place in 1926, with Puerto Ricans cast in the supporting roles. When restrictive immigration legislation in 1924 reduced the availability of alien labor from Mexico, the Arizona Cotton Growers' Association turned to the U.S. territory of Puerto Rico for additional hands to pick the cotton. Recruits and their families, along with dozens of stowaways, embarked on chartered steamships from San Juan to Galveston, Texas, where they transferred to chartered trains bound for Phoenix. Arizonans did not necessarily look upon the arrival of the Puerto Ricans with favor. The *Tempe News* noted that "the Porto Ricon can scarcely be classed as a desirable type of citizen but the cotton crop must be gathered and it seems the Porto Ricons are the only ones who will pick it. Let u[s] hope there will never be any regret to this experiment of importing that class of labor."[20]

If the residents thought their guests inferior, the new arrivals considered their hosts' accommodations even more deficient. Once in the Salt River Valley, the Puerto Ricans found the floorless tents and adobe houses unsuitable, the living conditions unsanitary, and the wages lower than promised. Although most had experience as agricultural laborers, none had picked cotton, making it difficult to earn enough to feed their families on a wage of $1.25 per hundred pounds. Worse still, the deduction for transportation costs amounted to as much as half a worker's wages. Encouraged by union organizers, the workers went on strike for a guaranteed wage of $2.00 per day and improved housing and sanitation. In response, the growers' association evicted striking workers from the labor camps, leaving the Puerto Ricans dependent on local charity for food and shelter. Although short-lived, the strike and the low productivity of the inexperienced cotton pickers quickly soured the growers on Puerto Rican labor. When the growers realized that the pickers would be unable to repay their share of the transportation costs, as much as $40.00 per capita, they decided to cancel a third shipment of workers. The experiment in importing a new, docile labor force had failed.[21]

Meanwhile, Arizona's cotton growers placed renewed emphasis on recruiting workers from the western cotton belt. This effort became particularly important after 1929 when new immigration restrictions and policies in the United States and Mexico encouraging the repatriation of Mexicans placed a premium on seasonal laborers.[22] As early as 1913, the newly formed Salt River Valley Egyptian Cotton Growers' Association had advertised in Oklahoma and West Texas to enlist competent cotton pickers. This initial campaign had attracted several hundred tenant farmers, many becoming permanent residents of Arizona.

In the 1920s, recruiters intensified their efforts to draw pickers from the western cotton belt. The concomitant shift

from Pima cotton to short-staple varieties, more familiar to
the cotton pickers from the south-central states, and the
development of good east-west roads made it possible for
labor scouts to tap a steady stream of migratory harvesters
bound for the fields of California. Most of these were "bind-
lestiffs," single men who rode the rails and thumbed the
highways to follow the crops. The Arizona Cotton Growers'
Association, however, did not leave labor procurement to
chance. To ensure that potential workers had the ability to
make the trip west, the association transported cotton pickers from the western cotton states directly to Arizona in
trucks and chartered buses and trains, the cost deducted
from each worker's wages. By the late 1920s, it distributed
gasoline cards throughout Oklahoma, Texas, and New Mexico to rebate transportation costs at the end of the season.
Moreover, the association maintained a mailing list to encourage pickers to return each year.[23]

It was during the Depression decade, however, that the
campaign to develop a new source of labor in the nation's
south-central region met great success. These efforts bore the
mark of a former cotton farmer, Arthur Earl Taber. An Iowa
native, he had come to Phoenix in 1918. He became the
manager of the Arizona Cotton Growers' Association in 1929
and directed its labor-recruitment activities. After 1933,
when the association was forced to suspend operations as a
result of a decline in financial support by cotton growers and
oil-mill operators, Taber continued his recruiting efforts as
head of the newly formed Farm Labor Service.

Organized as a committee of the Maricopa County Farm
Bureau and then reorganized as a separate agency, the Farm
Labor Service was in essence the creation of the major cotton
corporations of Maricopa and Pinal counties. Chief among
the founders was Western Cotton Products and its parent
firm, Anderson, Clayton and Company. The manager of

Western Cotton Products, P. W. Peden, served as chairman of the board, his company supplying more than one-third of the agency's operating costs in the 1930s. Colonel Walter O. Boswell, the local head of the J. G. Boswell Company, which provided another 23 percent of the agency's budget, and Kenneth B. McMicken, manager of Southwest Cotton Company, also served as directors. Cotton growers with smaller operations were active in the Farm Labor Service, but the major corporations and the Farm Bureau took the lead.[24]

The formation of the Farm Labor Service responded in part to a new development on Arizona's agricultural scene — labor unions. Labor organizers made inroads in the fields despite rising unemployment and reductions in cotton acreage brought about by the AAA. Steady decreases in wages fueled union sentiment. Picking rates took a nosedive between 1929 and 1930, from $1.50 per hundred pounds of seed cotton to 75¢. In 1932, responding to continued low commodity prices, the growers dropped the wage to a rate of 50¢ per hundred pounds. But as the 1933 harvest approached, the market price of cotton climbed rapidly, stimulated by federal production curtailments.

Many workers believed that the picking price should have risen commensurately and refused "starvation wages" of 50¢ per hundredweight, amounting to only 75¢ or perhaps $1 per day. Clay Naff of Glendale, local leader of the Communist Party–affiliated Cannery and Agricultural Workers Industrial Union (CAWIU), successfully negotiated with the state board of arbitration to raise the wage to 60¢ per hundred, but many pickers, principally local Hispanics, still refused to return to the fields. A similar protest against low wages took place the following year in the Casa Grande Valley, led this time by Lester Doane, organizer of the AFL-affiliated Federal Labor Union. Such actions, however, were merely temporary setbacks for the cotton industry.[25]

Taber proved adept in countering such threats by recruiting a large labor force from the south-central states through a
variety of approaches, including newspaper advertisements.
In September and October 1936, for example, he ran ads in
the "Help Wanted" column of the *Daily Oklahoman* calling
for thousands of cotton pickers. And he encouraged Oklahomans already living in Arizona to assist his campaign with a
notice in the *Arizona Republic*:

> TEXAS-OKLAHOMA PEOPLE
> If you have relatives or friends in drouth sections of
> Texas or Oklahoma who are looking for work, send
> them our AD in this section under
> COTTON PICKERS WANTED
> Write them to come early for four or five months
> work.[26]

The cotton industry's success in encouraging a bountiful
influx of seasonal labor became a perennial burden for the
state's relief system. Frances G. Blair, executive secretary of
the American Red Cross in Tucson, after interviewing social
workers in six Arizona cities, reported that the number of
migrant families seeking relief in early 1931 had grown by
leaps and bounds. Compared with the previous year, the
number of indigent transients had nearly doubled. Local
dairies and bakeries provided milk and stale bread, and relief
agencies provided gasoline and oil to send them on their way.
Until these funds arrived, however, migrant workers congregated in squatters' camps. A camp of makeshift shelters
thrived underneath the Central Avenue Bridge, which spanned
the Salt River just south of Phoenix. Home to fifty or sixty
families, many cotton pickers, the camp had acquired such a
sense of permanence that the residents had assigned numbers to the bridge piers as official addresses. Case records
revealed that a majority of the state's relief applicants were
transients, most of whom had responded to advertising for

seasonal labor. More of these people had come from Oklahoma than any other state. Of 4,628 transients who sought help from the Social Service Center in Phoenix, 35 percent were Oklahomans. Other evidence indicated that Oklahomans formed the bulk of the transient population in the Salt River Valley. A census of the first twenty-one piers under the Central Avenue Bridge found that all but four of the twenty-eight families were from Oklahoma.[27]

Arizona's growing transient problem elicited two important reactions, both representing a backlash against a much larger problem than that posed by migrant harvest labor. Arizona had long been a mecca for indigent health seekers, particularly tuberculars, and for the jobless seeking respite from colder climes. By the Depression decade, the care of these transient indigents had become a costly burden. The dissolution of the Transient Division of the Federal Emergency Relief Administration in 1935, which had maintained nineteen camps for transients in the state since the program's inception in 1933, rendered the issue of the transient poor more acute. While not the primary target of the actions against transients, migrant agricultural workers nonetheless found themselves caught in the cross fire.[28]

The first and most notorious response came from California in the form of the so-called Bum Blockade. Although erected primarily against hobos, unemployed men who hitchhiked or secreted themselves in empty boxcars, the blockade apparently also stopped poor migratory families moving on at the end of the cotton harvest. In February 1936 James E. Davis, the Los Angeles police chief, spearheaded the drive to keep indigents out of California. Stationed at Yuma, Needles, and Blythe along the west bank of the Colorado River, which formed the Arizona-California border, 136 Los Angeles police officers stopped indigent travelers, fingerprinted them, and turned them back across the Arizona boundary. In one

An Oklahoma migrant stops at the plant inspection station at Yuma, Arizona, on his way to California. At the Arizona and California borders, inspectors checked baggage for pests that could damage agricultural crops. In 1936, the Los Angeles police established a "Bum Blockade" at these ports of entry to keep poor migrant workers and hoboes out of California. Penniless migrants were fingerprinted and turned back across the Arizona border. (Photograph by Dorothea Lange, May 1937, courtesy of the Library of Congress.)

instance the police prevented the entry of an automobile filled with fourteen men, women, and children because the family had only $30.21, an amount insufficient to enter the Golden State. The group partially circumvented the blockade by purchasing train tickets to Los Angeles for the women and children.[29] Alfred Seabolt and his family were stopped at Yuma and detained until his brother arrived with proof that he had secured employment on a San Joaquin Valley farm.[30] John L. Sullivan, Arizona's attorney general, protested the Bum Blockade: "They want everyone to come to California; but they want to stop them at the state line, cull them out and take the best."[31] Still, those transients who elected to remain in Arizona as a result of the blockade found no sanctuary. Phoenix police raided squatters' camps and destroyed their shelters in an effort to keep indigents on the move.[32]

Arizona's broader reaction to its transient problem proved more significant and enduring for seasonal harvest laborers. In June 1937 the legislature enacted the state's first settlement law, requiring three years' continuous residence in the state to become a legal citizen of Arizona and providing that a person could establish eligibility for government relief only after living continuously for six months in the county of residence. Under the law, migrant workers from the south-central states, much like those from Mexico and Puerto Rico, became aliens in Arizona. For many of the poor, the state's open door of opportunity slammed shut.[33]

These events had little immediate effect on the Arizona cotton industry. Growers and ginners had relied for decades on the importation of a large pliant supply of labor that would expand and contract seemingly on command. By the mid-1930s, they had developed increasingly sophisticated methods of expanding their work force. They had thereby created, as they liked to boast, the most elastic supply of workers the world had ever known. Never mind the periodic warnings that the elastic might someday snap. As the 1937–38 harvest approached, the industry looked once again to the south-central region and its growing legion of former cotton farmers to pick the crop.

Chapter Four

Crisis in
the Fields

Cotton production boomed in 1937. The previous year, the U.S. Supreme Court had declared the AAA unconstitutional, suspending mandatory production restrictions. Planters in every leading cotton state responded by expanding their acreage, producing the largest cotton crop in the nation's history. In Arizona, growers in the Salt River and Casa Grande valleys set new records, enlarging the short-staple cotton fields by 72 percent to more than 230,000 acres. This trend was most pronounced in Pinal County where growers nearly doubled the irrigated acreage planted in cotton.[1] The industry thereby set the stage for a crisis in the cotton districts unseen since 1921.

As the harvest season drew near, Earl Taber of the Farm Labor Service launched his most ambitious recruiting campaign, aimed at cotton pickers from Oklahoma and the south-central states to ensure an adequate labor force to pick the bumper crop and discourage unionization. When floods in California's Central Valley prevented migrants from moving on at the end of the harvest to follow the ripening crops, the pernicious effects of the labor surplus, low wages, and substandard housing became apparent, yet neither the industry that had depended upon them nor the state relief system assumed responsibility for the welfare of the recruits. Only the intervention of the federal government averted disaster.

"Cotton Pickers Wanted"

As the season began, no one in the cotton industry anticipated that a labor surplus would bring misery to their midst. On the contrary, growers feared that an increased demand for labor in the southern cotton fields would retard the migration of harvest workers to Arizona, creating an acute labor shortage at the peak of the season. Taber estimated that as many as 20,000 out-of-state cotton pickers would be needed to augment the local labor force.[2]

Arizona's growers recognized that the flow of migrant workers would swell eventually as the southern harvest dwindled, but they were impatient to pick their crop rapidly as the bolls ripened. A delay in picking the cotton ran the risk of damage by the elements. Exposure to the sun deteriorated the color of the lint, and prolonged rain or heavy dew, common in Arizona from December through March, stained the fiber and destroyed its sheen. Any of these conditions would lower the grade and thereby the market value of the lint. Moreover, once the bolls opened, the cotton—valued by the pound—began to dry out and lose weight. And cotton could not be picked while wet, so a rainy spell could delay both the harvest and preparations for the next crop. Looking back on the previous season, a particularly rainy one, growers in the state's principal cotton districts intended to take no chances.[3]

Although cotton growers feared a potentially disastrous labor shortage, government agencies seemed bent on aggravating the situation. As the season got under way, the state farm bureau federation lodged a perennial complaint against the Works Progress Administration (WPA) for refusing to force laborers into the cotton fields by dropping all able-bodied workers from the relief rolls. The federation called for the suspension of all public-works projects until the end of the harvest. The WPA, however, insisted on releasing only those workers with agricultural experience, and even then the agency would not compel those on relief to accept wages less than what they received from the government.[4] Growers therefore blamed the WPA for the labor shortage. Upon hearing the news that state relief officials had requested more funding from Governor R. C. Stanford, exasperated growers protested that "the farmers will not stand for appropriating more money to feed people who refuse jobs harvesting our crops."[5]

To exacerbate the situation further, in early 1937 the state highway department began enforcing new license fees for common carriers transporting passengers into the state. Truckers, who had brought as many as 1,000 to 1,500 pickers from Oklahoma and Texas in 1936, reportedly found the fees prohibitive. A few truckers and labor contractors did manage to get past the highway department, and several growers took it upon themselves to transport pickers from Oklahoma and Texas to their fields. One grower near Sahuarita, twenty miles southeast of Tucson, brought a truckload of cotton pickers from Oklahoma on his own initiative, charging $10 a head. But after the arrest of another farmer for hauling workers without the required license, growers essentially abandoned the direct transportation of cotton pickers into the state as a technique for securing the necessary labor force.[6]

To compensate, Taber made an extraordinary effort to spread word of the demand for labor and direct the westward stream of unemployed workers toward the Salt River and Casa Grande valleys. At the beginning of the season he traveled to Oklahoma, Texas, and southern New Mexico urging employment services and relief agencies to encourage the jobless to look for work in Arizona. More significant, however, was the grapevine he established. Four labor scouts went to targeted states to spread the rumor of work, stopping at pool halls, saloons, grocery stores, auto camps, gas stations—anywhere that potential farm workers might congregate or pass through.[7] L. W. Goad, one of the scouts, described his activities to the La Follette Civil Liberties Committee: "I made one trip to Oklahoma in October of 1937, visiting the town[s] of Chickasha and Anadarko, Oklahoma City and Wewoka and Ardmore, Oklahoma[,] and returned to Phoenix by way of Lawton and Altas [sic] where I contacted prospective cotton picking laborers and gave them the information about conditions in Arizona with reference to the cotton harvest."[8]

Handbills were distributed, placards posted. A typical handbill disseminated in Oklahoma read:

COTTON PICKERS
5000 FAMILIES WANTED
240,000 ACRES COTTON . . .
BIG CROP. HEAVY PICKING.
Cabins or Tents Free—Good Camps
Several Months' Work—Warm, Dry Winters

The flyer went on to list the cotton towns in Maricopa and Pinal counties and advise prospective farm workers to apply at any gin or the offices of the Farm Labor Service. To reassure those who might doubt the authenticity of the offer, the leaflet noted that the Farm Labor Service operated in cooperation with the U.S. Farm Placement Service.[9]

Cotton Pickers

5000 Families Wanted
240,000 Acres Cotton

IN THE BIG COTTON DISTRICTS—NEAR

PHOENIX	SCOTTSDALE
BUCKEYE	GLENDALE
LITCHFIELD	PEORIA
AVONDALE	MARINETTE
GRIGGS	WADDELL
LAVEEN	QUEEN CREEK
TEMPE	COOLIDGE
MESA	CASA GRANDE
CHANDLER	FLORENCE
GILBERT	ELOY

Big Crop   Heavy Picking

CABINS OR TENTS FREE—GOOD CAMPS
SEVERAL MONTHS' WORK — WARM DRY WINTERS

APPLY AT ANY GIN—OR AT

28 West Jefferson Street
PHOENIX, ARIZONA

Farm Labor Service
CO-OPERATING WITH
UNITED STATES FARM PLACEMENT SERVICE

Handbill distributed by the Farm Labor Service.

Taber next sought to attract families already headed west. His workers posted placards along U.S. Highway 66 through northern Arizona and U.S. 70 between Lordsburg, New Mexico, and Phoenix. And they distributed handbills at the inspection stations near the state's ports of entry where labor scouts stood by to intercept California-bound migrants and direct them to Arizona's cotton fields. Taber ran newspaper advertisements in northern New Mexico aimed at gas-station operators and auto-court managers, on the assumption that

Three related farm families from Oklahoma are stalled on the highway near Lordsburg, New Mexico, on their way to Roswell to chop cotton. They have been following the migratory loop through Arizona and California. As a result of unsanitary conditions in the migrant labor camps, they have lost two babies to typhoid fever. One of the farmers said he "would go back to Oklahoma, but can't get along there.... Ain't made a crop there ... for five years." (Photograph by Dorothea Lange, May 1937, courtesy of the Library of Congress.)

A migrant family poses in front of their truck, stalled on the highway near Lordsburg, New Mexico. Although the license tag reads "Texas," the family is from the vicinity of Claremore, Oklahoma. (Photograph by Dorothea Lange, May 1937, courtesy of the Library of Congress.)

they would pass the word to customers. This tactic proved quite successful. In Las Cruces, New Mexico, for example, attendants at filling stations, lunch stands, grocery stores, and tourist camps reported to WPA researchers that good jobs could be had in the Arizona cotton fields for 75¢ to $1 per hundred pounds of cotton. Yet no one from the Farm Labor Service had visited the town.[10] This constant message that jobs lay just ahead raised the spirits of those Oklahomans now on the road who had seen a handbill or opened a newspaper to the classified ads and discovered that an employment bonanza awaited in the irrigated valleys of Arizona.

Advertisements had begun to appear in the Oklahoma City newspapers on Saturday, September 11, 1937. That day, the *Daily Oklahoman* "Help Wanted — Male" column listed only fifteen job openings, mostly for skilled trades requiring experience and good references. But a prominent notice at the center advertised a far greater demand: "COTTON PICKERS — Several thousand wanted near Phoenix and Coolidge, Ariz. Big crop; heavy picking; good prices; will yield 1 to 1½ bales per acre; several months work in ideal climate."[11] The same advertisement appeared in the *Oklahoma City Times*. The next Saturday, a new notice expanded on this theme but added that good pickers could make good money, with "houses or tents provided free."[12]

The initial response to Taber's newspaper campaign fell short of expectations. Attributing the sluggish flow of workers into Arizona to the continued harvest in the south-central states and competition from California where cotton growers offered higher wages, Taber tried to make his ads more enticing.[13] One version of his next string of announcements specified: "5,000 Pickers wanted near Phoenix and Coolidge, Ariz. . . . Growers paying 75¢ hundred. Good Pickers now getting 300 lbs. to 400 lbs. daily. Come soon for several months work. Picking lasts till February. Ideal climate, warm dry, sunshine Fall and Winter days. Houses or Tents provided free."[14] The theme of Arizona's temperate climate, reminiscent of appeals to health seekers and home seekers from the eastern frostbelt, was calculated to appeal to Oklahomans who were beginning to feel the nip of cold weather in the air.[15] In October, ads boasted of the "best fall and winter climate in [the] United States."[16]

Advertising continued until the middle of November. By then, Taber had deleted the amount of cotton a good worker could expect to pick since about one-third of the crop had been ginned. Nevertheless, as late as November 10, he trumpeted a need for 3,000 pickers in response to complaints of a continued labor shortage on large-scale farms.[17] One week later he discontinued advertising, explaining to his executive committee, "The indications were that the movement in here would be increasing daily and we would soon have about all the pickers coming that we could take care of. The measure of the success of our advertising and solicitation in the neighboring states is reflected in the ginning reports."[18] Taber exceeded his goal. An estimated 25,000 out-of-state cotton pickers arrived for the harvest. Most of them brought their families, swelling the migrant population to more than 40,000 people.[19]

Researchers with the WPA agreed with Taber's assessment of the campaign's success. In January and February of 1938, they interviewed more than five hundred groups of migrants as part of a series of studies of agricultural laborers in the Southwest.[20] While it seemed unlikely that down-and-out farm workers would have been much exposed to newspapers, almost 30 percent of the Oklahomans questioned cited advertising as a reason for going to Arizona. Some of these migrants had seen one of several United Press news stories about the labor shortage rather than paid advertising.[21] Another 20 percent had been persuaded by rumors of good wages in Arizona's cotton fields, rumors spread by advertising and labor scouts; and 8 percent simply "knew of cotton."[22] Classified advertisements and handbills had been taken quite seriously, the WPA found. In several of the cotton camps, groups of migrant families "had a single tattered but carefully preserved clipping among them. This bit of advertising, seen by one and shown to the others, had induced them all to come to Arizona."[23]

Migration patterns reveal the importance of the recruiting campaign as an inducement to move west. More than 60 percent of the migrants questioned by the WPA moved directly to Arizona without stopping to work en route. Only about 20 percent paused to pull cotton bolls on the high plains of Texas. Of those who left home after the first of November, by which time the campaign had been in full swing for nearly two months, almost 90 percent headed straight for Arizona.[24]

Not all the migrant farm workers were lured by the Farm Labor Service. Many came to join family or friends. Kinship had long been important in drawing Oklahomans to the cotton fields of central Arizona. Ned Gladden had come to work with his uncle, a foreman on George Sanders's farm near Marana, who likewise had joined a relative in the mid-1920s. Gladden returned home twice before settling in Arizona in 1936. Similarly, Betty Lyon had been encouraged by her brother, a hand on J. D. Stewart's farm, to twice come out for the cotton harvest before she and her parents decided in 1934 to make the Buckeye area home.[25] Like Lyon and Gladden, nearly 20 percent of the Oklahomans interviewed by the WPA in 1938 had received letters from friends or relatives living in Arizona encouraging them to come to the state. Another 8 percent of the migrants had previously visited Arizona.[26] The son of Thomas Higgenbottom, an eastern Oklahoma tenant farmer, had previously spent six

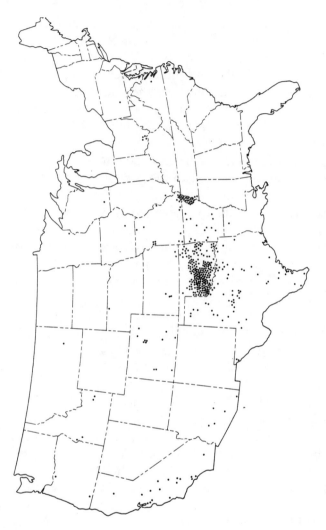

Map 4. Residence of 371 Arizona Cotton Pickers, January 1, 1937. Each dot represents one family or unattached person. (From WPA, *Migratory Cotton Pickers in Arizona*, 39.)

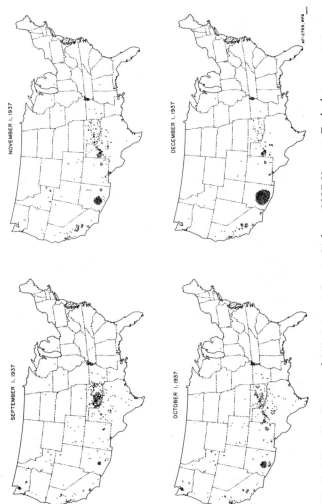

Map 5. Migration Pattern of 371 Arizona Cotton Pickers, 1937 Harvest. Each dot represents one family or unattached person. (From WPA, *Migratory Cotton Pickers in Arizona*, 76.)

months picking cotton in Arizona and returned to report that the Salt River Valley was "good cotton country." So one day in December 1937 the elder Higgenbottom and his wife, Maude, tired of just scraping by, loaded their five children into their Model A and with only $40 headed for the cotton town of Gilbert.[27]

That same month Marvin Montgomery, with his wife and four children, left his farm in eastern Oklahoma and struck out for California to join his son and daughter. He noted that his 1929 Hudson consumed so much gas and oil that "I got to where I had to blindfold it to get it past a filling station."[28] After two breakdowns the family was forced to stop at Eloy and pick cotton for five weeks to earn the money they needed to continue to California's Central Valley. Like the Montgomerys, some 10 percent of the Oklahoma migrants were on their way to California when they stopped in the Arizona cotton fields.[29]

And yet, Arizona's migrant farm laborers were not itinerant workers in the usual sense, perpetually following the crops. More than 70 percent had begun their westward migration after July 1937, and nearly half had been on the road for only three months when they were interviewed in early 1938. This pattern was confirmed by a study of nearly six hundred schoolchildren in the cotton districts of the Salt River Valley: 57 percent of the cotton-picker families had arrived in Arizona for the first time in 1937, and another 24 percent had come in 1935 or 1936 and never left the state. Only 19 percent had traveled from state to state, from crop to crop.[30]

A majority of those who had recently taken to the road were from Oklahoma. The WPA found that 54 percent of the migrants came from the Sooner State, that another 17 percent arrived from Texas. Aside from Arkansas and Missouri, collectively home to 14 percent, no other state provided an

Traveling across the desert on U.S. Highway 70, this family seeks work picking cotton. (Photograph by Dorothea Lange, May 1937, courtesy of the Library of Congress.)

appreciable number of migrant workers.[31] By comparison, 42 percent of the farm workers who had migrated to California's Central Valley between the fall of 1937 and October 1938 had come from Oklahoma, 16 percent from Texas (see Table 2).[32]

Most were young white farm families looking for a new start in life. According to WPA researchers, about 95 percent of the migrants were native-born whites. Many of those

Table 2. Origin of Migrant Farm Workers

ARIZONA	
State of Origin	Percentage
Oklahoma	54
Texas	17
Arkansas	8
Missouri	6
California	3
Colorado	3
All other states	9

CALIFORNIA	
State of Origin	Percentage
Oklahoma	42
Texas	16
Arkansas	11
Missouri	7
Arizona	5
New Mexico	2
Colorado	2
Kansas	2
Washington	2
All other states	11

Sources: WPA, *Migratory Cotton Pickers,* 23; FSA, *Study of 6,655 Migrant Households,* 14. The Arizona figures are based on 371 migrant groups interviewed in 1937; those from California reflect the origins of 6,655 migrant households in 1938.

enumerated as "white," however, may have been mixed-blood American Indian. Moreover, the researchers probably understated somewhat the number of blacks in Arizona's migrant population. Several large segregated camps for black laborers were located near Beardsley and Buckeye. And many

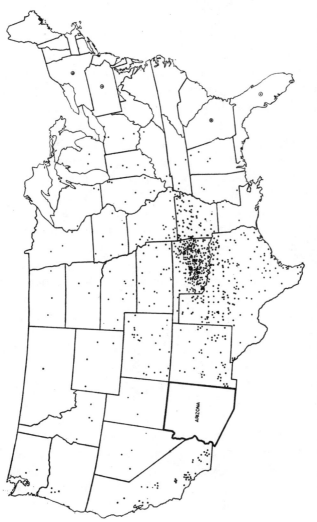

Map 6. Residence in 1930 of 3,889 Agricultural Families Moving to Arizona, 1930–39. Each dot represents five families. (From Tolan Committee, *Interstate Migration*, Pt. 6, *San Francisco Hearings*, 2285.)

single black men brought to Arizona from Oklahoma and
Texas by labor contractors lived in the slums of south Phoenix, traveling to the fields each day.[33]

Nonetheless, by all accounts, white native-born families of
European stock made up the vast majority of the migrants.
Sixty-five percent traveled with their families, small families
for the most part with one or two children. The majority were
in their prime working years. Nearly half had formerly
worked on cotton farms, mostly as share tenants or day laborers. Few had owned their own farms, and equally few had
been sharecroppers. Many of the rest had been employed as laborers on other types of farms. A 1940 study confirmed that
70 percent of the migrant farm workers in Arizona had at some
time been tenants, sharecroppers, or farm owners. Nearly one-
half of those who had farmed in the New Deal years left their
farms as a consequence of the Agricultural Adjustment Act,
and about 40 percent of the tenants had moved down the
ladder to become farm laborers between 1928 and 1936.[34]

Although uncertain about their final destination, most of the
migrants had left home for good, convinced that their prospects
were better in the West. When asked about their plans for the
future, only about one in five of those from the western cotton
states said they would return home, and one-fourth hoped to
stay in Arizona. Significantly, only a third said they intended to
move on to California. Whether or not they planned to go, however, proved irrelevant. As the cotton harvest neared completion, the migrants discovered there was little other work available. For most, the only choice was to move on, so in the early
months of 1938, encouraged by rumors of work in California,
the cotton pickers crossed the border in record numbers.[35]

"We Are Living Exactly Like Hogs"

Floods in the Central Valley drove many back to Arizona,
where they joined thousands more who had yet to leave.

Record rainfall in early 1938 caused the San Joaquin and Sacramento rivers to breach their banks, flooding agricultural land, destroying homes, isolating towns, blocking roads, halting trains, and rendering thousands of Californians and migratory workers homeless. As January turned into February and February into March, water continued to inundate California, leaving large numbers of migrant families virtually trapped in the cotton districts surrounding Phoenix.[36] Before long, the unemployed pickers grew desperate as their meager savings trickled away. By early March, Red Cross officials in Chandler, southeast of Phoenix, reported that conditions among the field workers were "very bad, with abject poverty and complete want an almost ordinary condition."[37]

On March 12 at least one hundred cotton pickers congregated at the Arizona state capitol to plead for help from Governor Stanford. A picture of thousands of families stranded without food or money emerged as they described their plight. Arthur Adams had traveled from Fort Smith, Arkansas, in answer to a newspaper advertisement. Now living in a cotton camp near Avondale, west of Phoenix, he had no money, and his family was starving, subsisting on beet tops purloined from nearby fields. T. J. Hanse of Edinburg, Texas, living at Goodyear's Litchfield camp, told the governor, "I have five in my family. We came here last August. I now have $1.50 and my two babies are sick. We are living exactly like hogs."[38]

Governor Stanford sympathized with the migrants but felt nearly powerless to cope with the emergency. Red Cross funds were almost exhausted, county and state relief coffers severely depleted. In October 1937 county relief agencies throughout the state had appealed for emergency funds for unemployment relief. Maricopa County had reported a $22,000 shortage in funds for the unemployed, and a Pinal County official had observed that many relief clients were in debt to merchants because the agency had insufficient funds for the jobless.[39] Clarence Finch, secretary of the Maricopa County Board of Social Security and Welfare, advised the governor that his agency had provided all the relief it could; indeed, in his opinion, shortages in funds for the unemployed had reached the point where food could not be given to nonresident families "even if someone were dying."[40] Similarly, the deputy commissioner at the Arizona Department of Social Security and Welfare, James R. McDougall, reminded Stanford that the state's three-year residency law prohibited the provision of relief to transients, adding that the agency had no funds to offer, even to emergency cases.[41]

Rebuffed by local welfare officials, Stanford wired President Franklin D. Roosevelt and Senator Carl T. Hayden for federal assistance. As early as February, when the harvest was nearly completed and an estimated twelve- to fifteen-thousand migrants remained in the Salt River Valley, he had anticipated such a crisis and had written Hayden for help. Now, with at least five thousand cotton pickers and their family members stranded in the valley, Stanford again appealed for funds for groceries and gasoline "so these transient people may be returned to their states."[42]

While the governor grappled with the emergency, local welfare officials resisted assisting the migrant farm workers. Federal relief, too, was unavailable at first since state residency laws governed the administration of WPA funds. State welfare administrators protested when officials at the WPA regional office in Salt Lake City announced that all indigents who had resided in Arizona for a year would be certified to receive surplus commodities and jobs on public projects. Relief officials argued that the program would take jobs from bona fide Arizonans waiting for work assignments, even though relatively few of the unemployed cotton pickers could have qualified under the more lenient residency standard since most had been in the state for only a few months. The officials therefore refused to comply until the governor compelled them to do so, citing the residency law's emergency clause. Even then, administrators insisted that commodities would be distributed to nonresidents for only a few weeks.[43] For Finch, helping the migrants meant "taking the food out of the mouths of Arizona residents."[44] Besides, he argued, the entire situation had been blown out of proportion. McDougall agreed. He maintained in testimony before the La Follette committee that although some of the farm workers did need assistance, "there was a lot that did not appear to be destitute."[45]

Governor Stanford confirmed the picture of widespread misery. Visiting one of the largest cotton camps, near Waddell, twenty-five miles northwest of Phoenix, he found disease and starvation. Taking emergency action, he dispatched six highway patrolmen to convey welfare workers to several cotton camps west of Phoenix and ordered the state welfare board to provide surplus commodities. The state superintendent of public health, Dr. Colt I. Hughes, who accompanied the governor, reported widespread illness, including typhoid fever, smallpox, measles, whooping cough, and infant diarrhea. He rushed three children afflicted by typhoid to the county clinic by ambulance. "The camp is in a deplorable state," he observed. "Most of the cotton pickers have sold everything they have, even their automobiles, and have eaten up the proceeds."[46]

Dr. Hughes concluded that malnutrition, poor sanitation, and other conditions in the camps bred illness and disease. Although most camps provided water piped from ranch wells, irrigation ditches served as the only source of drinking water at some, and often a single drinking cup served all the pickers in the field. As a result, dysentery was common.

Public health officials reported an epidemic of measles and limited outbreaks of smallpox, typhoid, pneumonia, and scarlet fever. Moreover, advertisements for cotton pickers stressing the state's warm dry climate had attracted numerous tuberculosis victims. Growers made no effort to segregate sufferers of this highly contagious disease in the camps, nor did they fumigate dwellings vacated by tuberculars before moving in new families. One physician reported seeing many lying sick in the camps. In February, all two hundred patients visiting his clinic had been cotton pickers. The true extent of disease among the farm workers remained unclear, however, since health practitioners made no regular visits to the camps and poverty generally precluded the luxury of medical care.[47] But even with limited knowledge, public health officials concluded that "immediate relief is an obvious humanitarian necessity."[48]

Health workers agreed that poor housing conditions underlay the migrants' health problems. The much-touted free housing typically consisted of unfurnished floorless wooden shacks or tents pitched in the desert. Living conditions at the cotton camps, unregulated by the state, varied with the whim of the grower. Camps associated with large-scale farms generally offered a better water supply, sanitary toilets, and refuse disposal; those operated by labor contractors were simply health hazards. One camp comprised more than two hundred pine shacks; although these closely built shelters had no floors, window glass, screens, or furnishings, the camp offered valued amenities such as running water, cold showers, and enclosed sex-segregated privies. A number of labor camps provided "tent-houses," sturdy army-surplus tents with screens and elevated wooden floors. But at most camps rivulets of water ran across earthen "floors" when it rained, and threadbare tents leaked.[49] Rosie Laird, who had stayed for three weeks in 1934 at J. C. Pennington's camp near Buckeye, recalled that the canvas was so thin, "you could see the stars through the tent." When it rained, the tent acted "like a sieve."[50]

Other camps were less sumptuous. One consisted of eighteen unscreened tents sited between a highway and an irrigation ditch and arranged around a square that served as a parking lot and garbage dump. The residents hauled their water from a source two miles distant and stored it in barrels rather than drink from the camp's contaminated well. An unenclosed open-pit toilet served all eighteen households. In a typical camp, entire families of as many as ten people crowded into tents measuring twelve by fourteen feet, and many cabins housed two families duplex-style. At least one grower provided barracks, subdivided by partitions, where thirty-six families found shelter. The less fortunate at the camps lived in makeshift accommodations. Dewey Phares spent several miserable weeks in an empty feed-storage tank, the only shelter available at an otherwise full camp near Perryville.[51]

When camps owned by growers or labor contractors filled to capacity, the migrants created squatters' camps along irrigation canals or roadways or in the open desert. The Farm Security Administration found as many as fifty families assembled in one of these improvised camps. In some instances the only shelter available was the family automobile, although many migrants traveled with their own canvas tents. Sanitation was absent. At a camp near Glendale, twelve families used an abandoned sedan body as a privy. At others, garbage and excrement littered the ground.[52]

Migrants who thought they had already hit bottom before leaving home found the filthy overcrowded conditions unspeakably wretched. Maude Higgenbottom, living with her family in a tin duplex with a dirt floor at an Avondale camp, took a peek into the next room through a hole in the common wall. She was horrified to see "a woman picking lice off her children," said her husband, "so we loaded right away and got out as quick as we could get, and headed for [California]."[53] Ruth Criswell and her husband, Albert, had planned to stay for a while in Arizona, where Albert's brother had already found work. But as Ruth later recalled, the tent houses at the camp were "so close together that you could hear conversations going on in the next tent. It had some of the awfullest people. You'd hear such awful language." Concerned about her three young daughters, Ruth told her husband, "I just can't keep my girls in a place like this." So they moved on to California to join another of Albert's brothers.[54] Dust plagued the migrants. A reporter for the *New York Times* noted that dust covered everything in the tents. "The food they ate was heavily seasoned with dust, the air they breathed was laden with it." In an effort to combat the dust, experienced migrants packed boards, sheets of linoleum, or (less effective) rugs to create makeshift floors.[55]

Not all the migrants lived in squalor. Those who were fortunate enough to find work with Cortaro Farms at Marana north of Tucson or at the Hodges or Mangham farms near Perryville west of Phoenix resided in relative luxury. These camps featured tent-houses on wooden platforms and adequate sanitation. One even offered a number of well-built one-room houses with glass windows and screens, and two were equipped with electric streetlights. The model camp at Cortaro Farms provided showers, laundry facilities, and nursing service. Some farm workers avoided the labor camps altogether. About 20 percent of the migrants resided on the outskirts of the cotton towns in inexpensive auto courts and trailer camps where they found somewhat better living conditions worth the rent. But for many, the comforts of a tourist court lay beyond their reach. Most had headed for Arizona with only a few dollars in their pockets. Their median income before beginning their migration that fall had been $224, much of it not in cash.[56]

Once in the Arizona desert, the migrants found the promise of high wages a mirage. Although advertisements claimed that good pickers could harvest three hundred to four hundred pounds per day, fewer than 3 percent of those interviewed by the WPA could pick that much, even though many of the migrants were experienced pickers. Only one-fifth of the families with *two* workers in the field twelve hours a day could meet that standard.[57]

Arizona growers required pickers to remove the seed cotton from the open bolls, keeping the "trash" like leaves and burrs to a minimum. Pickers called it "ginning in the field." "You really had to gin the cotton for them by hand," Ann Stephens recalled. "You didn't get no leaves or trash in it. If you did, you got fired. You didn't leave any cotton in the burr. If you did you got fired. And there was a row boss right there behind you all the time, checking the rows. And if you didn't pick a clean row, you didn't stay in the field. They fired you."[58] A "weigh boss" weighed the cotton and watched as pickers dumped the contents of their sacks into the cotton trailer. "If it had some green leaves in it they'd caution you about it the first time," Sam Cambron recalled. "If you went back the second time with some trash in it you got fired."[59]

To make matters worse, the cotton burrs were sharp and scratched the pickers' fingers and arms. For those used to picking cotton from open bolls, the larger Arizona bolls sometimes made it possible for workers to fill their sacks more quickly. But picking was slow work compared to the harvesting of closed-boll varieties of cotton in Texas and some parts of Oklahoma where laborers snapped the entire boll off the plant. The average worker could harvest only 140 to 175 pounds daily, much less if the cotton was sparse, as it inevitably was toward the end of the season.[60]

Migrant workers pick cotton at Cortaro Farms, near Marana. (Photograph by Dorothea Lange, November 1940, courtesy of the National Archives.)

With such slim pickings, earnings fell far below expectations. At 85¢ per hundred pounds of seed cotton, most pickers' wages ranged from $1.20 to $1.50 per day, the amount an unskilled WPA worker could earn in four hours. Families with one or two members working the harvest, the vast majority, brought in an average of $8.00 to $12.00 per week. That was considerably less than the $24.00 to $37.00 an experienced two-worker family had been led to expect.

Those households with children who were old enough to work alongside their parents of course earned more. The median weekly income for a family with four or more pickers amounted to about $18.00. Some fared much better. Marvin Montgomery and his family of six, picking cotton at Eloy, earned a daily average of $4.50. Like the Montgomerys, about 40 percent of those families with at least four workers in the fields brought in more than $20.00 per week. Although for many families that represented a sizable income, far more than they could have made at WPA work, once the cotton harvest ended, their savings dwindled rapidly. That was particularly true for those who had initially moved on to California only to be driven back by floods.[61]

Moreover, many found hidden costs in working the cotton fields. Employment was not always steady. A picker spent about one-fourth of his time moving from place to place searching for new fields or waiting out rain, according to Floyd G. Brown, secretary of the Pinal County Board of Social Security and Public Welfare. In isolated instances, some growers required workers to purchase groceries at camp commissaries at premium prices. Similarly, according to labor activist Carey McWilliams, those who worked for labor contractors often had to purchase food from the contractor's lunch wagon as a condition of employment. Others were not paid at all. Curtis Eslinger, a picker from Anadarko, Oklahoma, was fatally shot in front of eleven eyewitnesses

Pickers working near Eloy carry their tow sacks, laden with cotton, to the wagon where the sacks will be weighed. One hundred pounds of seed cotton earned a picker 75¢ for a morning's work. (Photograph by Dorothea Lange, November 1940, courtesy of the National Archives.)

after he reportedly resisted efforts to run him off a cotton field in the Buckeye district without his pay.[62]

Low wages and poor housing may have been at the root of the pickers' straitened circumstances, but growers and their agents made little effort to alleviate the situation. Some placed the blame on the laborers. Earl Taber refused to be held accountable for the welfare of his recruits. "Primarily it is expected that these pickers should be self-sustaining," he explained to his executive committee. "Indolence and folly are the chief causes of distress, and this is beyond the control of any one but the individual."[63] Similarly, R. W. Waddell, whose cotton camp had come under the scrutiny of the health department, blamed the conditions of the camps on the migrants. "With the price of cotton down," he admitted to a reporter, "we've had a hard time maintaining camps. . . . However, it's almost impossible to make these people observe rules of sanitation because laws, if there are any, aren't adequately enforced."[64] Public health officials contended that the workers' "ignorance and insanitary methods of living . . . is [sic] one of the most serious problems in preventive health measures."[65]

Regardless of who was at fault, residents of the cotton districts knew well the gravity of the crisis. From one end of the Salt River Valley to the other, civic leaders called for state or federal aid. Others took more direct action. Many residents of Buckeye acted with characteristic charity. The American Legion Auxiliary, headed by Edith Faver, the wife of a leading grower, Fred Faver, conducted a clothing drive. Lucille Beloat, the manager of the Liberty School cafeteria, near Buckeye, and wife of a prominent cattle rancher and farmer, Vernon Beloat, worked with principal Arthur L. Mercer to organize a breakfast and lunch program for migrant schoolchildren funded largely from the school coffers. Local farmer Mary Bales helped make the program a success by donating milk; June Woody, who with her husband, Cleo, operated a small dairy and hatchery, donated eggs; and various farm families pitched in to provide chickens and vegetables. But relatively few cotton growers and none of their organizations took it upon themselves to shoulder the burden of providing economic relief to those who had stooped in their fields. That initiative would have to come from the laborers themselves.[66]

On March 22, 1938, ten days after the crisis became apparent, farm workers demanding food marched to the county relief warehouse. These workers had formed a new alliance with the CIO-affiliated United Cannery, Agricultural, Packing and Allied Workers of America (UCAPAWA). Union organizers E. A. Kope and Louis Flavian had instigated the coalition when they approached a delegation of nearly two hundred cotton pickers, again rallying on the capitol grounds to demand food and medical attention for their families. The organizers then wired UCAPAWA and CIO headquarters in Washington, D.C., claiming that five hundred field workers were picketing the statehouse, "many of them starving to death," and inspired a flurry of telegrams to the governor. That evening, the pickers paraded peacefully through the streets of Phoenix from the CIO hall to the Maricopa County food warehouse. There they were met by county and state relief officials and twenty-eight police officers armed with tear-gas bombs and pick handles. No violence occurred. Instead, relief workers reluctantly doled out rations of vegetables, fruit, dried peas, and rice to the marchers, in accordance with an agreement with the governor.[67]

The following evening, using the threat of mob action as leverage, the union negotiated with the governor to speed aid to the stranded migrants. The police had responded twice that day to quell disturbances by pickers at relief headquarters, and officers had been stationed to prevent further trouble. That morning Kope and Flavian had led a group of more than a score of cotton pickers to the relief office. There they demanded food, threatening: "If we don't get what we want we'll take it."[68] A second disturbance reportedly took place that afternoon, and several score lingered about the statehouse grounds most of the day. In a third incident, a dozen men and women, led by an unidentified man who claimed affiliation with the Relief Workers Alliance, spoke with Governor Stanford, who helped secure food rations for the delegation. That night, as a crowd of unruly men formed at the CIO hall, Stanford summoned the UCAPAWA organizers to his office to review his relief plan with welfare officials, the chief of police, and the commander of the Arizona National Guard.[69] "On condition there is no more mob action and everyone goes home," he told the union leaders, "trucks will be sent out to the camps immediately to distribute food on the basis of investigations made by case workers and according to the need of the different families." Six welfare workers, each accompanied by a state highway patrol officer, would be sent to the cotton camps west of Phoenix to dispense emergency rations. Meanwhile, Stanford pledged to continue to seek funds to return the migrants to their home states. In return, Kope and Flavian promised to disperse the growing mob.[70]

Although the UCAPAWA claimed that its coalition with the migrants marked a turning point in its efforts to organize Arizona's agricultural workers, the union with pickers proved ephemeral. In a last-ditch effort to retain the loyalty of the migrants, Flavian and Kope apparently attempted to arrange for federal aid to be disbursed through the CIO office and made announcements to that effect. Governor Stanford quickly thwarted those plans. Once federal aid arrived, the pickers had no use for unions.[71]

Nevertheless, the brief alliance seemed to realize the growers' worst fears. In late February growers and other agricultural and business leaders in the Salt River Valley, spearheaded by Phoenix cattleman Kemper Marley, had formed the Associated Farmers of Maricopa County to combat organized labor. Cotton growers became prominent, although by no means dominant, among the Associated Farmers' membership and financial backers. Representatives of vegetable-, meat-, and fruit-packing companies; dairies; trucking companies; and agricultural-related businesses formed the core of the organization.[72]

A UCAPAWA-led strike in the lettuce fields of Yuma and the alleged use of strong-arm tactics by CIO organizers in the sheep-shearing camps near Phoenix provided the immediate spark to kindle the protective league, but the cotton industry helped gather the tinder. As early as 1936 Taber had contacted the Associated Farmers of California with the idea of establishing a counterpart. And as events unfolded over the next year, Taber's preparations seemed well advised. A strike led by UCAPAWA organizers at a Higley farm east of Chandler had forced one grower to raise the picking rate to $1 early in the 1937 season. By March 1938, rumor had it that some seventy members of the CIO were encamped along the Salt River below Phoenix plotting to dominate agricultural labor. Moreover, a shipping strike on the Pacific coast and a threatened longshoremen's boycott of Arizona cotton had caught the attention of those in the state's cotton industry. Many growers responded to these threats by throwing their support behind the Associated Farmers. Among the founding members were E. W. Hudson, Jack Bennett, Nat M. Dysart, C. O. Vosburgh, Harry A. Stewart, Fred Faver, Allen Belluzzi, and Walter O. Boswell—all leading cotton growers or ginners.[73]

But long-term support by the cotton industry proved weak. Unlike its California counterpart, whose violence against striking cotton pickers in Madera County became infamous, the Associated Farmers of Maricopa County never brought its forces to bear in the cotton fields, perhaps because the occasion never arose. Conflicts between the Teamsters Union and the trucking industry quickly became the focus of the Associated Farmers' efforts. By July 1938, the directors of the Farm Labor Service suspended monthly $100 payments to Marley's group because of questions about its financial and organizational plans. The Arizona Farm Bureau Federation withdrew its support after the association came under fire from the La Follette Civil Liberties Committee in January 1940. As it turned out, the UCAPAWA had ceased organizing agricultural field workers by 1939. The cotton industry had little need for a strike-breaking union.[74]

Few pickers joined forces with labor organizers, but their disinterest in unions did not mean acquiescence to their working conditions. On some farms, particularly those using labor contractors, scales were set to underweigh the cotton. Pickers protested dishonest scales by adding rocks or clods of dirt to their sacks; other showed their displeasure by walking out of the fields and looking for work elsewhere. Sometimes overworked hands sabotaged equipment. T. L. Cambron, working on C. O. Vosburgh's cotton and alfalfa farm, recalled purposefully running a rock through a piece of equipment to break the machine and thereby get an afternoon off. It was "the first day we'd gotten in forty days. I'd say they made slaves of us, but the thing is, if you didn't want the job, there would be ten more ready to take it." With these individual actions, field workers expressed their dissatisfaction with conditions in the fields. But as Cambron and his fellow laborers knew, the numbers of people desperate for work precluded organization.[75]

As the crisis wore on and the farm workers became more vocal, residents of the cotton districts began to grumble.

Their complaints no doubt reflected the growing presence of the laborers in the cotton towns as the harvest ended and the starving time set in. The *Chandler Arizonan* reported "quite a plentitude of panhandlers annoying the house wives of Chandler, begging for hand-outs, money, or what have you. They come down into the business district, too, and buttonhole men on the streets, and bother merchants who are waiting on customers in stores."[76] Although fewer than one migrant in four had been on relief before coming to Arizona, the Phoenix press began to portray the pickers as freeloaders moving from place to place in their ramshackle automobiles, becoming a burden to communities along the way wherever their cars broke down.[77] One resident summed up this image well when he observed that the migrants clamoring for relief had found Arizona "easy picking."[78]

Demands for relief were rewarded at last by the Farm Security Administration (FSA), which responded with a program to provide "subsistence grants" to distressed farm workers. Once again, however, conflict arose between federal administrators and state welfare officials, who were charged with certifying applicants as bona fide agricultural laborers. The governor and the welfare commissioner, Patrick R. Brooks, expected the migrant families to use their cash grants of $15 to $30 to purchase the food and gasoline they needed for a return trip home. To their dismay, James A. Waldron, the local FSA representative in charge of the program, had different intentions. He made it clear that his agency would not require the migrants to move on. After helping indigent farm workers get back on their feet, the federal program planned to continue to maintain those families wanting to stay in Arizona until the cotton-chopping season arrived three months hence. The grants would provide the unemployed with food, fuel, clothing, shelter, and medical care. Waldron hoped to use the resources of the federal government to create a stable labor force to meet the seasonal needs of the cotton growers and thereby prevent a recurrent tragedy.[79]

Despite resistance from the welfare board, relief for indigent farm workers began to flow into the state. Waldron took responsibility for certifying eligible recipients from Brooks, who protested that the program violated state policy restricting relief to the unemployable. By the end of April, more than 3,500 grants averaging $20 had been distributed, assisting an estimated 13,750 people. The funds triggered an exodus from the cotton districts. Within a week of the program's inauguration, about 30 percent of the pickers had packed up and gone. Still, many stayed. More than 1,700 families remained on the rolls throughout the summer awaiting the next harvest.[80]

Chapter Five

An Industry on Trial

The departure of the cotton pickers in April and May of 1938 brought the acute crisis in the irrigated valleys of central Arizona to a close. Migrant families, revived by FSA subsistence grants, repacked their rattletraps and headed for California or returned home, leaving behind only a cloud of dust.

Their story might well have been forgotten. But the magnitude of the migration of cotton pickers from Oklahoma and the south-central states and the publicity about their plight had exposed long-standing recruiting and employment practices. Growers came under fire from all quarters. Critics in Arizona, Texas, and California launched a volley of complaints against the growers. More important, a series of federal investigations from 1938 through 1940 revealed the exploitative nature of Arizona's cotton industry as well as abuses by federal and state employment agents. Leading the attack on the industry, the La Follette Civil Liberties Committee threatened to impose fundamental changes in labor practices. Fortunately for the growers, the distant sounds of a real war intervened.

At least "slaves were fed," wrote the editor of the *Arizona Labor Journal.*[1] Arizonans criticized the cotton industry for recruiting indigent laborers without providing them the means to support themselves. The low wages paid to cotton pickers, as some residents saw it, led to inevitable hardship. One man remarked that "with the present price of cotton picking in Arizona, I would like to see the picker who is able to earn enough for three meals per day."[2] Few critics were as caustic as the writer for the weekly labor newspaper, for most believed that the farmers simply could not afford to pay a living wage. Still, many Arizonans resented shouldering the relief burden the growers created.[3] "The ones who bring them here should be compelled to take care of them," a Phoenix man complained, "not the taxpayers who did not have anything to do with their coming here."[4] Likewise, relief agencies and private welfare organizations vigorously opposed the annual movement of thousands of cotton pickers into the state.

Opposition to the industry's recruiting practices arose outside the state as well. Fred Nichols, Texas labor commissioner, considered taking legal action against a group of growers from Buckeye whose advertisements for cotton pickers had been broadcast on radio stations in Texas. Similarly, administrators with the Texas State Employment Service complained that labor scouts from Arizona routinely violated state laws licensing emigrant agents. They lodged their complaint in a report to Congressman John H. Tolan of California, whose special committee was investigating the interstate migration of indigents. The Texas officials charged that recruiters for Arizona's growers lured pickers away from the Texas cotton fields with promises of abundant work to swell labor surpluses. Many of these workers returned to Texas later in the season with tales of misery. At the other end of the migrant road, the California State Chamber of Commerce blamed the Farm Labor Service, in part, for the oversupply of agricultural workers in that state. The Chamber called on the recruiting organization to help stem the tide of destitute migrants by discontinuing its activities in the south-central states. Governor Culbert Olson of California censured the Farm Labor Service and called for federal regulation of interstate recruiting activities.[5]

Federal investigators also denounced Arizona's labor recruiting practices. In January 1940 Senator Robert M. La Follette, Jr., pointed an accusing finger at Taber and the Farm Labor Service when he convened his Civil Liberties Committee in Los Angeles to examine charges of labor exploitation in western agriculture. Evidence indicated that labor scouts in Arizona — not California — were responsible for the infamous handbills that had lured agricultural labor westward. Taber's files were subpoenaed and hours of testimony compelled.[6] La Follette, the Progressive senator from Wisconsin and standard-bearer for the working class and the poor, presided over the inquiry, held in a federal courtroom. The proceedings often took on the tone of a trial as La Follette or his fellow committee member Senator Elbert D. Thomas of Utah posed questions to hostile witnesses. Leading the prosecution, as it were, La Follette focused his inquiry, in part, on allegations that Arizona's cotton industry had deliberately inflated the labor supply to depress wages and on the close association between the industry's recruiting arm and the federal Farm Placement Service.[7]

The agricultural labor division of the U.S. Employment Service had already launched its own investigation. The Farm

Placement Service, an agency of the Department of Labor, had been created by the Wagner-Peyser Act of 1933 to assist farm workers in finding jobs. O. D. Hollenbeck, director of the placement service in Washington, D.C., did not take lightly the news that the oversupply of migrant labor in Arizona had been lured with the cooperation of local representatives of his agency. The Farm Labor Service had printed "cooperating with the United States Farm Placement Service" on its letterhead and all its circulars, lending it an added air of legitimacy. Taber's private operation enjoyed a cozy relationship with the federal agency and the Arizona State Employment Service, as Hollenbeck quickly discovered.[8]

On the surface, everything seemed aboveboard. The three agencies coordinated their recruiting and placement activities as provided under the Wagner-Peyser Act; federal and state employment agents assumed responsibility for registering and referring recruits to farms.[9] But state and federal support of Taber's operations did not end with these legitimate functions. The Farm Labor Service shared an office with the two government agencies free of charge, courtesy of the state of Arizona. Far more questionable, Taber used the franking privilege when replying to written inquiries for work. When Hollenbeck learned of this commingling of operations in the summer of 1938, he issued orders that the use of his agency's name and franking privilege cease.[10]

Taber's use of the federal frank caught La Follette's attention. The senator called Ray Gilbert, acting supervisor for the Farm Placement Service in Phoenix, to join Taber at the witness table. In a classic example of La Follette's gift for interrogation, he allowed the witnesses to twist their entanglements of half-truths and evasions, baiting them with his wry wit before trapping them with their own words in black and white.[11]

Taber and Gilbert testified haltingly, apparently uncertain of the information that might be revealed in subpoenaed correspondence. Taber at first hedged that he was "not sure" whether he had used the franking privilege. La Follette refreshed his memory by introducing into evidence a letter from Taber to his executive committee. In the letter Taber reported the operational changes mandated by Hollenbeck: "We have just completed a setup with the State and Federal Employment Services to continue our working arrangements . . . with some modification of our using their names in our advertising and correspondence. This will require us to pay postage on our replies to inquiries instead of using their franking privilege, which will boost our cost for postage some."[12]

Taber and Gilbert, unnerved by the disclosure, attempted to pin responsibility for the impropriety on each other, lending an air of comic opera to the proceedings. Did Gilbert know about this franking privilege? La Follette queried. Gilbert's answer: "He never had no franking privilege." When asked to repeat his statement, Gilbert clarified that Taber had not been authorized to send franked mail.

Turning to the other man, La Follette inquired: "Well, do you remember who authorized it, Mr. Taber?"

"Yes, sir. Mr. Gilbert did," Taber replied, provoking laughter from the spectators in the courtroom.

Each man then cautiously revised his story, careful to avoid incriminating himself. Lewis Irvine, director of the Arizona State Employment Service, interjected that responses to out-of-state inquiries had been signed by a state employee, someone authorized to send franked mail. Taking his cue, Taber confirmed Irvine's account. La Follette remained skeptical, but he put aside the question of ethics and turned to issues of supply and demand.[13]

Labor experts Malcolm Brown and Orin Cassmore of the Works Progress Administration framed the central argument of La Follette's probe. Their study of migratory cotton pickers in Arizona had been one of a series of reports on agricultural laborers throughout the region. After examining a multitude of economic factors and interviewing hundreds of migrant workers, Brown and Cassmore concluded that the growers deliberately recruited an oversupply of labor to depress wage rates.[14] "A good many of them were on the point of starvation," Cassmore testified, describing the condition of the migrants when he arrived in Arizona in early 1938 to begin his survey. Cassmore maintained that the advertising campaign had been unnecessary and created needless hardship for farm workers, profiting the growers and gins. During his visit to Arizona he observed masses of cotton pickers in dire straits. "We found, I may say, that the primary cause of this difficulty was that these people have been recruited here in excess of the labor requirements."[15]

Cassmore believed that the crop could have been picked with about half as many workers. The harvest had peaked in early December with an estimated 37,000 cotton pickers in the fields. If Arizona's growers had been less eager to harvest the crop quickly and had spread the harvest evenly over the season using a constant supply of workers, Cassmore argued, only 16,000 to 20,000 pickers would have been needed. Growers had hired about half this number from the local labor force, and an estimated 13,750 farm workers would have come to the state without the campaign — a sufficient number to pick the crop. The presence of as many as 17,000 excess workers meant less work and less money for all and contributed to the misery at the end of the season, Cassmore contended.[16]

Cassmore gave little credence to the industry's point of view. Apprehension had shadowed the labor-recruiting campaign. At harvesttime the demand for labor on Arizona's cotton farms could increase by almost 700 percent. Growers always feared a shortage, particularly at the beginning of the season. The expansion of cotton acreage in 1937, which doubled the previous labor requirement, had heightened the growers' usual anxiety.

Indeed the pace of the harvest had lagged behind that of previous years. By the first of December, only about half of the cotton crop had been ginned, compared to nearly 70 percent the year before. Furthermore, the harvest was not the leisurely undertaking that federal critics implied. The growers felt compelled to pick the cotton as quickly as possible to keep lint grades high and protect the market value of the crop in a year of rapidly falling commodity prices. Growers had increased their cotton acreage in 1937 based on expectations of a stable price of 12¢ per pound of lint. By the beginning of the harvest, nationwide overproduction caused the price to crash to less than 9¢ per pound. Moreover, rural sociologist Elzer D. Tetreau would later argue that the industry needed nearly 75 percent more harvest workers than actual demand since, he maintained, the average cotton picker from the south-central states worked only about three and a half days per week. Tetreau contended that poor work habits, including an unwillingness to toil more than necessary to scrape by and nighttime drinking binges, kept many migrants from putting in full workweeks. He added that cotton pickers also spent time out of the fields looking for work, better pay, or better working conditions.[17]

By mid-November, however, the growers knew that sufficient labor would be available to harvest the crop. At that point, according to federal critics, the Farm Labor Service should have announced that no more workers were needed. But as jalopies full of migrant families continued to roll into the cotton districts, little was done to stop the influx. On Taber's advice, the federal and state employment services continued to refer all new arrivals to the fields.[18]

Taber's defense—that his campaign ended in mid-November—was disingenuous, or at least naive. It denied the inherent lag involved in the relocation of families, whom he preferred by his own admission. Moreover, the sustained appeal for thousands of cotton pickers created an image of an infinite number of jobs, as it was calculated to. Taber had predicated the entire campaign on the idea that the need for pickers would be spread by rumor. It was a pipeline with no cutoff valve.[19] When the flow did not stop, Taber shifted the blame to the workers. Much of the distress in the cotton fields, he told his superiors, was "caused by people coming in here too late in the picking season" and by the migrants' "indolence and folly."[20]

Taber's critics maintained that low wages, not indolence, caused the migrants' distress. Even Arizona's newly elected governor, Robert T. Jones, admitted that a migratory agricultural worker in his state could not earn "enough to maintain himself and his family according to our American standards of living."[21] Orin Cassmore testified that the oversupply of labor made it possible to complete the harvest while offering lower wages than those paid in California, where pickers earned an average of 95¢ per hundred and even more during the second picking. Had the Farm Labor Service been unsuccessful in soliciting a large labor force, Cassmore argued, earnings would have risen.[22] Furthermore, wages in Arizona were even lower than they appeared. At first glance, Arizona's wage scale ranked among the highest in the nation, second only to that in California. Yet in Texas and parts of Oklahoma, where the wage ranged from 10¢ to 20¢ lower than in Arizona, differences in the varieties of cotton enabled workers to pick at a faster rate, making their earnings somewhat higher.[23]

Cassmore had little evidence, however, to support the contention that depressing the wage rate had been the specific goal of the recruiting campaign. At the beginning of the 1937 season, growers throughout the Salt River Valley had met, as they customarily did, to establish a uniform wage and thereby discourage competition between growers. In setting the rate at 75¢ per hundred (the same rate as the previous year's despite a 26 percent decrease in the price of cotton lint), the growers considered the lower profit margins of the smaller operations as well as the prevailing wage in California. Yet labor supply did influence the rate of pay. Wages rose in October, when the supply lagged, as growers broke ranks from the "fixed" rate in competition for pickers. But once they established a higher rate of 85¢, the growers did not lower it, even during the subsequent deluge of workers. The practice of bidding the price downward as workers competed for jobs, reported in California, apparently did not occur in Arizona.[24]

More likely, the intent of recruiting surplus labor was to discourage unionization. Valley growers, fearing that a shortage of pickers could give labor the upper hand, kept an uneasy eye on the situation. In 1936 Taber had confided to John Phillips of the Associated Farmers of California: "It has been very quiet here . . . as far as labor troubles go, but we are on our toes all the time looking for anything that might arise. Through under-cover operatives who serve other interests here in this state, we keep constantly advised of the movements of Communist [CIO] leaders."[25]

With the presence of UCAPAWA organizers in the Salt River Valley in 1937, the cotton industry had more reason than ever to fear widespread labor unrest. Taber endeavored to withhold information from the press regarding the labor shortage and wage differentials, which could be used to provoke strikes. His diligence paid off. "So far as we know," he reported in December of that year, "there has not been any labor disturbance of consequence in the cotton camps. We have suppressed all newspaper publicity about picking conditions that has been requested from us, which we believe is the very best policy."[26] The continued influx of poor migrants from the south-central states would have undermined any effort by cotton pickers to protest their working conditions, even without media censorship. The inverse relationship between the supply of labor and worker unity did not escape the pickers. As the Mexican consul in Phoenix informed labor activist Carey McWilliams, the growers constantly warned the local Mexicans that "unless they toe the line 'we'll bring in more Okies.'"[27]

The debate Cassmore created over the relationship between labor supply and wages obscured a crucial point. The profitability of cotton throughout the United States depended on low wages to compete in an international market with Asian crops. The sharecropping southern states, which produced more than 90 percent of the nation's cotton, helped keep the wage scale low. In Arizona, harvest labor alone accounted for about 30 percent of the total cost of producing short-staple cotton. Moreover, any increase in wages had a threefold effect on the cost of producing lint since wages were based on the gross weight of seed cotton, which netted less than one-third lint after ginning. Arizona growers also had to cover an expense unknown to southern farmers—the cost of water to irrigate their farms. In the Buckeye Valley and parts of the Casa Grande Valley, where farmers had to use electrically pumped well water, irrigation accounted for almost 30 percent of production costs. Unable to lower their fixed costs of production, the growers protected their profit margins in the face of plummeting prices by paying labor as little as possible.[28]

However, Laurence Hewes, regional director of the Farm Security Administration, suggested to La Follette that low commodity prices were no excuse for exploiting workers. "Labor is one of the factors of production in industrialized agriculture, along with several other factors," he testified.

"The proprietors of these other factors are not asked to subsidize the industry, and there seems to be no logical reason why agricultural labor should take up the slack. Obviously, the industry cannot expect, for instance, a power company to accept a rate for power which would force such a company to operate to the verge of bankruptcy. . . . Consequently, the statement that the industry cannot pay higher wages cannot be accepted in good faith if labor is to be regarded as one of the real, permanent factors of production of this major industry."[29]

In his final report, La Follette censured Arizona's cotton industry, especially its recruiting practices, for exploiting migrant labor. His chief concern was the supportive role played by government employment agencies. In effect, he observed, the government had subsidized the Farm Labor Service by underwriting some of its operating costs. The senator took an especially dim view of the way the federal and state employment services handled referrals. In his opinion, Ray Gilbert of the federal Farm Placement Service and Lewis Irvine of the Arizona State Employment Service had contributed directly to the maintenance of low wages by failing to verify Taber's estimates of the numbers of pickers needed in the fields.[30] Indeed, the senator concluded, the record disclosed that "the public employment services in Arizona, financed by Federal funds, have been prostituted to the selfish purposes of those who seek to maintain an oversupply of cheap wage labor."[31]

However, La Follette's report had little effect on Arizona's cotton industry. For Taber and his colleagues, the probe had proved disconcerting, but to their relief, it resulted in few changes. The investigation had managed to illuminate a problem but failed to solve it. Circumstances frustrated La Follette's ability to institute new labor practices in agriculture. The senator called for a variety of reforms to improve the working conditions of agricultural laborers, including the regulation of private recruiting, adequate housing, and equal protection under the laws governing wages, unemployment compensation, and collective bargaining. But to no effect. Recruiting practices and low wage rates continued as before despite the outcry.[32]

True, the U.S. Farm Placement Service and the Farm Security Administration expanded programs initiated in the wake of the crisis. For a brief time, the select few who secured shelter in government camps found their lives improved. But no legislation emerged to redress the fundamental economic issues. By the time La Follette issued his report in 1942, World War II had intervened, offering jobs in the munitions industry, and the migrants from Oklahoma and the south-central states had left the fields. Congress turned its attention to more pressing matters than the workaday world of cotton pickers. And in the cotton fields of Arizona, age-old patterns remained unchanged.

Chapter Six

Migrant
Communities

In the spring of 1938 the federal government created a new partnership with the Arizona cotton industry, an uneasy alliance that continued until the Second World War. Federal agencies, particularly the Farm Security Administration (FSA), assumed an active role in caring for migrant farm workers and to a degree monitoring their numbers. The FSA introduced an ambitious plan to address the problems created by the massive migration from the south-central states to Arizona and California. By erecting migratory-labor camps and cooperative farms and providing relief funds, emergency rations, and medicine to those without legal residency, the FSA hoped to nurture the field workers and transform them from downtrodden migrants into upstanding citizens.

These well-meaning programs, born of necessity, had a double edge. On one hand, the federal camps became temporary havens for thousands of migrant families who continued to pour into the Salt River and Casa Grande valleys. There families could find respite from the hardships of migratory life and perhaps gain a toehold until they could make a home of their own. But in effect the federal programs subsidized Arizona's cotton industry to an extent far greater than La Follette had found so objectionable. They relieved many of the growers of any sense of obligation to provide for the well-being of their workers. They allowed the industry to continue business as usual.

"The Less It Is Discussed the Better"

Well-established recruiting patterns continued as before despite the watchful eye of New Deal emissaries. Indeed, disaster might have occurred again in the cotton fields in 1938 and 1939 had it not been for intervention by federal officials and local welfare administrators. Reinstatement of crop controls under the second Agricultural Adjustment Act had reduced the Arizona cotton crop in those years to nearly half that of 1937, thereby decreasing the demand for labor, while the forces expelling tenant farmers from Oklahoma and the south-central states continued with renewed vigor. An uncontrolled recruiting campaign could again have produced an overabundant supply of workers with its attendant social problems.[1]

Criticism of the 1937 advertising campaign and supervision by federal administrators encouraged Taber to modify his recruiting practices somewhat. As the director of the cotton industry's major labor-recruiting arm, Taber ostensibly cooperated with the efforts of federal officials to prevent a recurring calamity in the cotton fields by restricting the supply of migrant workers. "You can be sure of our fullest cooperation at all times," he wrote O. D. Hollenbeck, director of the U.S. Farm Placement Service, in the fall of 1938, "[since] it is the desire of this organization to handle our work to the most benefit of the farmers and the laborers and with the least distress and confusion to these transient workers."[2] But often, it seemed, Taber's cooperation was mere subterfuge. Confiding to the manager of a Buckeye gin, he warned: "As you probably know, we meet heavy resistance from the public, Government Officials and others on our advertising so the less it is discussed the better."[3]

The limits of Taber's cooperation quickly became apparent. At Hollenbeck's insistence, he agreed to restrict his newspaper advertising to the adjacent states of New Mexico and California. But when Hollenbeck suggested that Taber issue counterpublicity in late October to discourage continued migration from the south-central states, Taber resisted. The number of harvest workers was already sufficient, according to Lewis Irvine, director of the Arizona State Employment Service. Nonetheless, Taber insisted on waiting until the end of November to discourage workers from seeking employment in Arizona, by which time more than half the crop would be ginned. He refused to announce that the fields were full until abundant labor could be ensured. In an apparent veiled reference to the possibility of labor strikes, Taber told Hollenbeck that the danger in issuing counterpublicity "before the situation fully justifies it is that we might all get in bad if we should have something turn up that we do not know of at this time." It was the old refrain. Hollenbeck and Irvine therefore took the matter into their own hands and asked the state employment services in Oklahoma, Texas, Arkansas, New Mexico, and Colorado to tell their unemployed to stay home.[4]

The following year, new procedures, apparently implemented under pressure from Hollenbeck, called for closely coordinating recruitment activities through the offices of the various state employment services and the Farm Security

Administration. Taber (acting through Ray Gilbert, the local farm placement supervisor) issued "clearance orders" for a seemingly specific number of workers ranging from 500 to 1,500 to employment agencies and farm placement services in Oklahoma and other states. Newspaper and radio advertisements advised potential recruits to contact their state employment agencies, making it possible to regulate the number of migrants to correspond closely with labor demand. Implicitly, Taber's clearance orders assured that a job awaited each referral.[5]

But this time federal officials were wary of Taber's cooperative veneer. When he requested thousands of cotton pickers from California, Oklahoma, and the south-central states, officials in the Labor Relations Section of the FSA initiated an unofficial inquiry to determine the validity of the requisition. The FSA had felt betrayed the previous year, when in an effort to regulate the supply of agricultural workers in the Southwest and California the agency had assumed the role of labor dispatcher. Offering $10 transportation grants, FSA officials had encouraged migrants to relocate from areas glutted by workers to areas with reported labor shortages. In Arizona the results had proved exasperating. After the FSA had sent only 125 workers to the state in response to a request for 2,000 pickers from California, the agency received word that the migrants could no longer find employment. Understandably, then, the FSA looked upon this new request with skepticism. Officials sifted through conflicting reports about whether Taber had asked for 8,000 out-of-state pickers or only 3,000, which reflected actual need. This question was never clearly resolved, but the scrutiny must have hindered Taber's recruiting efforts.[6]

Meanwhile, welfare officials in California endeavored to retard the number of harvesters whose migratory routes needlessly crisscrossed the California-Arizona border in search of work. Ray Gilbert's requisition for 1,500 pickers issued to the California Department of Employment, along with a companion request from W. V. Allen, farm placement supervisor in Los Angeles, to supply gasoline to relief clients who wanted to make the trip, triggered an investigation by the California State Relief Administration. Welfare officials there conferred with the new commissioner for the Arizona Department of Social Security and Welfare, Harry W. Hall, who—balking at the prospect of having thousands of potential relief clients dumped on his state—maintained that there was no labor shortage in Arizona.[7]

Gilbert subsequently retracted his clearance order, evidently at Hall's behest. "We do not under any consideration want any of the people on the rolls of the Farm Security Administration or the State Relief Administration in California referred to the state for cotton picking," Gilbert advised Allen in an apparent contradiction of previous arrangements. "The only pickers we want referred out of your state are those who are in [a] position to come here under their own power and who when the cotton is picked out will be able to return to their homes under their own power. . . . We definitely do not want people who have to have funds advanced them in order for them to get here."[8] Recruitment through official channels in California thereby came to a virtual halt. As Allen confided to Taber, the position taken in Gilbert's letter, coupled with the inherently low harvest wages, "practically stymies us for, as you know, all cotton pickers are prospective relief clients within ten days after the cotton picking jobs are over."[9]

"A Restoration of Hope"
The FSA sought to encourage those who had already made the journey westward to remain in the Salt River and Casa Grande valleys while it endeavored to discourage the migra-

tion of indigent farm families from Oklahoma and the south-central states by curtailing Taber's operation. The retention of a resident population of seasonal harvest workers, administrators reasoned, would solve the perennial labor shortage and make recruiting efforts unnecessary. With this goal in mind, officials created an assortment of programs designed to relieve some of the hardships during the harvest and sustain the cotton pickers through the slack season.

The first of those programs, subsistence grants, gave sustenance to thousands of migrant families in the Salt River and Casa Grande valleys. Inaugurated in Arizona in late March 1938, the program had originally provided stranded migrant farm workers with small sums to purchase food and other essential goods such as fuel and clothing. These cash grants could make the difference between survival and misery, even for those who earned a hard day's pay in the fields. The relief rolls of the Farm Security Administration recorded the inadequacy of the picking wage and the overabundance of field labor. Even at the peak of the 1939 harvest, caseworkers found it necessary to provide assistance to nearly two thousand migrant families.

By that time, the FSA had modified the subsistence program. Most families waited until they were absolutely destitute before seeking this aid, partly because the grants carried the stigma of the dole. Consequently, the delay of a week or more while bureaucrats in San Francisco processed information and issued checks proved far too long. Already malnourished children cried with hunger. The FSA responded in September 1938 by replacing the cash grants with a commodities program for the most part. Caseworkers at each of the commissaries scattered throughout the cotton districts distributed food, soap, and other commonly needed items such as blankets, tents, stoves, shoes, and jackets to eligible families. The commodities program not only provided a greater number of provisions to needy families at less cost to the taxpayer since goods were purchased wholesale; it also decreased the opportunity for migrants to "chisel" the government or squander their money, as occasionally happened.[10]

For the migrants, however, the commodities program could be cumbersome. Although the FSA attempted to locate the commissary depots in the major cotton communities, many migrants had to travel as far as twenty-five miles to obtain their bimonthly allotment. When they arrived, they sometimes had to wait in line for hours before the warehouse staff could serve them. And the sacks of surplus foods containing rations of flour, corn meal, cereal, beans, dried fruit, bacon, shortening, peanut butter, sugar, syrup, cocoa, coffee, and tins of milk, tomatoes, and meat did not always suit the migrants' palates or offer a truly balanced diet. Some migrants got around the system by selling commodities to obtain the cash to purchase foods more to their liking.

The food stamp program, introduced by the Department of Agriculture in 1940, eliminated that problem. Certified migrants, as well as Arizona residents on relief, received orange food stamps to purchase edibles of their choice at any grocery store, bakery, or butcher shop. Blue commodity stamps were good for designated surplus foods, including eggs, butter, pork, flour, dried beans, fruit, and lard.[11] Commodity stamps seemed like charity, but sometimes they were a family's only means of survival. J. C. Harris arrived with his family just before Christmas of 1939 without a dime to his name. To make matters worse, it rained for three weeks, bringing the cotton harvest to a standstill. "It was the only time my family was ever on what you might call welfare," his son Mo recalled. "We got government food stamps. But as soon as we started picking cotton, why we quit getting them." Having to accept public assistance made the family feel "really, really bad."[12]

The FSA continued to issue cash grants for special programs. At Liberty School in the Buckeye Valley, the agency began funding the breakfast and lunch program that had been inaugurated at the height of the 1937–38 crisis and thereby helped the school continue to provide free hot meals to migrant children. In the cotton districts of the Casa Grande Valley, Hamilton N. Keddie, acting FSA grant supervisor for the area, developed a school-lunch program for migrant youth in 1940. At that time, school cafeterias were privately operated, and few migrant families could afford the cost of a prepared meal. To ensure that students received proper nourishment, the federal agency made cash grants of $3 per month per student to pay for the food. Local charities and agencies like the National Youth Administration donated the additional labor necessary to provide for the 450 eligible students. For those attending schools without lunchrooms, the cash grants could be used to purchase lunches from stores or restaurants. School superintendent R. A. Holy observed that the program markedly improved the health and academic performance of the students participating in the program.[13]

The subsistence grant programs, initially designed to meet the exigencies of the crisis in the cotton fields, quickly became an integral part of Arizona's cotton economy, a virtual unemployment-benefits package sustaining much of the work force from harvest to harvest. At the end of the 1938 season, the FSA relief rolls swelled to more than 3,800 migrant farm workers and their families, nearly two-thirds remaining under federal care until the next season. The following year, the caseload more than doubled, to about 10,000 families from Oklahoma, Texas, and Arkansas, representing a rising proportion of the total force of pickers.[14]

Although the subsistence grants helped to feed indigent farm workers, health care remained a persistent problem.

William P. Shepard, president of the Western Branch of the American Public Health Association, declared that aside from California, Arizona had the most severe migrant health problem in the West. In the winter of 1938–39 a smallpox outbreak in a growers' camp at Casa Grande spread throughout the district, as did an epidemic of typhoid fever. The smallpox epidemic cost Pinal County an estimated $10,000.[15] Even the *Arizona Producer* admitted that "every [labor] camp is more or less of a health menace to the entire community."[16] Nonetheless, the state health department, although empowered to aid nonresidents in emergency cases, provided no health care for transient agricultural workers.

In an effort to meet the medical needs of the migrant workers, the FSA developed a second program, the Agricultural Workers' Health and Medical Association. The nonprofit corporation, introduced to Arizona in November 1938, provided emergency and routine health care for those not entitled to the county and state programs available to legal residents. Migrants suffering from injury, disease, illness, or malnutrition and pregnant women needing prenatal care could visit one of the FSA clinics established in Phoenix, Chandler, Tolleson, and Buckeye or make use of a physician-referral service in Coolidge. Public-health nurses and local physicians, working in rotation, staffed the clinics and when necessary referred patients to private hospitals that had agreed to charge specific low rates. The migrants made a written pledge to repay the cost of the treatment as soon as they could. The clinics also provided vaccinations in an effort to prevent the sporadic outbreaks of communicable diseases that plagued the cotton districts.

The Arizona clinics (including the one in Yuma) treated nearly 35,000 cases in the second year of the program. In the Casa Grande Valley the financial burden for this program was shared by Pinal County, which hoped not to repeat the epidemic of 1938–39. The county established a twenty-six-bed hospital ward in the Lincoln Hotel at Casa Grande. By 1942, the FSA relieved the county of that responsibility and offered full medical services at Cairns general hospital at the Eleven Mile Corner migrant camp. The government hospital offered agricultural workers top-quality care at little or no cost. Naomi Durant, for example, gave birth to her second son at the Cairns hospital, and the FSA took care of her private doctor's fee. Together, the hospital, health clinics, and subsistence grants nurtured the mass of migrant workers.[17]

By far the most ambitious effort to address the needs of the workers, however, was the federal housing program created for migrant families. The Farm Security Administration adopted a variety of approaches to provide decent housing for migrant workers in Arizona. In 1939 and 1940 the agency opened "model" farm-labor communities on the outskirts of Somerton, near Yuma, and in the Casa Grande and Buckeye valleys. Mobile units were established in 1940, as well, in recognition of the shifting population of seasonal workers over the course of the harvest.

The administrators who designed the federal housing developments hoped to build demonstration projects to encourage a higher standard of shelter at grower-owned camps. Federal migrant camps could accommodate only a small fraction of the migrant population. Consequently, the general quality of migrant housing could improve only if growers themselves came to recognize the value of decent housing in attracting and retaining productive workers. But the government envisioned the camps as models in more ways than one. Idealistic New Dealers at the FSA viewed the permanent camps as tools of social reform: through these camps the FSA would bring the ignorant former sharecropper and tenant farmer from the backwater into the mainstream of American life.[18]

The Agua Fria farm-labor camp, constructed on the outskirts of Coldwater fourteen miles west of Phoenix near the
Agua Fria River, was the first such facility in Arizona. It
served the cotton pickers and other agricultural laborers
working in the environs of Avondale and Litchfield Park.
Planning for the camp, similar to those already operating in
California, began in late 1937. When the facility opened in
the spring of 1939, it provided housing for as many as 210
families; within months, an enlarged camp could accommodate 351 families, or as many as fifteen hundred people.

The camp offered two basic types of housing. A select
group of permanently employed farm laborers and their
families set up housekeeping in fairly substantial three-room
ranch-style cottages called Labor Homes, complete with
private indoor bathrooms and small garden plots. Most
families, however, lived in small fourteen-by-sixteen-foot
dwellings constructed of sheet metal with wooden or concrete floors. Although spare, these cabins were far superior to
the shacks the migrants themselves erected or the quarters
provided at most grower-owned camps. The FSA even tried
to effect a homey look: each prefabricated standing-seam
metal cabin was painted blue and featured a shaded four-foot
concrete porch in front. Unfortunately, in Arizona, where
temperatures generally remained above 100 degrees in the
shade from May through September, the sun could turn the
steel dwellings literally into ovens. To provide the migrants a
measure of comfort during the broiling summer months, the
houses had hinged sections on either side that could be
raised for ventilation.[19]

The camp resembled a small planned community set
against the backdrop of the Sierra Estrella. If the Agua Fria
Farm Workers Community appeared aesthetically sterile,
row upon monotonous row of sky-blue cabins shimmering in
the Arizona sand, it was nonetheless neat and orderly. A

The Agua Fria camp was the first in the federal program to provide cabins instead of tents. Unfortunately, they were ill-suited to the desert. In the summer the metal cabins became solar ovens. (Photograph by Russell Lee, May 1940, courtesy of the Library of Congress.)

The Agua Fria camp resembled a small, planned community, with rows of small, metal cabins. The camp also provided water pumps, bath houses and lavatories, a laundry, a community center, and a health clinic. (Photograph by Russell Lee, May 1940, courtesy of the Library of Congress.)

group of administrative buildings just inside the entrance gate included the camp manager's office, which also served as a gatehouse, and the manager's residence. A small health clinic, staffed by a nurse, and a dozen isolation units nearby for patients with communicable diseases completed the administrative complex.

The metal residences, arranged in a hexagonal pattern, surrounded a cluster of communal buildings. This central complex of modern sanitation and hygiene facilities included a bathhouse for hot showers and several lavatory buildings with flush toilets. A large community building offered space for social and educational activities, a library with several hundred volumes, sewing rooms, and a laundry with electric washers and large washtubs. A nursery cared for resident children while their parents worked in the fields, and in 1941 the workers established a cooperative store. The camp had its own water system and sewage plant, and electric light standards lined the oiled streets. Hydrants, one for every three or four houses, supplied water for drinking, cooking, and washing dishes. Migrant families, many unaccustomed to such amenities, found the camp a welcome refuge.[20]

A second camp, at Eleven Mile Corner, provided an oasis for 377 workers and their families, as many as eighteen hundred people. This model community, which opened in March 1940, was strategically situated on a section of desert amid the cotton fields of the Casa Grande Valley, eleven miles equidistant from Casa Grande, Coolidge, and Eloy. Migrant families working in the area could avail themselves of a variety of accommodations, including 215 steel cabins on concrete slabs, 78 concrete tent platforms, and 36 trailer spaces. Anyone fortunate enough to land a permanent job on one of the farms in the area could rent one of 48 Garden Home apartments. The two-story stucco-frame apartment buildings could house six families each and offered modern conveniences such as electricity, indoor plumbing, and air-cooling units.[21]

Those migrants who secured shelter at the federal labor camps found an opportunity for security hitherto unknown on the migrant road. As long as they were able and willing to work, they could remain for a year, though most stayed only a few months. For a fee of only 10¢ per day, a family had the use of a clean leak-proof cabin and all the camp amenities, including burial insurance, free health care, and beginning in 1941 free care at the Burton Cairns Convalescent Center, a small general hospital constructed at the camp. Unlike grower-owned camps, usually available only during employment at a particular farm, the FSA camps welcomed the unemployed. Those unable to pay the nominal fee were asked to work one hour per day helping to maintain the camp. But increased opportunities for wage employment proved a part of camp life. The hundreds of families residing in the federal camps formed a ready labor pool for the growers whenever the need arose.[22]

The camps meant more than sheltering or caring for the physical needs of the workers. Oliver M. Heflin, the kindly manager of the Eleven Mile Corner community, maintained that the purpose of the camp was to "rehabilitate" the migrants. And by that, he said, "I mean a restoration of hope." Heflin believed that his role was to nurture the social, educational, moral, and spiritual well-being of the migrants. The vicissitudes of life had profoundly affected the outlook of migrant farmers. By providing security, the FSA could renew the migrants' faith in the future. "Men and women," Heflin observed, "who, because of the depression and changed economic conditions, neither of which can they be held responsible for, have lost their homes and farms and have had to leave the places of their births and wander halfway across a continent and back time after time in order to get work by

which to live miserably, sometimes in the cold, rain and mud
and at other times in heat and dust, without the simplest
means of sanitation, or even decent cleanliness, cannot but
have become depressed and discouraged." The FSA camps
held the promise of transforming the downtrodden. "It is
hoped," he continued, "that a few months in one of the camps,
where they can be clean and happy and see their children
receive everything that normal boys and girls have, will
restore their hope—rehabilitate them psychologically."[23]

In Heflin the farm laborers encountered a man with empa-
thy. Typically the position of camp manager attracted young
idealists from urban backgrounds for whom the migrants often
seemed curiosities. But Heflin hailed from the south-central
states. Born in Missouri, he had been raised by his widowed
mother in Tyler, Texas. As a young man, he had served a stint
in the army, participating in the punitive expedition against
Francisco "Pancho" Villa under General John J. Pershing and
fighting in France during World War I. On returning home,
he had entered Southwestern Theological Seminary in Fort
Worth where he earned a bachelor's degree. With the advent
of the New Deal, Heflin was drawn into welfare work in
Arizona, where he had lived since 1927. He served for a time
with the state Board of Social Security and later as supervisor
of the FSA grant office in Casa Grande.[24]

The federal program of moral uplift that Heflin brought to
Eleven Mile Corner had its origins in the social-work movement of the Progressive Era, which sought to transform poor
urban immigrants into Americans with middle-class values.
Social reformers in the Farm Security Administration viewed
the migrants from Oklahoma and the south-central states
much like latter-day immigrants: backward, superstitious,
and culturally deficient. The migrants spoke in a quaint
dialect; consumed a strange diet of beans and cornbread,
black-eyed peas, grits, biscuits and gravy, and fried dough;

and practiced curious, enthusiastic religions. Moreover, in an age of interdependence, they tenaciously adhered to beliefs in individualism and self-reliance. Unlike Heflin, who recognized that the migrants were simply people long accustomed to living in rural poverty, some of the more paternalistic New Dealers viewed them as cultural anomalies. One purpose of the camps, then, was to acculturate the migrants into the modern American patterns of life—to teach them, for instance, the rudiments of good hygiene and nutrition and promote organized group activity.[25]

At the heart of the Eleven Mile Corner camp, literally and symbolically, stood the multifunctional community center. It was here that the acculturation program took focus with entertainment, educational programs, arts and crafts classes, and religious services. The large stuccoed bungalow-style structure featured a central auditorium flanked by reading rooms and classrooms. A wide old-fashioned fireplace lent the building "a homelike charm." When the folding doors to the side rooms were opened, the enlarged assembly hall could seat the entire population of the camp. At one end of the hall, a stage with dressing rooms accommodated theatrical productions. This area could be closed off by folding doors to convert it into a more intimate space for luncheons, banquets, club meetings, Sunday-school classes, and movie screenings. Meals could be prepared in the adjacent kitchen equipped with an electric range. Outside, a wide, recessed porch across the east facade provided a cool gathering place in the summer months.[26]

Under the guidance of the community managers and the governing camp councils, the camps at Eleven Mile Corner and Agua Fria came alive with activity, particularly in the summer months when work was scarce. Semiweekly motion pictures, especially Westerns and tales of military heroics, attracted large crowds. For a nickel or a dime, one could see

Tex Ritter on the *Utah Trail* or the *Cheyenne Kid* shoot-em-up. Children romped on the playground, equipped with swings, seesaws, and slides. The farm workers entertained themselves with amateur nights, dramatic productions, pie auctions, taffy pulls, treasure hunts, and box suppers. These entertainments attracted farm workers who lived elsewhere. On at least one occasion, Slim Rutledge and Roy Roper of Eloy performed on piano and guitar at the Eleven Mile Corner amateur night. And the "11-Mile Camp News," a regular column by camp resident Mary Swindell that ran in the *Casa Grande Dispatch,* encouraged readers to attend dances, amateur nights, and movies. Swindell often reported "lots of out of camp visitors."[27]

In various ways the camp managers endeavored to introduce new patterns of group activity to the migrants' lives. Most of the programs they developed had an educational focus. Lectures on health, first aid, family planning, and hygiene became a regular feature with such topics as "The Care of Children," "Baby Spacing," "Cleanliness and Sanitation," and "Keeping Our Camp Grounds Clean." Children and teenagers could participate in Girl Scout and Boy Scout troops, 4-H Clubs, and Young Peoples Clubs. And the Woman's Club at Eleven Mile Corner hosted home economics programs on such subjects as the art of rug making, led by an FSA home management supervisor.

Women at the camps banded together to assist their fellow migrants. At Eleven Mile Corner, the Woman's Club sponsored committees on camp aid, the nursery school, and social activities, which they financed by selling kerosene to the residents of the camp and staffing a booth at the community center where their fellow migrants could purchase drinks and confections. The Agua Fria community's "Camp Aid ladies" lent homemade quilts to those who needed them and provided food, lamp oil, and children's clothing to particularly needy families. Clubs and educational programs, however, while important to those who participated, attracted relatively few of those living in the camps.[28]

By far the most popular activities involved country music. The strong preference for old-fashioned fiddle music, cowboy singers, and Western swing bands reflected the origins of the migrants in Oklahoma, Texas, Arkansas, and Missouri, the so-called fertile crescent of country music. Music helped to bond the workers and reinforce cultural ties with their home states. Square and round dances featuring resident and visiting musicians and singers drew capacity crowds each week. Teenage boys and girls from miles around came to court and dance to fiddle music and Western swing. Weekly amateur nights also provided a showcase for those migrants with dramatic or musical talent. Accompanied by some combination of guitar, fiddle, banjo, mandolin, accordion, piano, or harmonica, the workers sang songs from the country radio stations, traditional Ozark folk songs, songs of poverty, songs of the migrant road.[29]

One musical group became a regular attraction at Eleven Mile Corner. The Weatherford Family String Band, which made its first appearance at the camp in the fall of 1941, was billed as being "well known as radio musicians in all the major centers of Oklahoma and Arkansas." The band's return to the farm worker community in June 1942, following a radio engagement with station KADA at Ada, Oklahoma, was the biggest news of the week. "From the day that their big cabin trailer came in the gate," reported the camp column in the *Casa Grande Dispatch,* "camp activity has taken a decided spurt." The Weatherford family played engagements throughout the Casa Grande Valley, including the Resettlement Club at Casa Grande Valley Farms and the Twenty-One Club in Coolidge as well as the weekly dances at the Eleven Mile Corner community center.[30]

The most popular social events at the camps involved country music. The strong preference for fiddle music, cowboy singers, and western swing bands reflected the origins of the migrants in Oklahoma and the surrounding states. Here the Agua Fria camp orchestra plays for a Saturday night dance. (Photograph by Russell Lee, May 1940, courtesy of the Library of Congress.)

Sports were also popular at the labor camps. Boxing and wrestling matches drew big crowds. And at a tri-camp "field day" between the Agua Fria, Eleven Mile Corner, and Yuma camps, about one thousand people watched various sporting events, including baseball, basketball, volleyball, foot races, boxing, croquet, and horseshoes. The migrants fielded boys' and girls' softball teams and boys' baseball clubs, which went to bat against school teams in the surrounding towns and teams from growers' camps and other federal camps. The ballclubs fostered camp pride and created increased opportunities for the farm workers to interact with the larger community. The Eleven Mile Corner baseball team played Casa Grande High School, Coolidge High, and the black team from Coolidge. The camp's volleyball team played area schools, and the Agua Fria basketball team joined the Palo Verde City League and competed against teams in Avondale and Litchfield Park.[31] The transience of the farm workers, however, could make it difficult to retain a winning team. After the Eleven Mile Corner baseball club scored a string of victories, the camp newspaper reported that "six of our ball team boys left Monday morning for California, but we hope to find some more good players to take their places until they come back."[32] Sporting events, musical entertainments, dances, and motion-picture shows broke the monotony, the drudgery of day-to-day existence in the cotton districts, but they created only a semblance of real community.

Holidays afforded a special opportunity for camp administrators to lighten the hearts of the migrants and impart a sense of belonging. At Agua Fria, about five hundred people, the entire population of the camp, turned out in 1939 for the Independence Day fireworks display and an evening of entertainment. About three hundred children hunted Easter eggs in 1941, and the camp's Halloween masquerade party that year attracted about four hundred camp residents and another one hundred people from outside the camp, who played games and danced to music by a WPA orchestra from Phoenix. At Eleven Mile Corner, the camp marked its first Christmas with a special celebration. The women of the camp decked a large tree and created a multitude of handmade toys—an assortment of dolls, hobbyhorses, and drums—which Santa Claus distributed to wide-eyed girls and boys. The following year, the Christmas for One-Third of the Nation committee, headed by actor Melvyn Douglas in Hollywood, assisted in underwriting some of the costs of the celebration.[33]

These diversions helped to reawaken the spirit of the pickers from the south-central states. Still, for many, the most important revivals took place not on the playing field or in the dance hall but in the church. Observers noted that on the whole, the migrant population was profoundly religious. Most of those from Oklahoma, Texas, Arkansas, and Missouri placed their faith in fundamentalist, evangelical religions, particularly the Southern Baptist church and to a lesser extent the Southern Methodist, Pentecostal, Nazarene, and Adventist denominations. On Sundays the camp community center became a house of God. Within a month of the opening of Eleven Mile Corner camp, the residents started a Sunday-school class, a Baptist young people's group, and a Tuesday-night prayer meeting. In the summer, children ages five through sixteen could attend Vacation Bible School at the camp. For a time, visiting ministers from nearby Baptist churches, affiliated with the Pinal County Ministerial Association, conducted services at the community center on Sunday afternoons. The camp had its own pastor by 1942, working under the direction of the nondenominational Migrant Gospel Fellowship.[34]

The Eleven Mile Corner camp also had its own school. At first, when the camp opened in March 1940, children and

Children living at Eleven Mile Corner camp attended classes at a school built by the Farm Security Administration. (Photograph by Russell Lee, February 1942, courtesy of the Library of Congress.)

Hot lunches are served to children at the federal Agua Fria camp school. (Photograph by Russell Lee, May 1940, courtesy of the Library of Congress.)

teenagers were bused to public schools in Casa Grande. But by the beginning of the fall term, the more than two hundred elementary students living at the camp were too many for the school district to accommodate. Consequently, J. J. Bugg, Pinal County superintendent for public instruction, arranged for a grammar school at the camp staffed by a principal and four teachers, who conducted classes in the community center. There the pupils learned music, handicrafts, and vocational agriculture in addition to the three R's. In 1941 the FSA constructed a sprawling building for the Eleven Mile Corner School.[35] Principal L. N. George found that the children did well despite having generally started school one year later than Arizona students. "The mentality of the children is fully equal to that of those who attend school every school day of their lives," he assured a reporter, "and they adjust themselves quickly to the grades." Moreover, segregation eliminated some of the social problems that sometimes occurred in the public schools, where children fresh out of Oklahoma and the south-central states suffered the taunts of their classmates. "No more than ordinary problems of discipline among them ever come up," George observed. "In fact, they seem a little more tractable than the average."[36]

One of the chief goals of the FSA migrant program was to eliminate the strong sense of individualism characteristic of the migrants from the south-central region. The program would reshape the migrants by instilling in them a collectivist spirit, teaching them to subordinate their individual interests to the commonweal. The official names of the camps, typically known as Farm Workers *Communities,* signified the approach by which reformers proposed to remake the antiquated agricultural worker.[37] The preamble to the standard constitution for each FSA camp further captured the idealistic republican vision the New Dealers held for their experiment:

> WE, THE PEOPLE OF THE _____ MIGRATORY LABOR CAMP, IN ORDER TO FORM A MORE PERFECT COMMUNITY, PROMOTE THE GENERAL WELFARE, AND INSURE DOMESTIC TRANQUILITY, DO HEREBY ESTABLISH THIS CONSTITUTION FOR THE _____ MIGRATORY LABOR CAMP.[38]

Democratic decision making lay at the foundation of the FSA experiment in community. At the Farm Workers Communities, camp councils governed migrant life, at least theoretically. The camps were divided into several residential units, each with its own council selected by popular vote at biannual elections. Women as well as men participated in camp government, at least at first. Each council was responsible to the camp management for the proper conduct of its subdivision. The combined unit councils constituted a general camp council, which determined how the moneys in the camp fund were spent; enacted and enforced rules and regulations regarding community safety, sanitation, and health; assigned maintenance chores to camp residents; and held at least token responsibility for developing educational and recreational programs. The general councils were also vested with the power to eject residents from the camp for failing to cooperate with fellow camp members. A community court consisting of a panel of "judges" selected by the members of the council arbitrated disputes between camp residents.[39] Heflin, the manager at Eleven Mile Corner, maintained that the council functioned as an autonomous governing body. He pledged not to take part in the deliberations of the council or interfere in any way in the government of the camp "as long as the requirements of good government" were met.[40] Nonetheless, if the experience of the Arizona camps was anything like that in California, paternalistic managers guided the councils to make "correct" decisions on matters of importance, leaving only trivial issues to the migrants.[41]

In a more aspiring effort to foster communal living at Eleven Mile Corner, the FSA created the Garden Homes tract in 1940. The Garden Homes, like the Labor Homes at the Agua Fria camp, were developed to encourage farm workers to settle down and improve their standard of living. But the goal encompassed more than stability. Those families who made their homes in one of these four-room partially furnished apartments participated in an experimental cooperative venture, first introduced by the FSA in 1938 at Chandler Part-Time Farms in the Salt River Valley. Residents of the Eleven Mile Corner Garden Homes apartments became members of a corporation, which leased the apartment complex from the government and a tract of land somewhat less than three-quarters of a section. The members farmed this land collectively part-time, growing vegetables, alfalfa, and assorted cash crops and keeping chickens and a herd of dairy cows.[42]

New Dealers envisioned the farm as something like a hybrid producers' and consumers' cooperative combined with the familiar practice of sharecropping. On their days off and during slack periods, association members worked the farm for cash wages, which circulated back to the corporation in payment for the apartment rent and food. They also filled their larders with vegetables from the garden free of charge. The FSA, as the mortgage holder for the cooperative, took a 25 percent share of the cash crops toward payment of certain operating expenses, including the lease on the land and interest on the government's operating loan for improvements (the corrals, barns, and silo, for example), livestock, and farm implements. The corporation sold the balance of the produce to its membership, the transient workers living at the Eleven Mile Corner labor camp, and the general public.

Members received the profits of these sales as an annual patronage dividend, prorated on the basis of their consumer purchases. However, the FSA conceived of the farm as a means for providing food and economic stability for the members, not as a source of income.[43]

This experiment in cooperative farming got off to a rocky start. Few of the farm workers who wanted a Garden Home qualified for the program, and those who did meet the requirements generally chose to live elsewhere for various reasons. The FSA limited participation in the cooperative venture to those who held year-round jobs on privately operated farms, working as irrigators, tractor drivers, and so forth. Moreover, an applicant had to be largely self-supporting, depending little on FSA grants, and able to afford the monthly rent of $8.20. Soon after the Garden Homes became available, Heflin reported that he could find no qualified applicants since most inquiries came from families who depended on the FSA for at least two-thirds of their income.

Nearly one year later only three farm workers and their families had settled into the forty-eight-unit apartment complex. The camp staff, including a group of girls working for the National Youth Administration, occupied another twenty-two units, and the rest remained vacant. Not until 1942 did the apartment complex become fully occupied and then only because the FSA had begun to allow a handful of families who did not work on farms to rent the apartments. Most permanent farmhands in the Casa Grande Valley chose to live in fairly substantial wooden or adobe houses provided by their employers. Although often inferior to the FSA apartments, which provided cooling units and indoor plumbing, these grower-owned houses offered two important advantages: they were close to the fields, and they were free.[44]

Casa Grande Valley Farms, the most ambitious of the cooperative farms conceived by New Deal administrators, proved somewhat more successful. Located midway between Coolidge and Florence, the farm occupied a 4,200-acre tract bordered on the north by the Gila River, which supplied irrigation water when it was available. The Resettlement Administration, precursor to the FSA, devised the experimental project, which began in October 1937, to test a number of new approaches to farming. The agency conceived the program in an effort to bring agriculture into the twentieth century and rid farming of a host of social and economic ills. Through an agricultural cooperative, the reformers in the Resettlement Administration believed, farmers would be able to compete with commercial agribusiness without acquiring a large indebtedness. They could achieve a richer existence by living in a village type of community rather than on isolated homesteads, and they could work more efficiently and receive an adequate wage for their labors. The cooperative farmers raised cotton as a cash crop, along with wheat, barley, and hegari. They also raised chickens, hogs, and cattle and operated a dairy, selling butchered meat, chickens, eggs, and milk to people in the surrounding community.[45]

Unlike a true producers' cooperative, however, where the workers controlled the means of production, the "settlers" worked under the paternalistic guidance of the federal government. The settlers had relatively little voice in the farm's operation, declarations by FSA administrators notwithstanding. A five-person board of directors, elected among the settlers, purportedly governed the cooperative, but the FSA made sure that the directors followed the agency's lead. The agency rather than the members created the corporate charter and bylaws, designed to protect the government's financial interest as much as to create a democratic government for the association. Federal administrators carefully selected member families, choosing those with ambition and relatively good farming experience, character, and health. Furthermore, a farm manager employed by the FSA and paid from corporate income supervised farm operations. In theory the cooperative members were to learn the fundamentals of modern industrial farm management through an agricultural collective. But in essence they functioned more like hands on a profit-sharing corporate farm. Nevertheless, according to Ewell Bennett, a settler at the cooperative, it was a "very good setup" that offered farmers an opportunity to learn new approaches and a chance at success. The farm proved increasingly profitable over the years, but the experiment ultimately failed, the result of a combination of factors, including declining political support for experimental New Deal programs, federal paternalism, some members' dissatisfaction with working conditions, and factionalism.[46]

Nonetheless, the residents of Casa Grande Valley Farms reaped the benefits of a generally improved standard of living. Many of the settlers had been destitute before joining the cooperative. Quite a few had come to Arizona as migrant pickers during the crisis season of 1937–38. Of the fifty-six families living on the farm in 1940, thirty-three were headed by former farm laborers. Nearly three-fourths of the settlers were from the south-central states, although not all of these had come for the cotton harvest: eighteen originated from Oklahoma, twelve from Texas, and eleven from Arkansas. Many of these families had been unable to secure adequate shelter on their meager wages as agricultural laborers. Ernie Bates, a former tenant farmer from Oklahoma, had moved to Arizona for his wife's health. When he signed up for the Casa Grande project, he was living in a tent in a cotton field looking for work. Martin King and his family, who had come from Texas in response to a handbill calling for cotton pickers, had been sleeping in a tent. George Cole, an Arkansas sharecropper who had come to Arizona for the 1937 cotton harvest, had last dwelt in a one-room shack without doors on the edge of a cotton field. Even Raymond Bowles and his family had been forced to make do with a two-room shack on a canal bank, despite the success of the former Oklahoma sharecropper and butcher in securing a steady income from a local dairy, which his wife and children supplemented by picking cotton.[47]

For these settlers, the Casa Grande cooperative offered an elevated standard of living and a renewed sense of self-esteem. Farm produce, available at cost, kept a bounty of food on the table. The men earned a steady income, which amounted to the prevailing wage for year-round farm labor, although it was less than some had been led to expect. They resided with their families in a cluster of small stuccoed adobe houses with concrete-block floors and galvanized-iron roofs. Screened porches provided a cool sleeping room in the summer, and the latest household appliances lightened the women's domestic chores. An adobe community center included a large hall for meetings, educational programs, and social affairs; a fully-equipped kitchen; a library; and sewing rooms. It even housed a nursery school staffed by the WPA and the National Youth Administration, making it easier for mothers to work outside the home or run errands without worrying about the children.[48]

The cooperative housing program, however ambitious, served only a handful of the workers who migrated to the cotton fields of central Arizona. Hundreds more found shelter at one of the FSA's mobile labor camps. After developing permanent housing facilities for the pickers, administrators with the FSA discovered the importance of proximity to the principal cotton fields under harvest, which shifted across the valleys as the bolls ripened. "A difference of a few miles in location may mark the difference between good occupancy and poor occupancy," Laurence Hewes observed.[49] To address this problem, in 1940 the agency created three mobile camps for Arizona, two in the Casa Grande Valley. Each ten-acre camp consisted of two hundred tent platforms and tent houses, privies, a number of trailers containing showers, a medical clinic, the camp manager's office and residence, and a power plant to provide electricity. When necessary, the mobile units were moved by trucks and trailers, but it required about ten days to disassemble and reassemble one of these camps. One of the so-called mobile units at Eloy became sufficiently permanent to acquire the name Friendly Corners.[50]

Administrators with the FSA viewed the agency's multifarious housing and subsistence program as a way to accomplish a number of goals. The program would break the dependence of the cotton growers on a migratory labor force, retain a sufficient supply of pickers in Arizona and thereby eliminate the need to import thousands of out-of-state workers each year, and create a more humane environment for those seemingly trapped by the harvest cycles. Growers generally embraced the program as a cost-free subsidy. The government housing projects, subsistence grants, commodities programs, and medical care in essence lifted the responsibility for the welfare of migratory workers from the shoulders of the agricultural industry.

In Arizona, growers praised the FSA camps, at least at first. That welcome contrasted sharply with the response in California where agribusinessmen viewed the camps as hotbeds for union organizing. An editorial in the *Arizona Farmer-Producer* noted that regardless of how well founded the suspicions in California may have been, "no such sentiments are heard in Arizona. The FSA's first Arizona camp, in the Avondale district, has been welcomed. . . . Everyone admits the deplorable lack of adequate housing for seasonal laborers and feels that the Government is partially filling a real need." Significantly, representatives from the Maricopa County Farm Bureau helped select the site for the Agua Fria camp.[51] In the

Casa Grande Valley, some growers considered the Eleven Mile Corner camp less of an asset. This negative opinion reflected problems with the location of the camp rather than the idea of federal housing. The growers thought the mobile camps to be of considerably greater value.[52]

The difference in attitude between the growers of Arizona and California toward the FSA housing program stemmed in part from the high regard of local residents for those administering the FSA programs in Arizona. The *Arizona Farmer-Producer* described James Waldron, state administrator for the FSA, as a man who "always means what he says and always knows what he is talking about."[53] Similarly, when R. A. Faul, a local farmer, was named manager of the Casa Grande Valley Farms, the *Coolidge Examiner* noted that the FSA had chosen wisely: "He has had the wide experience required to manage an enterprize of this kind," observed the editor. "He understands the actual problems of farming in this valley, and he knows what can be accomp[l]ished by co-operative methods."[54] The difference in attitudes from those in California may also have reflected the absence of an agricultural union in Arizona's cotton fields.

Furthermore, those on the FSA rolls formed a pool of workers ready to serve the growers when needed. At the beginning of the 1938 picking season when more than 1,700 migrant families remained on the subsistence rolls, the growers had a record-breaking supply of "local" pickers to begin the harvest. The following winter, growers in the Gilbert area turned to the FSA to recruit some 1,000 to 2,000 volunteers to eradicate the pink bollworm from heavily infested lands. Once the migratory camps and part-time farms were established, the government encouraged growers to contact the project managers to fill their labor needs. In numerous ways, then, the FSA programs helped the growers as well as the migrant workers.[55]

To a limited degree, the government also succeeded in extending its influence beyond the gates of the FSA camps and helped further improve the lives of agricultural workers. The manager of one of the mobile camps near Casa Grande observed that the federal housing program had inspired several growers to provide wooden cabins with concrete floors. The previous year, he claimed, a majority of the harvest workers in the area had lived in FSA camps rather than in the poorly equipped growers' camps. "The farmers found only one fault with this," he reported, "which was the fact that pickers could pick where they pleased and had no obligation to the grower." As a result, workers tended to stay on a farm only as long as the picking was good, then move to another farm with better cotton. By providing a nicer camp, some realized, a grower could attract a nucleus of workers who had to pick for him as long as they lived in his camp.[56] The *Arizona Farmer-Producer* proclaimed, with some exaggeration, that growers had improved their housing for migratory laborers in recognition that those who furnished the best shelter had their pick of the available workers.[57] But many observers recognized that the standards for migrant housing remained generally low. At least one leader in agricultural circles believed that the solution once again lay with the federal government. Rural sociologist E. D. Tetreau proposed to develop improved housing through a system of federal subsidies to all farm operators employing seasonal laborers.[58]

Most growers, Tetreau knew, failed to follow the government's example in providing improved housing for the cotton pickers. As a consequence, most migrants continued to live in squalor. The federal housing program served only a fraction of the migrants who streamed into the cotton fields of central Arizona. Many families chose not to live in the federal camps, which carried the stigma of the dole and remained

distant from major cotton fields. And even at their peak the
FSA camps could house only 1,266 families. The rest continued to live in growers' camps, commercial cabins, or ditch-
bank camps. Most growers' camps still consisted of tents
pitched on the open desert or small one-room cabins with
earthen floors and no lights, laundry or bathing facilities, or
proper garbage disposal.[59] The son of a Casa Grande Valley
grower later recalled that many of the camps in the area "were
filthy. I mean they'd just stink. When you'd go in there . . .
they'd just stink so bad you couldn't breathe hardly."[60]

An FSA survey of labor camps west of Phoenix extending
from Gila Bend to Tolleson was telling. The study revealed
that only three of the seventy-one grower-owned camps were
in excellent condition. One of these was for long-term workers like machinery operators, and the other two combined
had only twenty-eight cabins. About one-third of the camps,
primarily in the Avondale area, appeared to be in good shape.
Most of the camps, 58 percent, were deemed only fair. In
some instances the investigators may have been quite lenient
in bestowing that rating. At one such camp, garbage was
hauled from the site only once per year; at another, the
inspector noted that the dilapidated houses were "ready to
fall down." Those camps rated poor—17 percent, generally
clustered in the vicinity of Buckeye and Perryville—were
virtually indistinguishable from squatters' camps. Although
Miller's Camp near the Buckeye Gin had a capacity for more
than one hundred people in its five subdivided barns and
four tents, the garbage had not been removed in more than
one year. The inspector tersely described Abbott's Camp
south of the Buckeye Gin, a small camp without toilets, as
"very undesirable" and the Percy Camp near Perryville "a
regular hog pen."[61]

A similar picture emerged from surveys of other cotton
districts. In the East Valley, investigators found that more

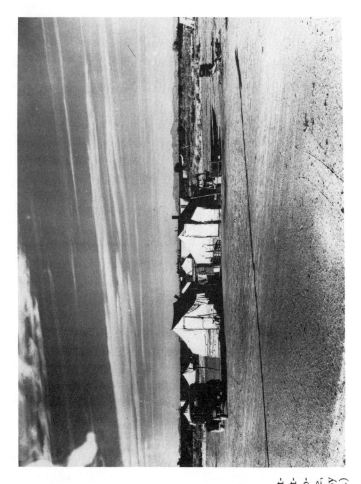

A grower's camp for cotton pickers on the outskirts of Eloy. (Photograph by Dorothea Lange, November 1940, courtesy of the National Archives.)

than one-third of the ninety-three grower-owned camps were in poor condition, principally in the vicinity of Gilbert; most were small camps with improvised toilets. A handful of these were owned by major agribusiness interests, including Goodyear, Dobson Ranch, and the Tovrea Company. Fewer than 10 percent appeared to be in good condition, and only one attained an excellent rating. Growers in the Casa Grande Valley apparently kept their camps in somewhat better shape. Of 286 camps in the area extending from Maricopa to Marana, only five were in unsatisfactory condition, lacking the most basic sanitation facilities. J. H. England owned three of those camps; one contained fifty tents, yet toilets were merely improvised.[62]

The grower-owned camps dotting the Salt River and Casa Grande valleys became in effect small villages, numbering as many as 150 tents. Farm folk accustomed to relative isolation or small-town life found themselves suddenly thrust into what amounted to urban slums. Privacy was almost unknown. With little distance between tents, conversations between husbands and wives could be heard by all, and at night shadows played on the walls.[63] Rosie Laird recalled that the J. C. Pennington camp near Buckeye "covered about a twenty-acre block of just nothing but tents—close enough together that all the room you had was to park your truck or your car in between your tent and the next tent."[64] Crowding and poverty strained tempers, often intensified by drink, sometimes resulting in ugly domestic disputes that could flare into violence.

For some families, the camps provided their first introduction to the unsavory aspects of lower-class culture long present in urban America. Drunkenness, gambling, fights, and prostitution made the camps frightful for many migrants.[65] Ruth Criswell recalled seeing "some single men just travelling around making more money with their gambling than anything else" at the Buckeye Valley camp where her family stayed. Warned that a couple of girls had been raped one night on their way to the privy, she would not let her daughters out of the tent alone after dark. "It's terrible when you have to live that way." But, as she explained, "We just had to stay there long enough to get a little ahead."[66] To fifteen-year-old Dorothy Price, a labor camp outside Phoenix seemed a cesspool of humanity, which she poignantly described in verse:

> The sun rises
> The hovel stifles
> The floor   a mattress
> Toilets run over
> Garbage heaps high
> Flies swarm
> Mosquitoes hum
> Children cry
> People hungry
> They couple and couple.[67]

A kind of class system developed in the larger camps, the more stable, hard-working, sober families often segregated from those who were more transient and those considered "riffraff." Workers who with a combination of ambition, persistence, and luck landed permanent jobs as irrigators, tractor drivers, and general hands and thus remained beyond the end of the harvest season formed the upper crust of the labor camps. If more substantial housing was not available, growers typically favored these families with two or three tents or cabins clustered together to create a more homelike environment, one tent serving as a kitchen and dining room and the others as bedrooms. At the bottom of the social scale, and the back of the camps, were those derisively referred to by the other camp residents as "transients," families who made frequent moves from farm to farm looking for greener pastures. Growers further segregated the camps by race and

ethnicity, putting Hispanic or African American workers in
separate camps or in separate sections at the insistence of the
white migrants from the south-central states.[68]

Whatever their social status in the camps, residents lived
depressingly similar lives as they struggled to survive. By day
a comparative stillness came over the tent cities as most adult
men and many teenagers and women, often taking their
young children with them, went into the fields. A few
enterprising women and their older children earned extra
money by outfitting lunch wagons and selling sandwiches,
hamburgers, hot dogs, milk, candy, and soft drinks to those
who toiled in the cotton. Back in the larger camps, peddlers
came through two or three times a day hawking vegetables
and fruit culled from local packing houses. When the laborers returned in the evening, the smell of kerosene and
burning wood wafted through the air as women prepared
meager dinners for their families and perhaps a handful of
single men boarding at their tables.[69]

Weekends offered a respite from the usual routine. On
Saturdays, after a half day of work in the fields, women
scrubbed the laundry against washboards, and family members bathed by turns in washtubs filled with water heated
over open fires. They then piled into trucks and cars and
headed to town to purchase groceries for the next week and
perhaps take in a motion-picture show. For Dennis Kirkland,
music became the highlight of Saturday visits to Casa Grande.
He and his father and brother would join others from camps
throughout the area for hoedowns in front of Joe Ackerman's
junk shop near Main Street. There the elder Kirkland and his
son Wilbur would play fiddle for the crowd, or father and
sons might listen to guitar pickers W. D. and David Durant,
Oklahoma Choctaws working on Charlie Pate's farm.[70]

Just as music reinforced cultural ties, so did religion. On
Sundays in some sections of the cotton district, itinerant

preachers came to the camps to preach the gospel. In the Buckeye Valley the "Cotton-camp Missionary," led by Rev. J. J. Frost and Albert C. Stewart, ministered to the cotton camps. Affiliated with the American Sunday School Union and financially supported by area churches and a handful of growers, they held services in tents and small wooden chapels. In some instances a preacher from the ranks of the cotton pickers themselves would offer Sunday sermons in a makeshift tent church. Others founded their own congregations. In 1931 a group of Pentecostal families from Oklahoma living in a cotton camp north of Palo Verde began holding prayer meetings in the camp. By the next year, attendance had become so great that a large shed was required to accommodate the worshipers. Four years later, when the migration of Oklahomans and others from the south-central states was in full swing, throngs of believers crowded into the Fisher Theater, and soon they founded the First Assembly of God Church. Throughout the cotton district, religion helped migrant families endure and forge long-lasting bonds.[71]

"Coolidge . . . the New Capital of Oklahoma"

As the Depression decade drew to a close, the continued stream of farm workers from the south-central states changed the complexion of the Arizona cotton districts. As early as 1936, nearly all of the non-Hispanic farm laborers not native to Arizona had come from Oklahoma, Texas, Missouri, and Arkansas. By the end of the decade, nearly one-third of the farm workers settled in southern Arizona were newcomers who had migrated to the state since 1935, mostly from the south-central region. Although the newcomers amounted to fewer than 3,900 farm laborers, they represented one-fifth of the population engaged in agriculture in southern Arizona.[72]

For most of the pickers from the south-central region, Arizona served merely as a way station.[73] Many families heading for California or other points west stopped for one or two seasons en route. For others, Arizona was simply one of several points along an established seasonal loop between their home states and California. A sizable number of agricultural workers, according to E. D. Tetreau, shuttled from Oklahoma and Texas to Arizona and California, taking their families with them wherever they went. Still others returned home for good, perhaps disillusioned by their experience in the West or full of longing for red clay and familiar faces.[74] A Bureau of Agricultural Economics survey of schoolchildren in January 1940 shed light on the transient residency of many agricultural workers in the state.[75] More than one-fourth of the farm labor families who had arrived in Arizona during the previous year expected to move: of these families, more than half intended to go on to California, 17 percent planned to return to Texas, and 11 percent thought they would head back to Oklahoma.[76]

The migrants who stayed in Arizona were similar in many respects to the larger agricultural population, particularly those who operated farms. Many of the migrant workers, some 40 percent, had been farm owners or operators (mostly tenant farmers) before coming to Arizona and shared the basic outlook of their employers. They accepted the social order that structured Arizona's farm society. At the top stood the large-scale farm operators, and below were the smaller farm owners, tenant farmers, farm managers, permanent hands, and seasonal laborers. Most of the migrants who had fallen to the bottom rung hoped to climb back up the ladder and some day, perhaps, own a farm of their own.

Moreover, the newcomers and their employers shared a cultural identity. More than half of Arizona's farm operators had originated in Oklahoma, Texas, Missouri, Arkansas, or the South, and by the mid-1930s almost one-third of the heads of all agricultural households had come from the

south-central region or New Mexico. Missouri natives had
long populated rural Arizona, and many residents of the
cotton districts had come from Texas beginning in the
mid-1910s and from Oklahoma in the mid-1920s. These
settlers had established a strong religious tradition in their
adopted state by the time the vast wave of migrants from the
south-central region arrived. Most were Baptists. In the
Buckeye Valley, the First Baptist Church of Buckeye and the
Palo Verde Baptist Church had been founded around the turn
of the century, and in the mid-1920s worshipers had organized the First Southern Baptist Church. Such cultural connections helped the migrants identify with their employers.[77]

The migrants were most dissimilar from resident farm
laborers. The principal difference was ethnicity: 50 percent
of the laborers in the Salt River Valley and 55 percent of those
in the Casa Grande Valley were Mexicans or Mexican Americans born in Sonora or southern Arizona. Native-born non-
Hispanic whites constituted only 37 percent of the farm
workers in the Salt River Valley and 33 percent of those in the
Casa Grande Valley, yet almost all of the migrant pickers,
some 97 percent, were white. Language and religious bar-
riers, along with residential segregation, divided these two
segments of the population.[78]

Although most of the migrants lived apart from the larger
agricultural community, at least until they settled down, they
were not wholly segregated from the people of nearby towns.
Much of the contact was informal. Men went to Casa Grande,
Coolidge, Buckeye, or Avondale for a drink or a game of
pool.[79] Those living at the Eleven Mile Corner or Agua Fria
camps, largely self-contained communities, took part in
structured activities designed to provide opportunities to
socialize with people outside the camps. Sporting competi-
tions in particular brought those in the FSA camps in contact
with residents of the surrounding towns.

Nevertheless, the newcomers did not blend easily into the community. Social stigma accompanied poverty. Few migrants and their children had the proper clothes to feel comfortable attending local churches or public schools. Even those living in well-established cooperative farming projects found it difficult to fit in. One woman at Casa Grande Valley Farms confided to a visitor: "I don't like to go to Coolidge even to church. Those people dress better, act a little different, and they just speak a different language than we do here. . . . I feel out of place there."[80] Intertwined with these tokens of poverty was the association of the pickers with popular images of sharecropping and the rural South. The WPA characterized the prevalent attitude toward the migrants as akin to racial prejudice, and indeed Arizonans associated the work of picking cotton with Mexicans, long racially disparaged in the Salt River Valley. But class was the principal demarcation line—class tinged with regional stereotypes.[81]

Many Arizonans regarded the migrants as "poor white trash," characters who had stepped off the pages of the novels of William Faulkner and Erskine Caldwell. When the touring production of the popular stage version of *Tobacco Road* played the Orpheum Theatre in Phoenix, the newspaper repeatedly asserted that Caldwell had portrayed a typical family of sharecroppers or tenant farmers.[82] Such stereotypes reinforced prevalent attitudes. One unnamed grower described the migrant farm workers to a WPA investigator: "You know they are poor white trash. They are naturally improvident. When they get some money, they spend it, blow it in. Then they wind up here broke, instead of going back home where they belong." Another grower observed: "Cotton-pickers have a gypsy streak in them. They like to wander. There isn't much you can do for people like that."[83]

For some locals, the migrants who drank and gambled on street corners each Saturday night colored their image of so-called Okies. One grower's son, then a teenager, recalled that Casa Grande's business district gained such a rough reputation that housewives "wouldn't go near downtown" on Saturdays.[84] A state official grumbled: "Look at how they have ruined the pretty little town of Chandler. It used to be a clean and decent place before the cotton pickers came in."[85] Others resented the invasion of the migrant hordes. Walter C. Smith, a Pinal County supervisor, complained to the Tolan committee that the migrants arrived in droves. "Then followed the 'in-laws' and the 'outlaws' and whole families descended upon us until the little town of Coolidge has become known as the new capital of Oklahoma."[86]

Such opinions were not necessarily universal. Many growers, depending on the cotton pickers for their own economic security, treated the migrants with a large measure of tolerance.[87] "I don't agree with those who say our pickers are undesirable," asserted one farmer. "They are fine people, and we give them a good living."[88] Some merchants also welcomed the farm workers. When the Eleven Mile Corner camp opened in 1940, the *Casa Grande Dispatch* ran a full-page advertisement: "Greetings and Best Wishes to Management and Residents of 11-Mile Camp from the People and Business Houses of Casa Grande."[89] Still, a woman living in Chandler, apparently not a cotton picker, complained indignantly to a local newspaper, "I hadn't been in this country a week when my neighbor told me confidentially that I must never admit that I came from Oklahoma, or folks would 'poke fun at me.'"[90] People often made jokes at the Oklahomans' expense. A standard joke held that you could always spot rich Okies: they were the ones with *two* mattresses strapped on top of their jalopies.

Schoolchildren suffered particularly from being treated as social outcasts. The children of farm laborers were generally older than their classmates and thus conspicuous. Rural children in Oklahoma tended to enter school a year later than students in Arizona. More than half did not begin attending school until they were between the ages of seven and nine. Moreover, migrant children changed schools frequently as their parents moved from harvest to harvest, and many stayed out of the classroom to work in the fields, despite laws to the contrary. As a consequence, the children of migrant workers, particularly those from the west south-central region, remained two years behind on average. Local schoolchildren taunted those who lived in the labor camps, wore bib overalls, or spoke with an Oklahoma twang.[91]

For Dennis Kirkland, such disdain made schooldays in Casa Grande almost unbearable at first. "Calling an Okie an Okie," he remembered, was "the closest thing to calling you a cuss word."[92] Kirkland eventually won acceptance from his classmates, but some children of pickers responded to prejudice by fighting or avoiding school altogether. Ellis Marshburn of the Home Missions Council observed that "migrant children, the equals of residents in intelligence and ability, are snubbed by classmates; become bitter, pugnacious, and trouble-makers who soon drift away from schools much to the relief of everyone."[93] Marshburn's observation notwithstanding, officials at some schools welcomed the migrant children. Members of the Avondale School District Board invited the students living at the Agua Fria camp to attend public schools, saying they considered the children "a desireable element of the community, which by no means should be segregated."[94]

Indeed prejudice against the migrants from the south-central states never reached the level in Arizona that it did in California's San Joaquin Valley, where a public official labeled the Okie a "subspecies" and a sign in a motion-picture theater commanded "Negroes and Okies Upstairs."[95] Apparently no such blatant expressions of hostility surfaced in the

Salt River and Casa Grande valleys. The pejorative "Okie" did not appear in the press; the migrants were always described by occupation. The origins the migrants shared with much of Arizona's agricultural population likely mitigated flagrant bigotry. Fred Faver, for example, a prominent grower and Missouri native, lived with his family in a cluster of tents near Palo Verde at the beginning of his successful farming career. "I've often thought," his daughter Flora Davis observed in retrospect, "maybe that made us look at the people differently because we came from kind of that way, you know. Not exactly like the migrant workers, but something like that."[96] The fairly small population of newcomers from the south-central states also helped keep overt hostility to a minimum. Relatively few destitute Oklahomans and their fellow migrants from Texas, Arkansas, and Missouri decided to settle in Arizona, compared to the burgeoning population of California's Central Valley. The newcomers posed little threat.[97]

Still, increasing numbers of agricultural migrants from the south-central states decided to transplant their roots in the Arizona sand. Of the 2,204 farm-labor families included in the BAE survey in 1940, more than four out of five had arrived in the state since 1936, and 84 percent had no plans to leave. Some had managed to distinguish themselves as hard-working, reliable employees and land one of the few year-round jobs available on farms. And many of those whose relatives had encouraged them to come to Arizona had used their connections to secure work as permanent hands. Phineas Leatherbury, a former Oklahoma tenant farmer, came to pick cotton on a farm owned by his uncle Charlie Yochum, who soon hired him as a year-round hand. Similarly, Ned Gladden took over his uncle Luther's job as foreman for George Sanders's operation when Luther bought his own farm. After their first couple of years in the state, farm-labor families tended to settle down and make homes for themselves. Indeed, more than 80 percent of the agricultural families who had lived in the state for two years or more had become residentially stable, according to the BAE survey. E. D. Tetreau, in a second study, also observed a high degree of stability among those who had become legal residents.[98]

As families like the Gladdens and the Leatherburys made their homes in Arizona, an increasing proportion of the state's nonnative population hailed from Texas, Missouri, Arkansas, and Oklahoma. In 1920, less than 30 percent of the Arizonans born outside the state had come from that region. By 1940, the proportion had risen to more than 40 percent. The percentage of Oklahomans among the newcomers to Arizona rose most dramatically during that period, from 3 percent to almost 12 percent, and the proportion of rural residents from the Sooner State was even more significant. By 1940, one in seven rural newcomers had been born in Oklahoma. Of those actually residing on farms, one-fifth were Oklahomans. The migration of cotton pickers contributed importantly to this growing population.[99]

With gumption, hard work, perseverance, and a bit of luck, many of the agricultural newcomers made good in their adopted state. Most settled in the cotton districts of the Buckeye or Casa Grande valleys. Not everyone had intended to stay. When Buck Owens, later famed as a country singer and guitar picker, set out from Texas in 1937, he and his parents headed for California. They stopped to pick cotton in Mesa, east of Phoenix, and stayed fourteen years. Lloyd Hamilton, a native of Headrick, Oklahoma, also arrived during the great migration of 1937 to pick cotton. In less than twelve months Lloyd found permanent work with the Buckeye Irrigation Company, a job that lasted forty-three years. During that time he also managed to acquire his own forty-acre farm. Similarly, Wesley Smalley, born on a farm near

Hulbert, Oklahoma, worked for twenty-three years as a farmhand for J. L. Hodge near Liberty and eventually bought his own farm. Ned Gladden, of Idabel, Oklahoma, established a dairy farm near Higley, southeast of Phoenix, with the help of his uncle and the Farmers Home Administration.

Harvey and Bertha Mae Cambron, who came to the Buckeye Valley from Cole, Oklahoma, in 1936, lived first in Palo Verde, then in Avondale where they worked for C. O. Vosburgh, a leading cotton grower. Two of the Cambron children became prominent members of the valley. Sam stayed on at the Vosburgh place as a permanent hand and eventually became superintendent of Vosburgh's operations. As a reward for years of loyal hard work, Vosburgh helped Sam start his own farm with a gift of more than 120 acres. Eventually Sam was farming some 2,000 acres, owned and leased. When he sold his land, he retired a millionaire. He also served for nearly three decades as a trustee for the Buckeye Union High School. His younger brother, T. L. Cambron, also played a significant role in the local education system, first as a teacher, then as the superintendent of Liberty School.

Few became millionaires or prominent community leaders, but many found solid work that provided them with economic security and entry into the middle class. Ewell Bennett, a farmer from Paden, Oklahoma, became one of the original settlers at Casa Grande Valley Farms. While there, he became acquainted with a man from the Bureau of Indian Affairs (BIA) who often came to the farm to buy produce. When the cooperative farm was dissolved, the man helped Bennett land a job as a meter reader for the BIA's San Carlos Project, a position Bennett held for thirty years. Dewey Phares, who in 1936 left his farm near Lula, Oklahoma, to work as a cotton picker in the Buckeye Valley, soon owned a vegetable trucking business in Tolleson. W. D. Durant worked as a hand and later foreman on Charlie Pate's farm near Casa

Grande for eleven years. When in the early 1950s a falling water table caused Pate, a native of Arkansas, to cease farming for a time, Durant received a bonus that enabled him to buy outright five acres of land and with it a sense of security. Durant quickly found work with O. S. Stapley Company, a supplier of International Harvester equipment, with whom he remained for more than three decades. Dennis Kirkland arrived from Oklahoma with his parents and three sisters in a cattle truck full of pickers recruited to work on Calvin Ethington's farm near Casa Grande. Kirkland parlayed his talent with the steel guitar into a successful business selling musical instruments. In these ways and others — as farmers, homemakers, teachers, business owners — the migrants from Oklahoma and neighboring states became a part of the rich fabric of their adopted communities.[100]

It had not been an easy road. The newcomers had faced many obstacles along the way. Had it not been for the efforts of the Farm Security Administration, providing succor, some may not have made the first step. Still, the FSA failed in its endeavor to transform living and working conditions for the mass of migrant agricultural workers. In the cotton fields of Arizona, old patterns persisted. Soon the changes wrought by war would reveal just how deeply entrenched those conditions could be.

Chapter Seven

Epilogue

World War II drew the migrants from the south-central states away from the cotton fields. And as the 1942 harvest approached, the Arizona agricultural industry began to search anew for a tractable, elastic labor supply. It would search in vain.

Almost immediately after the entry of the United States into the Second World War, the Department of Agriculture declared the production of long-staple cotton a vital crop for the war effort. The military needed long-staple fiber for the manufacture of parachutes, blimps, airplane fabric, camouflage material, machine-gun belts, and other supplies. The Arizona cotton industry responded by expanding the land planted in American-Egyptian cotton to 126,000 acres, an increase of 26 percent, far more than the modest 10 percent increase requested by the Department of Agriculture. Between 1940 and 1942, Arizona's growers increased the long-staple acreage by 94 percent. Much of that expansion took place in the vicinity of Eloy, which emerged as the center of long-staple production in Arizona.[1]

Such an increase meant a commensurately enlarged demand for cotton pickers. To exacerbate the situation further, the labor requirement to pick an acre of long-staple cotton far exceeded that of the short-staple fiber. But the labor supply had begun to contract in 1941, intensifying the growers' annual fear of a severe shortage of pickers. By the end of that season, nonetheless, growers had secured sufficient labor to harvest the crop. Migration toward the end of the season became so heavy that more than 10,000 unemployed migrant families turned to the FSA to secure what it termed the bare necessities of life. The next year, however, the growers' perennial fear became reality. Migrants in 1942 responded to rumors of defense work in California and passed through Arizona, not stopping to work the harvest. Others were kept home by tire rationing and later by talk of impending gas rationing. Some of those who migrated to the cotton fields instead found work constructing the Japanese Relocation Center near Sacaton and the military airport at Marana, near Tucson, both paying union wages nearly three times the rate paid for picking cotton. Growers reported a wholesale exodus of local farm workers to the Sacaton and Marana construction sites. Compounding the shortage of migrant laborers, many younger agricultural workers already living in Arizona left to take jobs in munitions factories on the West Coast, joined the armed forces, or found themselves drafted into military service.

Growers attempting to secure labor encountered obstructions at every turn. In an effort to overcome the migration obstacle imposed by tire rationing, growers advanced railroad or bus fare to pickers in Oklahoma, Texas, and Arkansas

who agreed to work the harvest, only to have them leave the
fields as soon as they earned enough to pay the union dues
necessary for work on federal projects. Growers who tried to
transport workers to the state in trucks were restricted by
wartime regulations requiring a full payload in each direction, although some managed to truck in workers anyway.
Calvin Ethington, a grower from the Casa Grande area,
brought a load of pickers from Oklahoma in a cattle truck
outfitted with benches. A handful of labor contractors also
managed to bring in crews of men. On the other hand, a
number of migrants who had traveled to Arizona's cotton
districts in their automobiles abruptly left the state just as the
harvest began out of fear that impending gas rationing would
leave them stranded. Arizona senator Carl Hayden offered
his assurance that migrants would be able to obtain gas and
oil for the return trip home under the gas-rationing program,
but to no avail.[2]

Arizona's cotton growers thus joined agricultural interests
in California, New Mexico, and Texas once again to call for
the importation of farm workers from Mexico. The result was
a new bracero program administered by the FSA. But when
the FSA announced the terms circumscribing the program,
the Arizona cotton industry balked.[3] The bracero agreement
between the United States and Mexico stipulated that participating employers would pay a fee of $5 per worker to offset
the cost of transportation and a minimum wage of 30¢ per
hour, or an .uivalent piecework rate. "Wages to be paid the
worker shall be the same as those paid for similar work to
other agricultural laborers," the agreement stated, ". . . but in
no case shall this wage be less than 30 cents per hour . . .;
piece rates shall be so set as to enable the worker of average
ability to earn the prevailing wage."[4] It further required
adequate housing, defined by the FSA as a leak-free building
or tent measuring twelve by fourteen feet for each family or

every three pickers who came without family members. The FSA also mandated that stoves, sanitary water, and a sufficient number of privies and showers be provided for each camp. Moreover, the agency required employers who obtained braceros to provide the same wages and accommodations to all harvest workers, including pickers from the south-central states. The minimum-wage and housing requirements also applied to those growers participating in a similar FSA program to transport surplus workers from the western cotton belt.[5]

Earl Maharg, secretary of the Arizona Farm Bureau Federation, called the FSA's plan to secure agricultural labor "absolutely unworkable" because of the "drastic provisions" for wages and housing.[6] A reporter for the *Casa Grande Dispatch* observed that few growers could comply with the housing requirements even if they wanted to, in part because of the difficulty of procuring lumber, stoves, and other necessary materials through the War Production Board. At the very least, it seemed to local growers, migrant workers from the south-central states could provide their own housing, as many had in the past.[7]

In the end, however, it was the issue of wages, not housing, that became the roadblock for Arizona's growers. They ignored the provision in the regulations that permitted payment of the piecework equivalent. Contending that the FSA contract required them to pay a wage of $3 for a ten-hour workday regardless of the amount of cotton a worker picked, growers refused to participate.[8] They stated that the minimum wage was also a maximum wage posing a disadvantage to industrious workers. As the *Casa Grande Dispatch* observed, "For the past 150 years cotton has been picked by piece work . . . and this has proven more satisfactory to both the picker and grower, since the more a man picks in 10 hours the more he can make."[9]

The growers' argument soon became absurd. The piece-work equivalent of the minimum wage amounted to $3.00 per hundredweight. But by the end of October, the labor shortage had forced growers to raise the prevailing wage for picking long-staple cotton to $4.00 per hundred. To earn the federal minimum wage, therefore, a worker needed to pick only 75 pounds of Egyptian cotton; yet the average worker could pick 100 pounds. Short-staple growers participating in the federal program, it is true, may have been required to raise the piecework rate slightly to guarantee a $3.00 minimum to the average worker. Short-staple cotton brought only $2.00 per hundredweight, but it could be harvested more quickly. The average worker could harvest 140 to 175 pounds per day, earning $2.80 to $3.50.

The quarrel over the minimum wage was only one absurdity. The growers' contention that it would allow inexperienced pickers to obtain more money than they had earned and would prevent particularly productive workers from earning more was erroneous. The bracero program provided for a lower wage for family members who proved less productive than the average because of their age or sex, and it stipulated that those who turned out to be unproductive, whether due to ill health, incompetence, or inexperience, would be returned to Mexico at no cost to the grower. More understandable, perhaps, was the growers' response to an FSA proposal to transport surplus workers from the south-central states. This plan not only established a minimum wage and a set number of workdays per month but also guaranteed payment for 75 percent of the contracted employment period, even when rain kept pickers out of the fields. The industry found this provision intolerable.[10]

The actual cost of complying with the terms of the federal labor program, however, was not really the issue. At the heart of the controversy was the right of Arizona's cotton industry to determine its labor conditions. Maharg charged that the 30¢ per-hour minimum demanded by federal programs nullified the exemption of farm labor from the Fair Labor Standards Act, which set a minimum wage for other industries. "By the terms of this policy," he contended, "the Department of Agriculture and the War Manpower Commission have seized on the shortage of farm labor to institute a program of minimum wages for farm labor."[11] Arizona's cotton industry refused to allow such a precedent.

"The time has come," Maharg proclaimed, "when we must kick the FSA clear out of Arizona."[12] The newly organized Arizona Cotton Growers' Cooperative Association turned down FSA contracts for pickers from Mexico and the western cotton belt, and the conflict over the labor contract soon grew into a general attack on the entire FSA program in Arizona. Growers had once welcomed the government's role in providing housing and food for their work force. But no more. The membership of the Casa Grande Farm Bureau maintained that the government was obstructing Arizona's growers from obtaining farm labor and called for the FSA to bow out of the labor scene. A. M. Ward, president of that organization, urged growers to stand united in their rejection of the government's attempt "to change a time-honored method of paying pickers."[13] Most growers held steadfast against the government's effort to dictate labor terms, and Arizona accepted none of the five thousand Mexican braceros sent in 1942 to pick cotton in the United States.[14]

A handful of growers in Maricopa and Pinal counties, however, eventually signed up for shipments of workers from the south-central states, as did growers in the Safford area. But the joint effort between the War Manpower Commission, the Farm Security Administration, the U.S. Employment Service (USES), and the Southern Tenant Farmers Union

(STFU) turned into one more fiasco for pickers and revealed the hypocrisy of federal administrators.

At the outset, though, no one anticipated what was to come. When STFU leaders learned of the federal program to import braceros at a wage higher than the prevailing rate for picking cotton in the South, they contacted the War Manpower Commission and offered to supply surplus pickers to the long-staple cotton fields of Arizona and other points west.[15] The STFU—which had been in organizational disarray after an ill-fated albeit short-term alliance with the United Cannery, Agricultural, Packing and Allied Workers of America—viewed its proposal as an opportunity to provide jobs to southern sharecroppers and tenant farmers at the end of that region's harvest, to regain visibility and prestige as a union, and to revitalize the union by enrolling all recruits as members. Moreover, the program seemed to offer a welcome solution to long-standing problems in synchronizing labor supply with demand in the West. Both labor and industry would benefit; the cotton pickers would be guaranteed work at a prearranged rate for a prearranged period of time, and growers would be guaranteed sufficient labor to harvest the crop.

The plan seemed simple. The USES issued a clearance order for two thousand cotton pickers, ostensibly based on actual requests by Arizona growers and the agency's independent certification of bona fide need. The STFU then recruited able-bodied pickers from Arkansas, Missouri, Tennessee, and Mississippi and gathered them at specified collection points where they were met by representatives of the FSA charged with administering the program. The FSA shipped the pickers and their families west by train and guaranteed their return transportation as long as they fulfilled the terms of their contracts.[16]

Contracts with the recruits specified a wage of $4 per hundredweight for long-staple cotton and $2 per hundred

for short-staple, housing meeting minimum federal standards, and free transportation and medical care. Furthermore, Section 3 of the contract stated that the government
would

> cause the Worker to be employed as an agricultural
> laborer . . . for at least seventy-five percent (75%) of
> the workdays (each day of the week except Sunday to be
> considered a workday) between the day after the Worker's
> arrival at the original point of destination . . . hereinafter
> called the "period of employment"; or, in the absence of
> such employment, make the Worker a minimum sub-
> sistence allowance of $3.00 per day for each workday
> within said minimum of seventy-five percent (75%) of
> the workdays that he is not so employed; provided,
> however, that no subsistence allowance shall be made
> for workdays in which the Worker is unemployed as a
> result of his refusal to work or his illness or other
> physical incapacity. The amount of such subsistence
> allowance, if any, shall be computed and the payment
> thereof shall be made at the end of the period of
> employment.[17]

In return, the pickers were to work eight to twelve hours per
day as agricultural laborers (with an implicit guarantee of an
average ten-hour day) and to perform satisfactorily all tasks
required by their employers. The contracts permitted union
organization but forbade strikes, lockouts, or work stop-
pages.

Once the pickers arrived in Arizona, they found their FSA
contracts all but worthless. Wages matched those advertised,
but housing and general working conditions did not. Cotton
could not be picked until the sun dried the morning dew,
which resulted in a shortened workday, and seasonal rains
kept workers out of the fields altogether. When pickers
complained that "we don't get to work half of the time," the
FSA refused to take responsibility for fulfilling contract

terms. Instead, Kay Meese, acting regional director of the
FSA, informed Harry L. Mitchell, general secretary of the
STFU, that Section 3 of the contract ensured only that work
would be "made available" and did not guarantee minimum
earnings.[18]

But some were not employed at all, despite their contracts.
B. V. Zachary and his family, of southeastern Missouri, had
sold all their belongings before boarding an FSA-sponsored
train for Arizona "with the thought in mind to have a
comfortable place to live and make some money too, but we
didn't find what our contracts called for." When Zachary, his
wife and seven children, and more than three hundred others
arrived at the railroad depot in Eloy, they found "a fine mist of
rain falling and no place to go." Only one grower in the area,
Jack Cobb, had signed up for the FSA's program, and he
needed only two hundred pickers. His workers found that
the government-approved housing consisted of "tents and no
floor and standing in 2 inches of mud and water." Zachary, his
wife, and four sons were not among those fortunate to find
work with Cobb. The family was lucky, however. They found
refuge in an FSA mobile camp. Some families were forced to
find shelter in boxcars; others slept on the ground. "Most of
this train load of people were men with familys and respectable," wrote Zachary. "I have seen some hard times and been
in some tough spots during my life time, but this is my first
time to be dumped off in the streets with my wife and seven
children (and 300 other people) like a bunch of hogs."[19]

Zachary and the other one hundred or so surplus workers
concluded that they would have to strike out on their own
and find work with other growers in the area, but they soon
discovered that such attempts to survive would be punished.
According to an FSA representative, pickers working for
growers other than Cobb would be in violation of their
contracts and consequently lose their free ticket home. Al-

though the FSA had brought them to Eloy with the promise of work, the agency offered no alternative but to return home.[20] Just as the Arizona cotton growers had lured pickers westward with falsehoods, so the federal government had reneged on its promise. True, there were differences. The FSA did provide many of the unemployed with decent shelter, food, and medical care at the mobile camp. But to Zachary, the FSA's labor recruitment program looked like "just another crooked deal."[21]

With few growers participating in the FSA's program for domestic pickers or braceros, the obstacles posed by wartime restrictions on travel, both real and perceived, combined with the attraction of alternative work in the war effort to create the smallest force of harvesters in the history of the Arizona cotton industry. Faced for the first time with an actual shortage of pickers, the cotton industry searched frantically for new sources of labor. A few growers employed Japanese internees from the Sacaton Relocation Center, with little success. Japanese workers were inexperienced in picking cotton, and many were unused to toiling in the intense desert heat. The amount of long-staple cotton gathered per Japanese worker ranged from fifteen to twenty-eight pounds per day, compared to the average of one hundred pounds typically picked by workers from the south-central states. Some growers arranged with the state prison in Florence to hire convicts but found those workers too slow; convict labor managed to pick only about 2 percent of Pinal County's long-staple crop.[22] In an attempt to encourage local residents to enter the fields, Eloy growers held a cotton-picking contest, awarding the winner, M. C. Peña, $100 plus his earnings of $1.16 for picking twenty-nine pounds of cotton in one hour.[23]

Patriotism, however, not financial reward, became the watchword for local recruiting efforts. Governor Sidney Osborn set the tone. Speaking to the crowd of spectators at the Eloy contest, he exhorted his audience: "You who are growing and picking this cotton . . . can rightfully consider yourselves in the Army of the United States, because without your product the army may fail."[24] In Casa Grande, the Chamber of Commerce and the Rotary Club formed a Victory Labor Battalion, calling on every able-bodied man, woman, and child to help the war effort by picking cotton. Employers closed their stores and offices for half a day each Tuesday, beginning in late October, so that they and their clerks could help with the harvest. The *Casa Grande Dispatch* suggested that each participant purchase a cotton sack and keep it as a memento "to show to their grandchildren in later years, proudly displaying it as the 'weapon' they used to defeat the axis."[25]

Similar programs were organized in Mesa and Phoenix, where volunteers were known as the Victory Labor Corps. Although thousands of patriotic residents participated in the Victory Labor programs, the effort proved largely unsuccessful. Inexperienced pickers found the work arduous and slow. In the end, growers lost an estimated twenty- to thirty-thousand bales of cotton because of an insufficient and inexperienced labor force. They preferred to lose part of the crop, it seemed, than agree to a minimum rate of pay and a minimum standard of living for the workers on whom they had long relied. There was, after all, a principle involved.[26]

The Arizona cotton industry performed a crucial role in encouraging the migration of agricultural laborers westward during the Great Depression. Many families would have made the journey anyway, attracted by California's legendary image as the land of milk and honey. But the immediate promise of jobs in Arizona touted in advertisements, on handbills, and by a well-greased rumor mill gave rural migrants from Oklahoma and neighboring states a strong sense of purpose. It made it possible for down-and-out farm families to set out with more than the vague hope for a better life that had guided so many waves of westward migration since the 1840s. More families left the region than might have otherwise. By holding out the lure of economic security, Arizona's cotton growers intensified the social and economic problems faced in their state and California during the Depression.

It is tempting to portray the story of the Depression-era migration of cotton pickers to Arizona in the classic mode of the grade-B Western movie. All of the archetypal characters would be present: the cotton growers would wear black hats; the farm workers would be hapless victims; and federal do-gooders would come riding to the rescue.

Such a characterization would create good melodrama, but it would be fictional. War rather than federal heroics saved the day. Moreover, the migrants proved quite resourceful themselves. Despite the hardships they faced in Arizona and California, many found their situation much improved compared to the one they left behind. They saw themselves not as victims but as survivors seeking new opportunity, looking for a step up. Many found it. As for the cotton growers, some even helped the migrants onto the first rung. Few if any were fully conscious that they exploited their workers. Their crime, if it may be characterized as such, lay in their general failure to see the mass of their workers as people like themselves rather than mere factors of production, commodities to be obtained at the lowest price.

The saga of the Oklahomans and their fellow migrants from the south-central states represented a continuum in the history of agricultural labor in Arizona. From the first days of Arizona's cotton industry, growers sought a cheap and elastic labor force. They cared not whether the fingers that picked the snowy fiber were brown or white so long as they were nimble. A popular notion holds that racism underlies the exploitation of agricultural workers.[27] But the experience of the migrant workers from the western cotton belt, overwhelmingly Anglo-American, demonstrated that neither race nor ethnicity played principal roles in determining the treatment of farm labor.

It was class. The migrants' enduring poverty—manifest in their tattered clothing, simple diet, backwoods manner of speaking, indeed their seemingly nomadic existence—set them apart from the rest of agricultural society. Back home, as tenant farmers living as poor people do the world over, they had been scorned as subnormal peasants. Arizonans likewise came to see the migrants as Jeeter Lester's kinfolk of *Tobacco Road* fame. The migrant life, with its attendant filth and absence of material wealth, came to be regarded by many growers as a matter of choice. Within this context, growers believed they merely maintained the status quo.

A look at the difference in attitudes toward the migrant workers and the Victory Laborers is revealing. E. D. Tetreau, Arizona's rural sociologist, argued that high wages would prove counterproductive in securing a reliable labor force because more money would encourage workers to spend less time in the fields and still get by. Migrants from the south-central states already exhibited a lackadaisical attitude toward work, in his opinion. To demonstrate his point, he related the observation of a "hard-bitten woman" from Oklahoma who had "seen men who were sound as a Missouri mule come 'belly-aching' in from the field at 3 o'clock on a late October afternoon because the sun was getting too hot."[28] Those men, it seemed, should have been capable of enduring October temperatures as high as 100 degrees. By contrast, organizers of Casa Grande's middle-class Victory Labor Battalion promised participants that they would not be asked to overexert in the late-afternoon sun, nor would workers be ridiculed for stopping for an occasional rest or leaving before the end of the workday.[29] What counted as laziness for one was mere prudence for another.

The importance of race and ethnicity cannot be discounted entirely, however, if we are to understand the experience of Arizona's cotton pickers in the Depression era. Race and national origin quite likely influenced the response of the federal government to the plight of the migrants from the south-central states. Brown-skinned Spanish-speaking people laboring in the fields for two decades under similar conditions attracted little public attention. But when large numbers of Anglo-American families took up residence in ramshackle farm-labor camps or squatted along the side of the road, people noticed. John Steinbeck wrote *The Grapes of Wrath*. The WPA sent investigators. And the FSA erected safety nets. Certainly the attention afforded the migrants from the western cotton belt grew out of the general spirit of the times and the influence of sociologists, social workers, and liberal sympathizers during the New Deal. Yet one cannot help but wonder whether the same spotlight would have been focused on Arizona's cotton pickers had their dominant skin color been brown or black.[30] Race and ethnicity also probably played a part in the eventual acceptance of the migrants in the communities they settled in. Unlike many Mexican American farm workers, most of the pickers from Oklahoma and the south-central states moved up the agricultural ladder and out of poverty.

The migration from Oklahoma and the south-central states was but one episode in the unbroken past of the American Southwest.[31] The widespread use of the mechanical picker after World War II virtually put to an end the exploitation of workers in the cotton fields of Arizona. But the seasonal influx of harvest workers into the state continued. Only the details varied. Consider a news report of late. Mexican laborers waged a strike in the citrus groves at Arrowhead Ranch near Phoenix, owned in part by Robert Goldwater, brother of Senator Barry M. Goldwater. They demanded (among other things) the installation of latrines and showers in the groves where they worked and slept, medical care, advance warning of insecticide spraying, full payment of wages, and an end to the use of Border Patrol raids and deportation to suppress strikes.[32] The story remained essentially the same. Only the names had changed.

Notes

Abbreviations

ACGA	Arizona Cotton Growers' Association, Phoenix
ADL	Arizona Department of Library, Archives, and Public Records, Phoenix
AHS	Arizona Historical Society, Tucson
ASSW	Arizona State Board of Social Security and Welfare
ASU	Arizona State University, Tempe
BAE	U.S. Department of Agriculture, Bureau of Agricultural Economics
CAC	Carl Albert Congressional Research and Studies Center, Norman, Oklahoma
CGVHS	Casa Grande Valley Historical Society, Casa Grande, Arizona
COP	California Odyssey Project, California State University, Bakersfield
FHA	U.S. Department of Agriculture, Farmers Home Administration
FSA	U.S. Department of Agriculture, Farm Security Administration

LC   Hearings, La Follette Committee, U.S. Congress, Senate, Committee on Education and Labor
NA   National Archives, Washington, D.C.
ODL   Oklahoma Department of Libraries, Oklahoma City
OMP   Oklahoma-Arizona Migration Project, Arizona Historical Society, Tempe
RD   Resettlement Division
RG   Record Group
SL   *U.S. Statutes at Large*
SRP   Salt River Project, Tempe, Arizona
STFU   Southern Tenant Farmers Union Papers, University of North Carolina Library, Chapel Hill
TC   Hearings, Tolan Committee, U.S. Congress, House, Select Committee to Investigate the Interstate Migration of Destitute Citizens
UA   University of Arizona, Tucson
WPA   Works Progress Administration

Chapter 1

1. *Arizona Republic*, 13 Mar. 1938, p. 8.

2. Lange and Taylor, *American Exodus;* see also Cox, ed., *Dorothea Lange;* Fleischhauer and Brannan, eds., *Documenting America.* Lange's photographs of migrant farm workers were published in *American Exodus* and in national magazines such as *Life.*

3. John Steinbeck, *Grapes of Wrath.*

4. McWilliams's *Factories in the Field,* a factual companion piece to Steinbeck's novel, also helped to stimulate congressional interest in the migration.

5. Gregory (*American Exodus: The Dust Bowl Migration and Okie Culture in California*) and Stein (*California and the Dust Bowl Migration*) have produced the most thoughtful analyses of the migration to California. Other useful studies include Manes, "Depression Pioneers" (diss.); Sherman, "Oklahomans in California" (diss.); Gilbert, "Migrations of Farm Population" (thesis). Aside from the chapter "Arizona: Migrant Way Station" in McWilliams, *Ill Fares the Land,* the only examination of the issues surrounding Arizona's Depression-era migrants is provided by Pendleton (a student of economist Paul S. Taylor), "History of Labor" (diss.).

Chapter 2

1. Descriptions of household goods taken on the road westward may be found in the California Odyssey Project, a collection of interviews with Oklahoma migrants conducted in 1981, California State University, Bakersfield (hereinafter COP); see especially the transcripts for Loye Lucille Martin Holmes, Vera Ruth Woodall Criswell, Vivian Leah Barnes Kirschenmann, Hattye Rankin Shields, Byrd Monford Morgan, Rosie Lee Harlas Laird, and Dorothy Louise Price Rose. Similar descriptions are contained in my interviews with Oklahoma migrants in 1992, collected as the Oklahoma-Arizona Migration Project, Arizona Historical Society, Tempe (OMP); see particularly the interviews with Thomas Lawton Cambron, Samuel Orvel Cambron, and Betty Lyon McGrath.

2. A provocative interpretation of the failure of the farming frontier in eastern Oklahoma is found in Thompson, *Closing the Frontier.* Manes, "Depression Pioneers," viii, argues that the Depression migration simply represented another wave of westward expansion.

3. Bogue, Shryock, and Hoermann, *Subregional Migration,* vol. 1, *Streams of Migration,* table 1; Oklahoma Agricultural Experiment Station, *Population Trends in Oklahoma,* 10, 19; U.S. Department of Commerce, Bureau of the Census (hereinafter, Bureau Census), *Fifteenth Census of the United States: 1930: Population,* vol. 3, pt. 2, *Reports by States . . . Montana-Wyoming,* 541, 941. In the 1940 census respondents were asked for the first time where they had been living five years previous. A total of 308,838 persons residing outside Oklahoma stated that they had been residents of Oklahoma in 1935. This figure excludes those who had migrated from the state during the period but returned before April 1940. Conversely, it includes those who were living outside the state when the census was taken but returned to Oklahoma shortly thereafter. By comparison, Texas (with a 1930 population nearly 2.5 times that of Oklahoma) lost only 282,988 people as a result of migration; most of that state's population movement was internal.

4. Bogue, Shryock, and Hoermann, *Subregional Migration,* table 1. By comparison, only about 68,000 Texans went to California, and another 15,000 moved to Arizona. Gregory, *American Exodus,* 31–33, argues that migrants often made the decision to move west casually, counting on an easy trip along the modern U.S. Highway 66. Although that may have been true for middle-class migrants with dependable transportation, few tenant farmers had the luxury of a reliable car.

5. Bogue, Shryock, and Hoermann, *Subregional Migration,* table 1; Arizona Agricultural Experiment Station, *Volume and Characteristics of*

Migration to Arizona, 1930–39, 301–3, 310–11, *Statistical Supplement to Volume and Characteristics of Migration to Arizona, 1930–39,* 17–18. For an excellent discussion of the two migration streams to California, see Gregory, *American Exodus,* 15–17, 39–62. Estimates of the number of people who migrated in the 1930s from Oklahoma's farms to California and Arizona are complicated by inadequacies in the data. None of the published census data distinguish rural migration streams from their urban counterparts; moreover, the available information does not cover the first half of the decade. The study of migration to Arizona is particularly problematic since the statistical subregion that encompasses the state's major agricultural areas includes its major urban centers, Phoenix and Tucson.

6. From September through November 1937, every issue of the Oklahoma City *Daily Oklahoman* carried at least one and as many as four advertisements for transportation to California or, far less frequently, Arizona. The quotes are from 3, 10 Sept. 1937; see also the interview with Hazel Oleta Thompson Smalling, COP.

7. Taylor, "Covered Wagon," 348–51; see also Gregory, *American Exodus,* 11, 81. Historians continue to refer to the exodus as the Dust Bowl migration even as they seek to dispel the myth.

8. Guthrie, *Dust Bowl Ballads;* Bogue, Shryock, and Hoermann, *Subregional Migration,* table 1; see also Worster, *Dust Bowl,* 16, 28–31, 49, 61. It is not possible to estimate the percentage of Oklahomans who fled the Dust Bowl to California and Arizona with any accuracy. Less than 1 percent of the state's westward migrants hailed from the panhandle. Another 3.4 percent came from the statistical subregion containing Harper and Ellis counties, also within the Dust Bowl. However, that subregion includes six counties east of the Dust Bowl. Moveover, data on interstate migration exists only for the second half of the decade.

9. Bureau Census, *Sixteenth Census of the United States: 1940: Population, First Series: Oklahoma,* table 3; Bogue, Shryock, and Hoermann, *Subregional Migration,* table 1.

10. Oklahoma Agricultural Experiment Station, *Socio-Economic Atlas,* 111, *Farm Tenancy in Oklahoma,* 23; Bureau of Census, *Fifteenth Census of the United States, 1930: Agriculture,* vol. 3, pt. 2, *Southern States,* 937–42. Hurt, *Dust Bowl,* discusses the various federal programs that helped Dust Bowl farmers survive. Bonnifield, *Dust Bowl,* examining postal receipts, closings of banks and public institutions, and school enrollment, argues that no mass migration from the Dust Bowl area took place (see especially 93–94, 106–7).

11. Quoted in Ganzel, *Dust Bowl Descent*, 20. For a good discussion of the indomitable spirit of the people of the Dust Bowl, see Hurt, *Dust Bowl*, chap. 4.

12. Bogue, Shryock, and Hoermann, *Subregional Migration*, table 1; U.S. Department of Agriculture, Farm Security Administration (FSA), *Study of 6,655 Migrant Households Receiving Emergency Grants, Farm Security Administration, California, 1938*, 20; Oklahoma Agricultural Experiment Station, *Socio-Economic Atlas*, 6, 34; Morris, Goins, and McReynolds, *Historical Atlas*, maps 3, 9. For a discussion of the different cultural dynamics governing the settlement of the eastern and western regions of the state, see Bonnifield, *Dust Bowl*; Thompson, *Closing the Frontier*. Also useful is Nall, "King Cotton," 37–55.

13. U.S. Works Progress Administration, Division of Social Research (WPA), *People of the Drought States*, 76–77; Bureau Census, *Fifteenth Census: Agriculture*, vol. 3, pt. 2, 1284–89, *United States Census of Agriculture, 1935: Oklahoma, Statistics by Counties, Second Series*, county table 4, *United States Census of Agriculture, 1945*, vol. 1, pt. 25, *Oklahoma, Statistics for Counties*, county table 5; Gilbert, "Migrations of Farm Population," 46–47, 53, 59, 77, 83–88; McMillan, "Some Observations," 334, 338–40; U.S. Department of Agriculture, Bureau of Agricultural Economics (BAE), *County Variation in Net Migration from the Rural-Farm Population, 1930–1940*, 33–34; Oklahoma Agricultural Experiment Station, *Recent Population Trends in Oklahoma*, 8, 11. Manes, "Depression Pioneers," 135, 346–52, asserts a relationship between the westward migration and Route 66.

The percentage of farm population loss in LeFlore County is calculated by me based on the 1930 population; it does not take into account the gain in farm population experienced during the first half of the decade. Population loss between 1930 and 1935 is based on census data, which do not distinguish population change due to migration from that due to natural increase or decrease. The figures on net migration between 1935 and 1940 were estimated by the Bureau of Agricultural Economics based on differences between the expected and the enumerated population.

Care must be taken not to confuse migration from farms with outmigration from a county or the state. Not all migrants from Oklahoma's farms left the state. Internal migration was also significant: more than 262,000 Oklahomans, nearly half of those who changed residence, stayed in the state (see Bogue, Shryock, and Hoermann, *Subregional Migration*, table 1, cxx). Indeed most of eastern Oklahoma, including LeFlore County, actually grew in total population (urban and rural nonfarm residents) during the period, partly the result of internal migration. Moreover, net loss of farm population did not necessarily mean a comparable loss of farms. LeFlore County had only 10 percent fewer farms by the end of the decade, but 30 percent fewer farm residents.

14. Hearings, Tolan Committee, U.S. Congress, House, Select Committee to Investigate the Interstate Migration of Destitute Citizens (TC), *Interstate Migration*, pt. 6, *San Francisco Hearings,* 2216.

15. TC, pt. 7, *Los Angeles Hearings,* 2817.

16. Ibid., 2903–4.

17. Interview with Vera Ruth Woodall Criswell, 22, COP.

18. FSA, *Study of 6,655 Migrant Households,* 33, table 2-A.

19. Graves, "Exodus from Indian Territory," 188–91; Nall, "King Cotton," 38; Hale, "People of Oklahoma," 44, 46; Fite, "Cotton Industry," 349, 351–52; interviews with Hadley Leon Yocum and Lula May Quinn Martin, COP; U.S. Congress, House, National Resources Committee, *Farm Tenancy: Report of the President's Committee,* 89, 94, 99; Oklahoma Agricultural Experiment Station, *Farm Tenancy in Oklahoma,* 7, 10–11; "Proceedings of Oklahoma Farm Land Tenantry Conference, State Capitol, Oklahoma City, October 22, 1936," 9, Oklahoma file, box 21, project files, Records of the Land Tenure Section, Records of the Bureau of Agricultural Economics, Record Group 83 (BAE, RG), National Archives, Washington, D.C. (hereinafter NA); Bureau Census, *Fifteenth Census: Agriculture,* vol. 3, pt. 2, 937–42. The freedmen mentioned here were former slaves in the Creek, Cherokee, Choctaw, Chickasaw, and Seminole nations who received land allotments as enrolled tribal members.

The percentage of tenants on all farms held roughly steady between 1930 and 1935. Although the figure for the cotton belt includes black and Indian renters, the numbers closely reflect the level of tenancy among whites. Relatively few blacks and Indians operated farms, and the percentage of tenants among them was roughly equal to that of whites (see Bureau Census, *Census of Agriculture, 1935: Oklahoma Counties,* state table 2).

Information on the race of tenant farmers is complicated by the way American Indians were reported by the agricultural census. Enrolled Indians and those readily identifiable as Indians by census takers were counted as "colored," undifferentiated from those enumerated as African Americans; those not enrolled and not readily identifiable as American Indians were counted as "white."

20. Oklahoma Agricultural Experiment Station, *Farm Tenancy in Oklahoma,* 15–16. In 1935 about 75 percent of all tenants rented on a

share basis, 14 percent paid cash, and only 10 percent worked as sharecroppers.

21. "Report of the Working Division on Government Program," Muskogee Convention of the Southern Tenant Farmers Union, 14–17 Jan. 1937, 5, reel 4, *Southern Tenant Farmers Union Papers,* University of North Carolina Library, Chapel Hill (STFU).

22. "Proceedings of Oklahoma Farm Land Tenantry Conference, 1936," 30–31, Oklahoma file, box 21, project files, Records of the Land Tenure Section, "Farm Tenancy Conference, Dallas, Texas, Jan. 4, 1937," 38, Oklahoma City file, box 29, hearings files, Records Relating to the President's Special Committee on Farm Tenancy, Records of BAE, RG 83, NA; Oklahoma Agricultural Experiment Station, *Farm Housing in Southern Oklahoma,* 10–21.

23. Interview with Dennis Elems Kirkland, 3, OMP. See also the interview with Thomas Cambron.

24. Interview with Terry Bennett Clipper, 3, COP; see also the interviews with Martha Lee Martin Jackson and Vivian Barnes Kirschenmann. On the other hand, landlords often complained that their tenants wrecked farm buildings by neglecting their upkeep and scavenging them for firewood. For example, see Mahala Sullivan to Henry A. Wallace, Secretary of Agriculture, box 29, Miscellaneous Correspondence, Records Relating to the President's Special Committee on Farm Tenancy, Records of BAE, RG 83, NA.

25. Interviews with James Edward Gladden, Thomas Cambron, Ewell Bennett, W. D. Durant and Naomi Marie Dixon Durant, Lucille Peck Henry, OMP; Terry Clipper, James Harrison Ward, Joyce Vernon Seabolt, Hadley Yocum, Lillie Counts Dunn, Esta Mae Lewis Rymal, COP.

Pellagra, caused by a niacin deficiency, remained a problem in rural Oklahoma, although its incidence in the state was lower than in the South. The prevalence of other nutritional problems, however, is difficult to ascertain because of poor medical record keeping; see Brown, "Hard Times for Children."

26. Oklahoma Agricultural Experiment Station, *Cotton Experiments at the Lawton (Oklahoma) Field Station, 1916–1931,* 9–11; *Oklahoma Farmer-Stockman,* 1 Sept. 1934, p. 5. The "Crop Outlook" column of the *Farmer-Stockman,* 1930–1934, provides insight into the vicissitudes of Oklahoma weather and the effect on crops in each county; see also the interviews with Loye Lucille Martin Holmes, Vera Ruth Woodell Criswell, James Ward, Juanita Everly Price, Lillie Ruth Ann Counts Dunn, Thomas J. Smith, Martha Lee Martin Jackson, Ethel Oleta Wever Belezzuoli, Joyce

Vernon Seabolt, Terry Clipper, Hattye Rankin Shields, COP; Ewell Bennett, OMP.

27. "Crop Outlook," *Oklahoma Farmer-Stockman,* 15 Aug. 1934.

28. BAE, *Oklahoma Cotton: Estimated Acreage, Yield, and Production, 1928–1937, by Counties,* 6–9; the quote is from an interview with Alvin Bryan Laird, 2, COP.

29. Quoted in Taylor, "Covered Wagon," 349.

30. *Oklahoma Farmer-Stockman,* 15 Nov. 1930, p. 6, 15 Feb. 1935, p. 3; *Daily Oklahoman,* 24 Sept. 1939, sec. D, p. 2; Graves, "Exodus from Indian Territory," 189, 191; Fite, "Cotton Industry," 352–53; Oklahoma State Planning Board, "A Compendium of Graphic Studies Relating to Farm Tenancy," box 1, Oklahoma Industrial Development and Parks Department records, State Archives, Oklahoma Department of Libraries, Oklahoma City (ODL); U.S. Department of Agriculture, Bureau of Chemistry and Soils (hereinafter, Bureau Chemistry Soils), *Soil Survey of Le-Flore County, Oklahoma,* 2, 6, 7, 10, 14–15, 25–26, *Soil Survey of McIntosh County, Oklahoma,* 2, 9, 11–12, 17, 36, *Soil Survey of Pittsburg County, Oklahoma,* 1, 5–6, 8, 11, 21; the quote is from the Pittsburg report, 7. Also consult the interviews with Lillie Counts Dunn, Byrd Morgan, Ethel Wever Belezzuoli, COP.

31. *Oklahoma Farmer-Stockman,* 15 Nov. 1930, p. 6, 1 May 1937, p. 8; U.S. Department of Agriculture, Bureau of Plant Industry, *Soil Survey of Pontotoc County, Oklahoma,* 12, 13, 15, 29, 31, 39, *Soil Survey of Washita County, Oklahoma,* 8, 10, 17, 19, 20; Bureau Chemistry Soils, *Soil Survey of Carter County, Oklahoma,* 12, 16, 18, 23, *Soil Survey of Tillman County, Oklahoma,* 22, 23, *Soil Survey of Greer County, Oklahoma,* 11, *Soil Survey of Kiowa County, Oklahoma,* 23.

32. Bureau Chemistry Soils, *Soil Survey of McIntosh County,* 30; *Farmer-Stockman,* 15 Feb. 1935, p. 8; Moore, "Farm Tenancy" (thesis), 42; "Minutes of the Oklahoma Farm Tenancy Committee Held in the State Capitol Building, Oklahoma City, Oklahoma, December 19, 1936," 1–2, reel 3, STFU.

33. Oklahoma Agricultural Experiment Station, *Social Aspects of Farm Mechanization in Oklahoma,* 7, 11, 16–17, 20, 22, *Cotton Growing in Southwestern Oklahoma,* 25; Goke and Hollopeter, "Influences of Soils," 55; *Oklahoma Farmer-Stockman,* 15 Jan. 1930, p. 5, 1 Mar. 1930, p. 3, 1 Sept. 1930, p. 6, 7 July 1940, sec. D, p. 4; Bureau Census, *Fifteenth Census of the United States: 1930: Agriculture,* vol. 2, pt. 2, *Southern States,* 1316–21, *United States Census of Agriculture, 1935: Reports for States with Statistics for Counties,* vol. 1, pt. 2, *Southern States,* 731–37, *Census of Agriculture,*

1935: Oklahoma Counties, county table 4, *Census of Agriculture, 1945: Oklahoma Counties,* county table 6; *Daily Oklahoman,* 2 Apr. 1939, sec. D, p. 8, 7 July 1940, sec. D, p. 4; letter, S. D. Crouch to H. L. Mitchell, 23 Jan. 1939, reel 10, STFU.

To a limited extent, mechanical sleds or strippers were also used in the southwest for the last picking to salvage late-ripening bolls too scattered for hand snapping. But efficient methods of mechanical harvesting did not become available until after World War II. See Hurt, "Cotton Pickers," 30–42.

34. Oklahoma Agricultural Experiment Station, *Cotton Growing in Eastern Oklahoma,* 15; TC, pt. 5, *Oklahoma City Hearings,* 2105, 2124.

The Oklahoma Tenant Farmers Union (OTFU) should not be confused with the Oklahoma branch of the Southern Tenant Farmers Union (STFU). The OTFU was organized in 1939 by Odis Sweeden, formerly the Oklahoma organizer of the STFU, and Donald Henderson of the United Cannery, Agricultural, Packing and Allied Workers of America after a schism developed between the national STFU and Henderson's organization, with which the STFU briefly federated. Soon after Henderson dispatched Otis G. Nation to help Sweeden with organizing efforts, Sweeden broke from the OTFU and again professed loyalty to the STFU.

35. Bureau Census, *Fourteenth Census of the United States: 1920,* Bulletin, *Agriculture: Oklahoma: Statistics for the State and Its Counties,* county table 1, *United States Census of Agriculture, 1925: Reports for States, with Statistics for Counties,* pt. 2, *The Southern States,* 1038–47, *Fifteenth Census: Agriculture,* vol. 2, pt. 2, 1284–89, *Census of Agriculture, 1935: Reports for States,* vol. 1, pt. 2, 716–22, *Census of Agriculture, 1935: Oklahoma Counties,* 8, *Census of Agriculture, 1945: Oklahoma Counties,* county table 5; Agricultural Adjustment Act, *U.S. Statutes at Large* (SL) 48, ch. 25, 31–41; *Oklahoma Farmer-Stockman,* 15 June 1930, p. 6, 15 Dec. 1933, pp. 3, 18, 1 Jan. 1934, pp. 4, 9, 14; Oklahoma Planning Board, "Compendium of Graphic Studies Relating to Farm Tenancy," box 1, Oklahoma Industrial Development Department, State Archives, ODL; BAE, *Oklahoma Cotton,* 6–9; Ganger, "Impact of Mechanization" (diss.), 140–41; Graves, "Exodus from Indian Territory," 205. For an analysis of the socioeconomic problems created by tenant farming, see McDean, "'Okie' Migration," 77–91.

The reduction of the tenantry accelerated even more after 1940. Between 1935 and 1940, the tenant population declined by nearly 25,000 farmers, or 20 percent. Over the course of the next five years, however, the tenant population dropped by one-third more, some 32,000 fewer people renting or sharecropping.

36. *Farmer-Stockman*, 1 June 1935, p. 8, 1 Jan. 1936, p. 10; the quote is from the former.

37. Quoted by Lange and Taylor, *American Exodus*, 80. See also *Oklahoma Farmer-Stockman*, 1 Dec. 1934, p. 4.

38. The customary verbal contract made the length of tenure uncertain, and it proved difficult to enforce an oral contract in any event. Generally, only those leasing land owned by corporations, the State School Land Commission, and American Indians under the supervision of the Indian Service held written tenant contracts. See Oklahoma, Agricultural Experiment Station, *Legal Aspects of Landlord-Tenant Relationships in Oklahoma*, 12–15, *The Economic and Social Aspects of Mobility of Oklahoma Farmers*, 11–12, 33–38.

39. *Oklahoma Farmer-Stockman*, 15 Jan. 1934, p. 7; see also the interview with Martha Lee Martin Jackson, COP.

40. Grubbs, *Cry from Cotton*, 39; Bureau Census, *Census of Agriculture, 1935: Oklahoma Counties*, 9; interview with Lillie Counts Dunn, COP. This figure was significantly higher for sharecroppers than for renters, lower for black and Indian tenants. About 70 percent of all sharecroppers had lived on their farms for one year or less, compared to 53 percent for renters. Blacks and Indians were more likely to remain on their farms from year to year, perhaps because they perceived fewer opportunities for upward mobility or they more frequently fell into peonage (a condition, however, that was much less prevalent than in the South). About 66 percent of black and Indian sharecroppers and 44 percent of black and Indian renters had lived on their farms for one year or less. Grossman, *Land of Hope*, 28, observes that throughout the South black tenants tended to be more stable than whites.

41. TC, pt. 5, p. 1933.

42. Graves, "Exodus from Indian Territory," 205; Bureau Census, *Fifteenth Census: Agriculture*, vol. 2, pt. 2, 1284–95, *Census of Agriculture, 1935: Reports for States*, vol. 1, pt. 2, 716–26, 731–37; WPA, *People of the Drought States*, 76–77; TC, pt. 5, 2125; the quote is from the *Oklahoma Farmer-Stockman*, 15 Jan. 1934, p. 7. Due to a population influx from other areas of the state, the central and eastern regions of the cotton belt recorded an increase in the total number of tenant farms and cotton farms as more marginal lands were put into production between 1929 and 1935. This increase statistically masks the dislocation of tenants already living in the area.

43. *Oklahoma Farmer-Stockman,* 1 Feb. 1934, p. 7.
44. Bankhead Act of 1934, *U.S. Statutes at Large* (SL) 48, ch. 157, pp. 598–607; Soil Conservation and Domestic Allotment Act, SL 49, ch. 104, pp. 1148–52; Agricultural Adjustment Act, SL 52, ch. 30, pp. 31–77; *United States v. Butler et al.,* 297 U.S. Reports 1–88 (6 Jan. 1936); BAE, *Oklahoma Cotton,* 7, [15]; *Oklahoma Farmer-Stockman,* 1 Jan. 1935, p. 7; *Daily Oklahoman,* 30 Apr. 1939, sec. D, p. 8; Duncan, "Rural Shifts," 88, 91; McMillan, "Oklahoma Population Movements," 334; Bureau Census, *Fifteenth Census: Agriculture,* vol. 2, pt. 2, 1284–89, *Census of Agriculture, 1945: Oklahoma Counties,* county table 5; interviews with Alvin Laird and Rosie Harlas Laird, COP.
45. Scales and Goble, *Oklahoma Politics,* chaps. 9, 11; Fossey, "'Talkin' Dust Bowl Blues'", 23–25; Patterson, *New Deal,* 54; TC, pt. 6, 2120–21, pt. 7, 2874.
46. Elm Grove, between Pennsylvania and Exchange avenues among a cluster of elm trees, was the name the residents gave the Oklahoma City Community Camp. The term "transient camp" was a misnomer. According to a survey of 235 families living at Elm Grove in 1936, nearly 75 percent had resided in the camp for more than one year, and 41 percent had lived there for more than three years. For a description of the camps and the characteristics of the residents, see Gibson, "Dependent Family" (thesis); Dean, "Social Forces" (thesis); Replogle and Tibbitts, eds., *Welfare Activities,* 205; Appel, *People Talk,* 414–21; *Daily Oklahoman,* 8 May 1935, p. 1.
47. TC, pt. 6, 2410; see also *Daily Oklahoman,* 2 June 1940, sec. A, p. 13, *Tulsa Tribune,* 2 June 1940, p. 12.
48. Moore, "Farm Tenancy," iii, 55; *Oklahoma Farmer-Stockman,* 15 Oct. 1935, p. 4; Grubbs, *Cry from Cotton,* 15, 126.
49. *Tulsa Tribune,* 23 Sept. 1938, p. 26.
50. The history of the STFU is well documented. The standard work on the subject is Grubbs, *Cry from Cotton.* Insight into the Oklahoma chapter is provided by Dyson, *Red Harvest,* chap. 8. H. L. Mitchell, one of the founders of the STFU in Arkansas, provides a personal look in *Mean Things.* My account is based on the STFU Papers, available on microfilm (see especially reels 3, 4, 6, 9–12, 19). Also consult Oklahoma Agricultural Experiment Station, *Legal Aspects of Landlord-Tenant Relations,* 5; "Getting at the Bottom of Oklahoma's Landlord-Tenant Problem," *Extension Service Review,* 162; *Oklahoma Session Laws of 1936–1937,* ch. 53, pp. 391–93; *Oklahoma Session Laws of 1939,* ch. 53, p. 341; TC, pt. 5, 2029–30.

51. FSA, *Study of 6,655 Migrant Households,* table 3A. No statistics were kept regarding the sums the migrants had upon leaving home. Interviews with migrant tenant farmers during the Tolan committee hearings, however, provide some insight; see TC, pt. 6, 2211, 2698, pt. 7, 2817, 2904. See also the interviews with Masuria Ann McCandless Stephens, OMP; Dorothy Price Rose, Talmage Lee Collins, Alvin Laird and Rosie Harlas Laird, Lillie Counts Dunn, COP. In the latter collection, the interviews with Joyce Vernon Seabolt and Byrd Morgan provide insight into the difficulty of leaving friends and family.

Chapter 3

1. The lay of the land in Arizona's agricultural valleys is somewhat complicated. The Buckeye Valley lies west of the confluence of the Salt and Gila rivers but is still considered within the Salt River Valley.

2. Carey McWilliams, a leading labor activist in California, coined perhaps the most vivid phrase describing industrial agriculture in his muckraking book *Factories in the Field.*

3. Mawn, "Phoenix, Arizona" (diss.), 13–16, 43–44, 80–94, 107–14; Duchemin, "Introducing Urban Form" (thesis), chap. 3. Parallel developments took place south of the Salt River and in the Buckeye Valley; see, for example, Lewis, "Tempe Canal Company," 227–38.

4. The most complete study of the development of the Salt River Project is provided by Smith, *Magnificent Experiment;* chaps. 2, 3, 7 are particularly useful. Donald Worster provides a provocative analysis of reclamation in the Salt River Valley in *Rivers of Empire;* see especially chap. 5. Also helpful are a study of the environmental history of the region, Dunbier, *Sonoran Desert,* especially chaps. 5, 9; Mawn, "Phoenix, Arizona," chap. 6, 497–98.

Not all of the Salt River Valley fell within the boundaries of the Salt River Project. The Buckeye Valley, west of the Agua Fria River, for example, lay on the periphery of the Salt River Project. Growers in the Buckeye Valley and other peripheral areas organized into several irrigation districts that purchased project electricity to pump groundwater for surface irrigation.

5. K. K. Henness, "A History of Agriculture in Pinal County," and James M. Smithwick, "Casa Grande: From Mining to Agriculture: Population Growth and Economic Expansion," both in the vertical files of the Casa Grande Valley Historical Society, Casa Grande (CGVHS); U.S. Department of the Interior, *Annual Report of the Commissioner of Indian*

Affairs to the Secretary of the Interior for the Fiscal Year Ending June 30, 1930, 22; *Engineering News Record* 102 (Feb. 1929): 239; Bureau Census, *Sixteenth Census of the United States: 1940: Agriculture,* vol. 1, pt. 6, *Statistics for Counties,* 399.

6. U.S. Congress, House, Committee on Immigration and Naturalization, *Seasonal Agricultural Laborers from Mexico,* hearings, 69th Cong., 1st sess., 1926, 32.

7. McGowan, *Extra-Long Staple Cottons,* 53, 78–81; Schetter, *Litchfield Park,* 3, 22. Also useful is Smith, "Litchfield Park and Vicinity" (thesis). The Goodyear Ranch developed near Chandler and later known as Ocotillo should not be confused with the town of Goodyear, established in 1964 west of Phoenix. The Southwest Cotton Company changed its name to Goodyear Farms in 1943.

8. Kotlanger, "Phoenix, Arizona" (diss.), 56–57, 64–65, 78; Luckingham, *Phoenix,* 74, 76; McGowan, *Extra-Long Staple Cottons,* 80, 84, 89–91; *Arizona Republic,* 29 Dec. 1929, sec. 8, p. 7; Arizona Department of Agriculture, Crop and Livestock Reporting Service, *Arizona Agricultural Statistics, 1867–1965,* 8, 12, 14, 25, 31; Hearings, La Follette Committee, U.S. Congress, Senate, Committee on Education and Labor (LC), *Violations of Free Speech and Rights of Labor,* pt. 53, *Open-Shop Activities,* 19560.

The cotton-production percentages for Maricopa and Pinal counties are rough averages for the 1930s. During the latter part of that decade, Pinal County increased its percentage of the state's cotton production from 19 percent in 1936 to 30 percent in 1940.

9. Bureau Census, *Fifteenth Census of the United States, 1930: Agriculture,* vol. 3, pt. 3, *The Western States,* 345, 347, *Sixteenth Census: Agriculture,* vol. 1, pt. 6, 401, 403; interviews with Lee Theron Faver and Flora Elizabeth Faver Davis, Thomas Cambron, Samuel Cambron, OMP; Arizona Agricultural Experiment Station, *Agricultural Land Ownership and Operating Tenures in the Casa Grande Valley,* 282–88; TC, *Interstate Migration,* Report of the Select Committee, 432. See also Minutes, Pinal County Land Use Planning Committee, 24 Jan. 1941, 2, Pinal County file, box 56, Regional Files, 1937–42, Arizona State Office, Memo—Pinal Co., Records of the Arizona State Representative, Records of State Offices, Records of BAE, RG 83, NA.

10. *Arizona Producer,* 1 Oct. 1929, p. 10, 15 Oct. 1937, p. 20; WPA, Federal Writers' Program, *Arizona: A State Guide,* 355–56; LC, pt. 53, 19556–57, 19720, exhibit 8791, pt. 72, *Supplementary Exhibits,* 26586, exhibit 13333; Arizona Crop and Livestock Reporting Service, *Arizona*

Agricultural Statistics, 8; Anderson, Clayton and Co., *This Is Anderson, Clayton,* 15–16, Arizona Collection, Arizona Department of Library, Archives, and Public Records (ADL), Phoenix; Bureau Census, *Fifteenth Census: Agriculture,* vol 3, pt. 3, 345; "A Survey of the Migratory Agricultural Labor Population and the Program of the Agricultural Worker's Health and Medical Association in Maricopa and Pinal Counties, Arizona, November 1939," typescript, table 18, folder 217, carton 6, Regional Office 9 Correspondence and Papers, FSA Collection, Bancroft Library, University of California, Berkeley (hereinafter, Bancroft Library); interviews with Fred Faver and Flora Faver Davis, Edwards Young Hooper, Jr., OMP. Anderson, Clayton & Company traced its beginnings to Oklahoma City, where William L. Clayton, Frank E. Anderson, and Monroe D. Anderson formed a cotton merchant partnership in 1904. The number of gins operated by Western Cotton Products and J. G. Boswell Company varied from year to year. During the 1938 and 1939 harvest seasons, Western Cotton Products had six gins in Maricopa County, and J. G. Boswell operated four; the Miller Gin Company ran three, and Farmers Mutual owned two; another ten gins were independent operations.

11. McGowan, *Extra-Long Staple Cottons,* 39–40, 63; *Tempe News,* 28 Feb. 1913, index to the *Tempe News,* Tempe Historical Society, Tempe; *Associated Arizona Producer,* 15 Mar. 1922, pp. 3–5, 7; Nall, "King Cotton," 50–53; Arizona Cotton Growers' Association (ACGA), Board of Directors Minutes, 8 July 1930, Arizona Cotton Growers' Association office, Phoenix. Growers in Texas fixed wages in a similar fashion. See Montejano, *Anglos and Mexicans,* 198.

12. The most detailed study of Arizona's bracero program during World War I is Peterson, "Cibola" (thesis), especially iii, 20–22, 177. Also useful is Scruggs, "Mexican Farm Labor," 319–26; Maciel, "Mexican Migrant Workers," 188.

13. Quoted in WPA, Division of Research, *Migratory Cotton Pickers in Arizona,* 65.

14. Scruggs, "Mexican Farm Labor," 321, 325; Peterson, "Cibola," 32, 39, 45, 48–50, 55–57; *Arizona Labor Journal,* 6 Aug. 1920, p. 1.

15. Much of the information on the 1921 crisis in the cotton fields provided in this chapter is drawn from Peterson, "Cibola," chap. 6. Kotlanger provides background on the cotton-market bust and the stranded Mexicans in "Phoenix," 56–61. See also *Tucson Citizen,* 22 Jan. 1921, p. 8, Mexico Consulate, Phoenix, "Partial Report . . . regarding the Conditions of the Mexican Cotton Pickers Brought to the Salt River Valley by the Arizona Cotton Growers' Association," Arizona Collection, ADL.

16. Mexico Consulate, "Partial Report," Arizona Collection, ADL, [18].

17. Ibid., 2, [6]. The quote is from the latter.

18. Ibid., [23].

19. *Arizona Labor Journal,* 24 Feb. 1921, p. 1, 3 Mar. 1921, p. 1, 10 Mar. 1921, p. 1, 31 Mar. 1921, p. 1; *Tucson Citizen,* 24 Feb. 1921, pp. 1–2, 25 Feb. 1921, p. 2, 27 Feb. 1921, p. 3, 26 Apr. 1921, p. 10, 21 May 1921, p. 2; Tempe City Council Minutes, 22 Apr. 1921, Office of the City Clerk, Tempe City Hall; Peterson, "Cibola," 66–69, chap. 5. Mayor C. H. Tinker of Glendale, Guy Vernon of the Maricopa County Board of Supervisors, and Phoenix City Manager Avery Thompson led the local effort to pressure the cotton growers' association to repatriate the destitute Mexican cotton pickers. The association held that it repatriated 20,651 Mexicans. Still more than 1,000 contract workers, along with many who had crossed into Arizona illegally, remained in the state, adding to the growing Hispanic population.

20. 18 Sept. 1926, index to the *Tempe News,* Tempe Historical Society.

21. *Arizona Republican,* 1 Mar. 1926, p. 6; "Report of the Porto Rican Situation," typescript, n.d., folder 18, Labor Relations file, box 33, Carl Trumbull Hayden Collection, Arizona Collection, Arizona State University, Tempe; *Arizona Labor Journal,* 25 Sept. 1926, p. 1, 2 Oct. 1926, p. 1, 9 Oct. 1926, p. 1, 4 Dec. 1926, p. 1; Pendleton, "History of Labor," 160–79. The Arizona Cotton Growers' Association contracted with the Munson Steamship Company and the Southern Pacific and Santa Fe railroads to transport 1,500 workers in three shipments at a total cost of $56.40 per full fare. Only 1,000–1,200 Puerto Ricans were actually sent to Arizona. It is unclear whether the union organizers came from the ranks of the Puerto Ricans or from Arizona's labor unions. Once the strike was in progress, the Phoenix Central Labor Council came to the aid of the workers, providing food and shelter at the council hall. The AFL, however, claimed no responsibility for initiating the strike. The growers' association maintained that it had proof otherwise.

22. Maciel, "Mexican Migrant Workers," 190; *Arizona Producer,* 1 Sept. 1929, p. 4; TC, *Interstate Migration,* 354–55. In the early 1930s, importation of Mexican labor continued, although to a lesser degree. Those who could document residence in the United States before 1921 could crisscross the border fairly easily. Moreover, considerable numbers of Mexicans remained in Arizona and other southwestern states. Many followed a migratory loop through the fields and formed a large portion of

the local labor force, along with American Indians from nearby reservations, who were preferred in the long-staple fields because of the meticulous care they took in separating the fiber from the leaves and stems, known as "trash." On this last point, see the interview with James Edward Gladden, OMP; U.S. Department of Agriculture, Office of Markets and Rural Organization, "Handling and Marketing," 2.

23. McGowan, *Extra-Long Staple Cottons,* 68; form letter, E. J. Walker, acting general manager, Arizona Cotton Growers' Association, [c. 1923], Arizona Collection, ADL; WPA, *Migratory Cotton Pickers,* 64, 67; Manuscript Census, Maricopa and Pinal Counties, Ariz., 1920, NA; LC, pt. 53, 19560; ACGA, Minutes, 10 June 1930, 11 Sept. 1930, 10 July 1931, 13 Oct. 1931, 17 Nov. 1931. According to Gregory, *American Exodus,* 9, by 1917 growers in California's Imperial and San Joaquin valleys began advertising for cotton pickers in Oklahoma and Texas and in some cases paying their railroad fares. Land companies helped spread the word of the growing cotton industry and urged farmers from the western cotton states to settle newly opened farmlands in the Golden State.

24. *Arizona Republic,* 29 Dec. 1958, 16; LC, pt. 53, 19553–54, 19718, exhibits 8788, 8789, pt. 72, 26601, exhibit 13353-A; interview with Kenneth Earl Taber, OMP; ACGA, Minutes, 13 Dec. 1932, 15 Apr. 1933.

25. Agricultural Workers of Buckeye District to Moeur, folder 18, box 6, Cotton Strike Arbitration Committee, Minutes, 28 Sept. 1933; F. Cornejo (?) and F. Saria (?) to President F. Roosevelt, 3 Oct. 1933; CAWIU Protest Resolution, 4 Nov. 1933; C. B. McDonald, President, Roosevelt Commercial Company, to Gov. B. B. Moeur, 22 Sept. 1934; all in folder 1, box 5A, Governor B. B. Moeur Papers, State Archives, ADL. See also *Arizona Daily Star,* 26 Sept. 1933; Kotlanger, "Phoenix," 74–75; LC, pt. 72, 26608, exhibit 13353-I; Daniel, *Bitter Harvest,* 179, 181–94; *Arizona Labor Journal,* 30 Aug. 1934, p. 1, 13 Sept. 1934, p. 1, 15 Nov. 1934, p. 1; "Interview with Paul Aldridge, Fruit Tramp and Former Organizer, Phoenix, October 24, 1940," typescript, folder 1, carton 1, Regional Office 9 Correspondence and Papers, FSA Collection, Bancroft Library. The 1933 strike, which also took place in the Yuma Valley, preceded a major cotton strike in California's Central Valley by a week. Some cotton growers agreed with the pickers' demands for wage increases proportionate with increases in the price of cotton. C. B. McDonald, president of the Roosevelt Commercial Company, argued for a picking wage of 75 cents per hundred in 1933 but was voted down by the vast majority of the cotton growers.

26. The quote is from the *Arizona Republic,* 2 Sept. 1936, sec. 2, p. 7. See also *Daily Oklahoman,* 19 Sept. 1936, p. 12, 3 Oct. 1936, p. 15, 25

Oct. 1936, sec. B, p. 1, 15 Nov. 1936, sec. B, p. 1. Also that year an individual grower or contractor placed an ad in the Oklahoma City newspapers, as did a labor scout who may or may not have been affiliated with the Farm Labor Service.

27. National Association of Travelers Aid Societies, *Transient Families in Arizona*, 2–7, 16–17, Arizona Collection, ADL. See also ACGA, Minutes, 12 Nov. 1930, 17 Nov. 1931. Tuberculars and other transient health seekers, for whom Arizona had long been a mecca, were excluded from Blair's study. Blair did not attribute the increase in the number of migrant families to the influx of cotton pickers; in fact, she discounted any correlation. Yet the first six months of the year, the boom period, corresponded precisely to the months when pickers would have become unemployed and in need of relief.

Curiously, 43 percent of the Oklahomans recorded by the Social Service Center in Phoenix were black. As we shall see, almost all of the Oklahoma cotton pickers in the latter half of the decade were white. This disparity may indicate that African Americans were expelled from tenant farms early on and did not thereafter claim residency in Oklahoma. Interviews with growers and migrant workers indicate that few blacks picked cotton in Arizona in the 1930s.

About middecade, relief officials abandoned the practice of providing gas and oil once they realized that transients used the fuel to move westward rather than to return home. Instead, the Transient Division of the Federal Emergency Relief Administration, which in 1933 began providing aid to transients in Arizona, gave migrants bus or train tickets to their home states and kept their decrepit automobiles in exchange. Migrant workers who intended to push on to California were forced to obtain transportation money from some source other than local relief agencies; see WPA, *Transient Camps: Emergency Relief Administration of Arizona*, 34, Arizona Collection, ADL; Lowitt and Beasley, eds., *One-Third of a Nation*, 245. The practice may have been revived after 1935 when the federal transient camps closed their gates, if the claims of California officials during the Bum Blockade of 1936 can be believed; see *Arizona Republic*, 5 Feb. 1936, p. 4, *Los Angeles Times*, 7 Feb. 1936, p. 4, for examples of this argument.

28. WPA, *Transient Camps*, 39, Arizona Collection, ADL; Lowitt and Beasley, *One-Third of a Nation*, 246–48.

29. *Arizona Republic*, 5 Feb. 1936, pp. 1, 4, 6 Feb. 1936, p. 1, 7 Feb. 1936, p. 1, 8 Feb. 1936, p. 1, 11 Feb. 1936, p. 1, 12 Feb. 1936, p. 1, 14 Feb. 1936, p. 1; *Los Angeles Times*, 7 Feb. 1936, p. 1, 11 Feb. 1936, p. 1; *Yuma*

Daily Sun and Yuma Arizona Sentinel (hereinafter, *Yuma Daily Sun*), 3 Feb. 1936, p. 2, 4 Feb. 1936, p. 1, 5 Feb. 1936, p. 1, 6 Feb. 1936, p. 1, 7 Feb. 1936, p. 1, 8 Feb. 1936, p. 1, 10 Feb. 1936, p. 1, 11 Feb. 1936, p. 1. Although this family may not have been in Arizona to pick cotton, the apparent financial standard would have prevented the migration into California of most farm-worker families without employment contracts. Ironically, Yuma had tried the same type of blockade at the beginning of the decade only to have the action stopped by the federal government at the behest of California officials. See Capt. MacCardie to Moeur, 9 June 1935, Moeur Papers, State Archives, ADL.

30. Interview with Joyce Vernon Seabolt, COP. Sympathetic people in Yuma took the Seabolt family into their home for refreshments and then to a neighborhood park to await the arrival of Alfred's brother. The practice of requiring proof of employment to enter California apparently continued after the Los Angeles police officially disbanded the Bum Blockade; see interview with Alvin Laird, COP.

31. *Arizona Republic,* 5 Feb. 1936, p. 4.

32. Kotlanger, "Phoenix, Arizona," 259; *Arizona Republic,* 12 Feb. 1936, p. 1. Just prior to the Bum Blockade, the Phoenix police had raided a "hobo jungle" and "deported" 143 men and a woman by taking them thirty miles in the direction of their choice and ordering them to keep moving; see *Yuma Daily Sun,* 17 Jan. 1936, p. 1.

33. *Laws of Arizona, 1937,* ch. 18, sec. 1, p. 34. The passage of the residency law came about in response not only to the problems created by migrant field laborers and the transient unemployed but also to the increasing burden of the indigent sick, particularly victims of tuberculosis who flocked to Arizona for the curing effects of its dry air. Since the 1890s, Phoenix boosters had sought health seekers by promoting the city as a "lunger's mecca." By the Great Depression, however, the care for and burial of penniless consumptives had become a financial burden. See Mawn, "Phoenix, Arizona," 281–88; Kotlanger, "Phoenix," 223–26; Arizona Board of Public Health, *Public Health in Arizona,* 38, 45, 48; Harry L. Hopkins, Administrator, Federal Emergency Relief Administration, to Sen. Carl Hayden, 31 Oct. 1933, Oct.–Dec. 1933 file, box 11, Arizona Transients; Esther C. Friedman, Case Consultant, Arizona Board of Public Welfare, to Charles H. Alspach, Director, Transient Activities, 16 Mar. 1936, Complaints (A–C) file, box 12, Arizona Transients; both in Federal Emergency Relief Administration Records, Records of WPA, RG 69, NA.

Chapter 4

1. *U. S. v. Butler,* 1–88; Saloutos, *American Farmer,* 124, 236–37; Ganger, "Impact of Mechanization," 301–2; Bureau Census, *Cotton Production and Distribution, Season of 1937–38,* 4, 20; Arizona Crop and Livestock Reporting Service, *Arizona Agricultural Statistics,* 12, 24, 30, 36. The 1937 harvest proved especially fruitful: production in Pinal County more than doubled, and that in Maricopa County increased by more than 75 percent compared to the previous year. Altogether, Arizona's cotton growers produced more than 300,000 bales of upland cotton.

2. *Casa Grande Dispatch,* 27 Aug. 1937, p. 1; *Chandler Arizonan,* 27 Aug. 1937, p. 1; *Arizona Producer,* 15 Oct. 1937, p. 7; *Arizona Republic,* 2 Nov. 1937, sec. 2, p. 1; LC, pt. 72, 26603, exhibit 13353-D.

3. LC, pt. 72, 26590, exhibit 13338, 26593, exhibit 13343; *Arizona Farmer-Producer,* 30 Sept. 1939, pp. 1, 13; Arizona Agricultural Experiment Station, *Growing Upland Cotton in Arizona,* 11, *Upland Cotton Production in Arizona,* 18; Brown and Ware, *Cotton,* 422–23; Carl V. Feaster, SuPima Association, interview with author, 3 Aug. 1988; interviews with Kenneth Taber, Edwards Hooper, OMP; Salt River Project, *Annual History,* 1936, 1937, 1938, temperature and precipitation tables, Research Archives, Salt River Project (SRP), Tempe.

4. *Arizona Republic,* 17 Oct. 1937, p. 8, 19 Oct. 1937, sec. 2, p. 7; *Arizona Daily Star,* 27 Mar. 1938, p. 2; LC, pt. 72, 26595–96, exhibit 13348; WPA, *Migratory Cotton Pickers,* 62. In Pinal County, agricultural leaders requested that the WPA workers, even cotton pickers, constructing the road between Casa Grande and La Palma be retained to complete the market route. According to the WPA, all other agricultural laborers in the cotton counties were released from its rolls during the harvest.

5. *Arizona Republic,* 17 Oct. 1937, p. 8.

6. LC, pt. 53, 19731, exhibit 8805; *Laws of Arizona, 1937,* ch. 67, sec. 1672, pp. 266–67; *Laws of Arizona, 1933,* ch. 100, sec. 1, pp. 472–73; WPA, *Migratory Cotton Pickers,* 68–69, 74. Arizona law defined a "common carrier" as any vehicle hired to transport three or more persons at a time.

7. LC, pt. 53, 19565–66, 19729, exhibit 8803, 19730, exhibit 8804; WPA, *Migratory Cotton Pickers,* 71, 73; *Daily Oklahoman,* 23 Sept. 1937, p. 9; interviews with Kenneth Taber and Murrel Harris, OMP. In Oklahoma, Neil Addington, director of the state public welfare administration, told Earl Taber that he could not help since the growers in his own state had a labor shortage. A WPA study found that few people who arrived

for the cotton harvest had been encouraged by relief agencies to make the trip.

8. LC, pt. 72, 26588–89, exhibit 13336.

9. Facsimile in WPA, *Migratory Cotton Pickers,* 72. Taber also conducted leaflet campaigns to attract American Indians from nearby reservations and Hispanics from southern Arizona and southern California; see LC, pt. 53, 19561–62.

10. LC, pt. 53, 19563–65, 19728, exhibit 8801; WPA, *Migratory Cotton Pickers,* 71, 73–74; interview with Kenneth Taber, OMP.

11. *Daily Oklahoman,* 11 Sept. 1937, p. 11. This advertisement ran for the next two days. Similar notices appeared in newspapers in towns along the migratory routes through northern Arizona and New Mexico and in Arkansas, Colorado, Texas, and Utah. For a summary of the advertising campaign, see LC, pt. 53, 19722–25, exhibit 8797.

12. *Daily Oklahoman,* 18 Sept. 1937, p. 10.

13. LC, pt. 53, 19730, exhibit 8804.

14. *Daily Oklahoman,* 23 Sept. 1937, p. 15. This series ran for five days the week of September 23. Later advertisements reported earnings of 85¢ per 100 pounds of cotton. In Texas, Taber advertised a need for 7,000 cotton pickers throughout the month of October.

15. Mawn, "Phoenix," 121, 172; Luckingham, *Phoenix,* 110; LC, pt. 53, 19730, exhibit 8804; *Daily Oklahoman,* 19 Oct. 1937, p. 1.

16. *Daily Oklahoman,* 15 Oct. 1937, p. 19.

17. Bureau Census, *Cotton Production, 1937–38,* 12; *Arizona Producer,* 15 Oct. 1937, p. 7; *Chandler Arizonan,* 15 Oct. 1937, p. 1, 10 Nov. 1937, p. 1, 12 Nov. 1937, p. 1; *Daily Oklahoman,* 10 Nov. 1937, p. 17; LC, pt. 53, 19723–24, exhibit 8797.

18. LC, pt. 53, 19731, exhibit 8805. By early December, 70 percent of the cotton in the vicinity of Chandler had been harvested, and all three gins were operating full time. Other areas continued to experience labor shortages. In the Buckeye area, only one-third of the crop had been ginned by the first week of December, and ginning capacity had yet to be reached. See *Arizona Republic,* 4 Dec. 1937, sec. 2, p. 7; *Chandler Arizonan,* 5 Nov. 1937, p. 1; *Buckeye Valley News,* 9 Dec. 1937, p. 1.

19. LC, pt. 53, 19566, 19574–75, 19773, exhibit 8824; Taylor and Rowell, "Refugee Labor Migration," 241; Arizona Agricultural Extension Service, *Arizona's Farm Laborers,* 334. Estimates ranged from a low of 20,000–22,000 provided by Taber and E. D. Tetreau, rural sociologist for the Arizona Agricultural Extension Service, to a high of 30,000 provided by the U.S. Department of Labor. The figure used here was derived by the

WPA based on daily ginning figures and the assumption that it took ten workers to pick a bale of cotton per day.

20. The WPA selected a sample of 518 household units from thirty "representative camps" of all sizes in Maricopa, Pinal, and Pima counties. Through interviews and questionnaires, researchers from the WPA and the University of Arizona created personal histories of each migrant group for the period between January 1 and December 31, 1937. During the course of the study (January–February 1938), the migrant population dropped from about 30,000 to an estimated 15,000. See WPA, *Migratory Cotton Pickers,* xii–xiii, 103–4, for a description of the methodology and facsimiles of the questionnaire schedules.

21. News stories about the labor shortage appeared, for example, in the *Anadarko Daily News,* 23 Sept. 1937, p. 1; the *Wewoka Times-Democrat,* 23 Sept. 1937, p. 10; and the *Lawton Constitution,* 23 Sept. 1937, sec. A, p. 8. The article in the Anadarko paper was based on a press release that mimicked paid advertising. The other stories, from the UP wires, reported Taber's unsuccessful request for help in securing labor from the Oklahoma Public Welfare Administration.

22. WPA, *Migratory Cotton Pickers,* 29–30, 71; draft manuscript of "Migratory Cotton-Pickers in Arizona, 1937," 15 Mar. 1938, 24–25, general file, box 12, Arizona records, Records of the Rural Rehabilitation Division, Records of the Farmers Home Administration (FHA), RG 96, NA (hereinafter, Draft WPA Report). See also *Phoenix Gazette,* 23 Mar. 1940 (Blue Streak ed. unless otherwise indicated), p. 9; LaRue McCormick, International Labor Defense, to Franklin D. Roosevelt, 17 Feb. 1938, Governor R. C. Stanford Papers, State Archives, ADL.

In the WPA study, 498 groups reported their reasons for coming to Arizona; of these, 211 came from Oklahoma. Those who cited advertising referred to newspapers, radio, and handbills, not to placards seen along the road. An even greater percentage of Texans were attracted by advertising, although their numbers were fewer. Of the 69 Texans who responded to the question, 42 percent were attracted to Arizona by advertising, and 22 percent had heard rumors of jobs picking cotton. Many Texans had heard appeals for cotton pickers broadcast on radio stations in Texas, an advertising strategy devised by a group of growers in Buckeye under the auspices of the Buckeye Chamber of Commerce. See LC, pt. 53, 19730, exhibit 8804; WPA, *Migratory Cotton Pickers,* 74.

23. WPA, *Migratory Cotton Pickers,* 30.

24. Ibid., 99. These percentages refer only to the 371 migrant groups in the study who started their migration in 1937.

25. Interviews with James Edward "Ned" Gladden and Betty Lyon McGrath, OMP. In the same collection, see also interviews with Dewey George Phares and Donel O'Neil Leatherbury.

26. WPA, *Migratory Cotton Pickers*, 29. See also the interview with Loye Lucille Holmes, COP, and interviews with Ewell Bennett, Dennis Kirkland, Samuel Cambron, Thomas Cambron, OMP.

27. TC, pt. 7, 2817.

28. Ibid., 2904–5.

29. WPA, *Migratory Cotton Pickers*, 29. For a similar story, see the interview with Dorothy Price Rose, COP.

30. WPA, *Migratory Cotton Pickers*, 21–22, 98. School authorities in the Dysart and Liberty school districts in Maricopa County provided this information to WPA researchers.

31. WPA, *Migratory Cotton Pickers*, 23. These figures refer to the 371 migrant groups in the study who had left their states of origin in 1937. Specific information on the origins of the 147 groups who began following the crops earlier is not available.

32. FSA, *Study of 6,655 Migrant Households*, 14. These figures refer only to the farm laborers who received assistance from the FSA in 1938. According to Paul Taylor and Edward Rowell, only 24 percent of the unemployed laborers (including nonagricultural laborers) who entered California in 1937 had come from Oklahoma, 10 percent from Texas. These percentages, however, probably understate the proportion of Oklahomans and Texans among the migrants to California since they are based on a count of license plates made at the plant quarantine stations at the ports of entry. Those who stopped for the Arizona cotton harvest in 1936 and stayed through April 1, 1937, would have been required to purchase Arizona license plates. In fact, most migrants with Arizona tags entered California between April and July. Nearly 12 percent of the vehicles enumerated at the California line bore Arizona plates. Assuming that half of these migrants were actually Oklahomans, the Sooner State supplied 30 percent of those entering California in 1937. See Taylor and Rowell, "Refugee Labor Migration," 242–43.

33. WPA, *Migratory Cotton Pickers*, 24; draft manuscript of "Migratory Cotton Picker in Arizona," 1 Mar. 1938, p. 12, folder 27, carton 1, Regional Office 9 Correspondence and Papers, FSA Collection, Bancroft Library. Other studies confirmed the predominance of whites in the migrant population. About 93 percent of the unemployed laborers entering California in 1937 were white, as were 92 percent of those applying for assistance from the FSA in California during 1938. Of those migrants from

Oklahoma, Arkansas, and Missouri, nearly 96 percent were white (see Taylor and Rowell, "Refugee Labor Migration," 245, FSA, *Study of 6,655 Migrant Households,* appendix, table 6). Mixed-blood American Indians, however, could have been difficult to discern, and since the census classified American Indians as "white," no statistical information on their interstate migration during the Depression is available. However, interviews with Oklahoma migrants in California and Arizona lend credence to the idea that many of the migrants were mixed-blood American Indian. About one in six of the Oklahomans interviewed for the California Odyssey Project were mixed-blood Cherokee, Choctaw, or Creek. Of those interviewed by me as part of the Oklahoma Migration Project, one in three were mixed-blood Cherokee, Choctaw, or Kiowa-Comanche. The total number of interviews with migrants, however, is far too small to offer statistical reliability. Few of the families identified themselves as American Indian during the Depression, largely to avoid discrimination. Among those I interviewed, only Donel Leatherbury, a Kiowa-Comanche, and W. D. Durant, the proud grandson of Choctaw leader Dixon Durant, could be identified readily as American Indian (see also the interviews with Vivian Smith Estes, Dennis Kirkland, Ewell Bennett, OMP; Joyce Vernon Seabolt, Loye Lucille Martin Holmes, Lillie Counts Dunn, Vivian Barnes Kirschenmann, Byrd Morgan, Clarence William Graham, Martha Lee Martin Jackson, COP). As for the number of African Americans, the WPA did not include black migrants living in the slums of south Phoenix in its study. At the beginning of the decade, 43 percent of the Oklahomans seeking travelers' aid in Phoenix were black. However, by all accounts, African Americans did not become a significant part of the overall agricultural work force until the 1940s (see National Association of Travelers Aid Societies, *Transient Families in Arizona,* 4, Arizona Collection, ADL; McWilliams, *Ill Fares the Land,* 87–88; Kotlanger, "Phoenix," 448–49).

34. WPA, *Migratory Cotton Pickers,* 25–26, 95–96; Arizona Agricultural Experiment Station, *Arizona's Agricultural Population,* i, 62. The median family size was about four persons. Stereotypes notwithstanding, nearly one-fourth of the migrant families consisted of only two persons, usually a husband and a wife. Still, nearly one-third of the families were fairly large, consisting of six or more people. More than 65 percent of the family heads were less than forty-five years old. Not all were farmers by the time they left Oklahoma. Some migrant families had left cities, towns, and oil fields. More than one-fourth of the men interviewed by the WPA had been employed in construction, manufacturing, or industry.

35. WPA, *Migratory Cotton Pickers,* 45–47, 100; Taber to Moeur, 7 Mar. 1936, folder 37, box 7, Moeur Papers, State Archives, ADL; Janow and Gilmartin, "Labor and Migration," 24; interview with Samuel Cambron, OMP. Some growers, like C. O. Vosburgh, encouraged their pickers to leave while they still had money. These figures refer to the migrants who resided in one of the western cotton states in January 1937. When those already on the road at the first of the year were counted, only one quarter of the respondents intended to go on to California. This difference indicates that a higher percentage of those who had already been to California did not know where they would go next. Only one in seven of the Oklahomans (including those who had left home more than a year before the survey) planned to return to the Sooner State.

36. WPA, *Migratory Cotton Pickers,* xi; *Arizona Republic,* 12 Feb. 1938, p. 1; *Yuma Daily Sun,* 11 Feb. 1938, p. 1, 14 Feb. 1938, p. 1, 3 Mar. 1938, p. 1; *Daily Oklahoman,* 13 Feb. 1938, sec. A, p. 8, 14 Feb. 1938, p. 1. By Mar., the Imperial Valley experienced flooding rains as well. These floods, which created new misery for already destitute migrant laborers, provided the backdrop for John Steinbeck's *The Grapes of Wrath.* Importantly, they precipitated the development of an anti-Okie hysteria in California; see Stein, *Dust Bowl Migration,* 75–77; Benson, *True Adventures,* 368.

37. *Chandler Arizonan,* 11 Mar. 1938, p. 1.

38. *Arizona Republic,* 13 Mar. 1938, p. 8; *Arizona Daily Star,* 13 Mar. 1938, p. 1.

39. *Chandler Arizonan,* 11 Mar. 1938, p. 1; *Arizona Republic,* 31 Oct. 1937, p. 9.

40. *Arizona Republic,* 13 Mar. 1938, p. 8.

41. LC, pt. 53, 19569.

42. *Arizona Republic,* 13 Mar. 1938, p. 8; see also Stanford to Hayden, 10 Feb. 1938, folder 18, box 10, Stanford Papers, State Archives, ADL.

43. *Yuma Daily Sun,* 15 Mar. 1938, p. 1; *Arizona Daily Star,* 15 Mar. 1938, p. 1; LC, pt. 53, 19570; WPA, *Migratory Cotton Pickers,* xii; Pendleton, "History," 240. The state residency law (*Laws of Arizona, 1937,* ch. 18, sec. 1, p. 34) provided that "nothing herein shall prevent the granting of relief or aid in emergency cases."

44. *Arizona Republic,* 24 Mar. 1938, p. 3.

45. LC, pt. 53, 19570. McDougall's case workers maintained that conditions were not as acute as reported by the cotton pickers. A reporter for the *Phoenix Gazette* found conditions in some camps as serious as

represented; in others "they appeared to be no worse than usual" (see *Phoenix Gazette,* 23 Mar. 1938, pp. 9, 10). As we shall see, however, the "usual" condition of the cotton camps could be squalid.

46. *Arizona Daily Star,* 22 Mar. 1938, p. 1; *Phoenix Gazette,* 21 Mar. 1938, p. 3; the quote is from the latter.

47. WPA, *Migratory Cotton Pickers,* 9–10; Draft WPA Report, 36, Records of FHA, RG 96, NA; "Survey of the Program of the Agricultural Worker's Health and Medical Association," 9, folder 217, carton 6, Regional 9 Correspondence and Papers, FSA Collection, Bancroft Library; TC, pt. 7, 2819; *Arizona Republic,* 2 Apr. 1938, p. 5.

48. "Cotton! Cotton!," *Arizona Public Health News,* 2.

49. Ibid.; WPA, *Migratory Cotton Pickers,* 5–7; Evans, "Housing," 2; reports in Farm Labor Housing Surveys file, box 53, regional files, correspondence—Flood Control, Records of the Arizona State Representative 1937–42, Records of State Offices, Records of BAE, RG 83, NA; McWilliams, *Ill Fares the Land,* 86; interviews with Edwards Hooper, Lee Faver, Dewey Phares, Betty Lyon McGrath, Thomas Cambron, Samuel Cambron, Donel Leatherbury, Dennis Kirkland, OMP. In 1939 nearly 70 percent of the pickers in central Arizona lived in one of nearly 200 grower-owned cotton camps or in camps established by labor contractors.

50. Interview with Rosie Harlas Laird, 42, COP.

51. Interview with Dewey Phares, OMP.

52. McWilliams, *Ill Fares the Land,* 87; interviews with Masuria Ann McCandless Stephens, Betty Lyon McGrath, Thomas Cambron, Samuel Cambron, Jarrell Eugene Bowlan, OMP. In 1939 at least 10 percent of the migrants lived in squatters' camps. In Maricopa and Pinal counties, the FSA enumerated 716 squatters' camps, home to more than three thousand migrants. Considering the probable difficulty in locating small squatters' camps, however, it is quite likely that this figure is low.

53. TC, pt. 7, 2820.

54. Interview with Vera Ruth Woodall Criswell, COP.

55. *New York Times,* 5 Mar. 1940, p. 25. See also McWilliams, *Ill Fares the Land,* 86; Draft WPA Report, 36, Records of FHA, RG 96, NA; TC, pt. 7, 2819; Banfield, *Government Project,* 69; WPA, *Migratory Cotton Pickers,* 6.

56. WPA, *Migratory Cotton Pickers,* 5–6, 15; McWilliams, *Ill Fares the Land,* 86–87; TC, pt. 7, 2818; interview with Vivian Smith Estes, OMP. Some motor courts were just a step above the average cotton camp. Thomas Higgenbottom remembered that an Eloy tourist camp was "mighty filthy" despite the $8–$10 monthly rent.

57. WPA, *Migratory Cotton Pickers,* 1–3.

58. Interview with Masuria Ann McCandless Stephens, 14–15, OMP.

59. Interview with Samuel Cambron, 13, OMP. See also the interview with Thomas Cambron, OMP; Alvin Laird, COP.

60. WPA, *Migratory Cotton Pickers,* 2–3; LC, pt. 53, 19594; *Daily Oklahoman,* 7 Oct. 1937, p. 1; interviews with James Edward Gladden, Masuria Ann McCandless Stephens, Thomas Cambron, W. D. Durant and Naomi Dixon Durant, Dennis Kirkland, OMP; Alvin Laird, COP. In areas of Oklahoma where cotton averaged one-fourth to one-half a bale an acre, workers snapping bolls reportedly averaged about 350 pounds per day.

61. The data on cotton pickers' earnings comes from WPA, *Migratory Cotton Pickers,* 1–3, 14–16, 94–95; see also Draft WPA Report, 29–32, Records of FHA, RG 96, NA. The information on wages for WPA workers is provided in W. J. Jamieson, State Works Progress Administrator, to Stanford, 20 Jan. 1937, 2–3, folder 3, box 11, Stanford Papers, State Archives, ADL. Marvin Montgomery's weekly earnings are reported in TC, pt. 7, 2905. Those who had entered the migration stream in 1937 had earned an average of only $156 after leaving home, raising their average total earnings to $424. By comparison, per capita income in Arizona for 1937 was $482. For nonseasonal farm labor, the average annual wage without board in Arizona amounted to $648, whereas the annual wage for an unskilled laborer employed by the WPA, assuming year-round employment, came to $527. For per capita income, consult *Arizona Statistical Review, 1948,* 6. The average annual farm wage is calculated from BAE, *Farm Wage Rates, Farm Employment, and Related Data,* 94. The interview with Dennis Kirkland, OMP, provides insight into workers' expectations.

62. McWilliams, *Ill Fares the Land,* 87–88; TC, pt. 7, 2955; *Yuma Daily Sun,* 5 Jan. 1938, p. 3; *Buckeye Valley News,* 6 Jan. 1938, p. 1; *Phoenix Gazette,* Home ed., 30 Mar. 1938, p. 10, Blue Streak ed., 30 Mar. 1938, sec. 2, p. 4, 31 Mar. 1938, p. 5; *Arizona v. Bill Walker, Bill Walker v. Arizona,* Criminal Record 14538, Maricopa County Superior Court, Maricopa County Courthouse, Phoenix. The extent of grower-owned commissaries was limited, although some growers, such as Roy and Jim Fansler, operated them. On Saturdays, the workday usually ended at noon, and many farm workers went to town to buy groceries (see WPA, *Migratory Cotton Pickers,* 8; interviews with Fred Faver, Dennis Kirkland, OMP; Bertha Wallace oral history, excerpted in the newsletter of the Coolidge Historical Society, Oct. 1988).

63. LC, pt. 53, 19732, exhibit 8806. Some migrants squandered their earnings on wine or gambled them away. For observations on the subject, see the interviews with Masuria Ann McCandless Stephens, Dennis Kirkland, OMP.

64. *Phoenix Gazette,* 23 Mar. 1938, p. 10.

65. "Cotton! Cotton!" 2.

66. *Chandler Arizonan,* 11 Mar. 1938, p. 1; *Buckeye Valley News,* 17 Mar. 1938, p. 8, 31 Mar. 1938, p. 1; *Phoenix Gazette,* 23 Mar. 1938, p. 10; *Arizona Producer,* 1 June 1938, p. 8; interviews with Lee Faver and Flora Faver Davis, Arthur Linville Mercer, OMP.

67. *Arizona Republic,* 23 Mar. 1938, p. 1; *Arizona Daily Star,* 23 Mar. 1938, p. 1; *Phoenix Gazette,* 23 Mar. 1938, pp. 5, 9. Telegrams and letters to the governor were sent by Donald Henderson, president of UCAPAWA (23 Mar. 1938); C. H. Jordan, secretary of the Los Angeles Industrial Union Council (24 Mar. 1938); H. Stuyvelaar, secretary of the San Francisco District Industrial Union Council (23 Mar. 1938), and officials at UCAPAWA District 2 and the West Coast Regional Office of the CIO (both 23 Mar. 1938); these missives and the governor's replies are in folder 2, box 8, Stanford Papers, State Archives, ADL; see especially Stanford to Henderson, 26 Mar. 1938. As for the actual size of the crowd at the capitol, estimates reported by newspapers ranged from sixty to two hundred men. In sworn testimony, however, McDougall put the figure at about two hundred persons.

68. *Phoenix Gazette,* 23 Mar. 1938, p. 5.

69. *Arizona Daily Star,* 24 Mar. 1938, p. 1; *Arizona Republic,* 24 Mar. 1938, p. 3; *Phoenix Gazette,* Home ed., 23 Mar. 1938, p. 9, Blue Streak ed., 23 Mar. 1938, p. 5, 24 Mar. 1938, sec. 2, p. 10. The *Arizona Labor Journal,* 24 Mar. 1938, p. 1, published by the Arizona Federation of Labor, commended the restraint of the Phoenix police in maintaining order during the various disturbances "without using clubs, guns, or gas bombs."

70. *Arizona Republic,* 24 Mar. 1938, p. 1.

71. U.S. Department of Labor, Bureau of Labor Statistics, *Labor Unionism in American Agriculture,* 200–202; Pendleton, "History of Labor," 264; *Phoenix Gazette,* 26 Mar. 1938, p. 2; *Arizona Daily Star,* 27 Mar. 1938, p. 14. A personal account of Kope's organizing efforts by someone who worked with him is in "Interview with Paul Aldridge, Fruit Tramp and Former Organizer, Phoenix, October 24, 1940," folder 1, carton 1, Regional Office 9 Correspondence and Papers, FSA Collection, Bancroft Library.

72. *Arizona Producer,* 1 Mar. 1938, pp. 1, 12. The subpoenaed exhibits contained in LC, pt. 58, *Open-Shop Activities,* 21706–23 and

21725–28, pt. 71, *Supplementary Exhibits,* 26227–46, constitute a rich source of information on the activities of the Associated Farmers of Maricopa County. The press frequently referred to the organization erroneously as Associated Farmers of Arizona. Pinal and Yuma counties also organized Associated Farmers groups.

73. *Chandler Arizonan,* 1 Apr. 1938, p. 2; correspondence in folder 28, box 8, Stanford Papers, State Archives, ADL; *Arizona Republic,* 17 Feb. 1938, p. 1, 9 Feb. 1937, p. 4, 12 Feb. 1937, p. 2; *Phoenix Gazette,* 24 Feb. 1938, p. 10; *CIO News,* 12 Mar. 1938, p. 1; Pendleton, "History of Labor," 265–68, 271–75; Bureau of Labor Statistics, *Labor Unionism in Agriculture,* 200; WPA, *Migratory Cotton Pickers,* 59. Information regarding the role of cotton growers in the Associated Farmers is in LC, pt. 72, 26598–604, exhibits 13351-A, -B, exhibits 13353-A, -B, -C, -E.

74. LC, pt. 72, 26604, exhibit 13353-F, pt. 58, 21716, exhibit 9348, 21719, exhibit 9351; *Arizona Labor Journal,* 11 Jan. 1940, p. 1. After 1939, following unsuccessful efforts to organize strawberry and lettuce pickers, UCAPAWA concentrated on organizing packing-shed workers, not field laborers. Nonetheless, in October 1939 Lawrence Andrews, the field secretary of the Associated Farmers of Maricopa County, wrote to Hugh T. Osborne, the secretary-manager of the Associated Farmers of Imperial County, seeking the "low down" on the Madera strike, particularly the names of the "agitators" who participated.

75. The quote is from the interview with Thomas Cambron, 30, OMP; also see the interviews with James Edward Gladden, Donel Leatherbury, Betty McGrath, Kenneth Taber, Samuel Cambron, Murrell Harris, Lee Faver and Flora Faver Davis, and Masuria Ann McCandless Stephens. Even farmers who were fair with their workers could be targets. Fred Faver, who by all accounts was scrupulously honest with his pickers, caught one man who had lined his cotton sack with a quilt to increase the weight.

76. 11 Feb. 1938, p. 1.

77. *Phoenix Gazette,* 23 Mar. 1938, p. 10.

78. *Arizona Republic,* 27 Mar. 1938, sec. 2, p. 4.

79. Ibid., 25 Mar. 1938, p. 1, 26 Mar. 1938, p. 5, 27 Mar. 1938, p. 4; *Arizona Daily Star,* 26 Mar. 1938, p. 3, 27 Mar. 1938, p. 14; *Phoenix Gazette,* 25 Mar. 1939, p. 2, 26 Mar. 1938, p. 2, 2 Apr. 1938, p. 5, 5 Apr. 1938, sec. 2, p. 4; LC, pt. 53, 19571.

80. *Arizona Republic,* 10 Apr. 1938, p. 6; Laurence I. Hewes, Jr., regional director, to C. B. Baldwin, assistant administrator, FSA, 24 Jan. 1940, 1, "Arizona Grant Program" attachment, both in Grants file, box 11, General Correspondence 1934–43, Records of Region 9, Records of the

Resettlement Division (RD), Records of FHA, RG 96, NA; LC, pt. 72, 26587, exhibit 13335. The FSA required recipients to be former farm owners, tenants, or sharecroppers who had labored in Arizona's agricultural fields. Inevitably, however, indigents who did not meet these requirements managed to slip through, inflating the apparent number of distressed cotton pickers remaining in Arizona.

Chapter 5

1. 24 Mar. 1938, p. 2.

2. *Arizona Republic,* 24 Oct. 1937, sec. 3, p. 8.

3. Ibid., 3 Apr. 1938, sec. 3, p. 8; LC, pt. 53, 19732, exhibit 8806; Draft WPA Report, 25–26, Records of FHA, RG 96, NA.

4. *Arizona Republic,* 17 Oct. 1937, sec. 2, p. 3; see also 27 Mar. 1938, sec. 2, p. 4.

5. TC, pt. 5, 1820, 1825, 1885, pt. 6, 2475; LC, pt. 53, 19582, 19730, exhibit 8804, pt. 72, 26589–90, exhibit 13338, pt. 47, *California Agricultural Background: Subpena Hearing,* 17264; Robinson, *Migrants,* 20, 27–28. Californians did not decry Arizona's recruiting activities until 1940, after La Follette's investigation of agricultural conditions in California motivated them to focus the blame elsewhere. Moreover, Texans did not complain out of altruism. For a discussion of the measures Texas farmers took to avoid "labor theft," see Montejano, *Anglos and Mexicans,* 207–13.

6. The location of the original file of subpoenaed documents is unknown. A search of the La Follette committee's files, the papers of Robert M. La Follette, Jr., and the files of the Arizona Cotton Growers' Association and the Maricopa County Farm Bureau (parent organizations of the Farm Labor Service) failed to uncover the documents. Nor did Taber's son, Kenneth, know their whereabouts. Access to the records of the Arizona Farm Bureau Federation, for whom Taber subsequently worked, was denied. Those documents that were printed as part of the hearing record form the foundation of this study.

7. A good analysis of the committee's work is provided by Auerbach, *Labor and Liberty.* The La Follette committee, a subcommittee of the Senate Committee on Education and Labor, examined civil liberties violations throughout the nation — specifically anti-union activities — from 1936 through mid-1940. In California, La Follette focused on the activities of the Associated Farmers of California. The Associated Farmers of Maricopa County in Arizona also came under scrutiny. Committee mem-

ber David I. Walsh, senator from Massachusetts, did not participate in the California hearings, nor did he help prepare the hearing report.

8. Wagner-Peyser Act, SL 48, ch. 49, pp. 113–17; LC, pt. 53, 19580, 19582, 19769, exhibit 8815.

9. Under the regulations governing the administration of the Wagner-Peyser Act, which created the U.S. Employment Service and the Farm Placement Service, the federal and state employment services were required to cooperate with any private employment agency that did not charge a fee. The Farm Labor Service was financed by cotton gin operators, not by workers or growers. However, Taber's operation did not fulfill all the requirements of a "cooperating agency." Employment services working in affiliation with the U.S. Employment Service were to be governed by public boards or agencies, not private boards of directors (see "Cooperation of United States Employment Service and State Employment Agencies," *Code of Federal Regulations,* title 29, pt. 21, 1938 ed.).

10. LC, pt. 53, 19561, 19566, 19576–82, 19767–69, exhibits 8812, 8813, 8814, 8815; WPA, *Migratory Cotton Pickers,* 68; John N. Webb, Coordinator of Urban Surveys, WPA, to Philip McGuire, Director of Rural Rehabilitation Division, FSA, 18 Apr. 1938, Arizona file, General Correspondence, Records of the Rural Rehabilitation Division, Records of FHA, RG 96, NA. Taber also maintained a private office in the annex of the Physicians Building on Monroe Street, the address that appeared on the letterhead of the Farm Labor Service. But all of his advertising carried the Jefferson Street address of the Arizona State Employment Service and the U.S. Farm Placement Service. Investigators with the WPA voiced concern that casual observers had no way of distinguishing between the federal Farm Placement Service and the growers' recruiting organization.

11. See Auerbach, *Labor and Liberty,* 80, for a discussion of La Follette's interrogation methods.

12. LC, pt. 53, 19578.

13. Ibid., 19576–81.

14. Weekly Progress Reports binder, 1937–1939, Records of the Division of Social Research, Records of WPA, RG 69, NA; WPA, *Migratory Cotton Pickers,* xxi, 63, 78; LC, pt. 53, 19574–75; Brown and Cassmore, "Earnings," 10–12. The WPA began its study of Arizona's migrant cotton pickers in December 1937, months before the crisis arose. The WPA files reveal no hidden agenda in selecting the Arizona cotton industry for study.

15. LC, pt. 53, 19573.

16. Ibid., 19573–75; WPA, *Migratory Cotton Pickers,* xiii, 29, 61, 93. Cassmore's estimates were rough approximations. Peak employment

may have been closer to 30,000, based on Taber's estimate of an average of 175 pounds of cotton picked per worker in December. The number of local cotton pickers ranged from 5,000 to 10,000 persons according to Taber; the WPA estimated 7,000–10,000 local workers (see LC, pt. 53, 19773, exhibit 8824, pt. 72, 26603, exhibit 13353-D). The WPA estimated that about 55 percent of the migrants would have come to Arizona without the recruiting campaign. They "knew of cotton," had been contracted to work, had been to Arizona in previous years, were passing through the state, came at the urging of friends or relatives, or came for other reasons, such as health.

17. WPA, *Migratory Cotton Pickers*, 53–55; Arizona Agricultural Experiment Station, *Hired Labor Requirements on Arizona Irrigated Farms*, 199, *Wanted—Man Power for Arizona Farms: Seasonal and Year-Round Farm Labor Requirements, Arizona, 1935–42*, 15–6; Bureau Census, *Cotton Production, 1937–38*, 12, 15; *Arizona Republic*, 14 Mar. 1937, sec. 4, p. 1; *Chandler Arizonan*, 17 Sept. 1937, p. 1; *Daily Oklahoman*, 9 Oct. 1937, p. 2. Cotton pickers confirmed that at least some of their fellow farm laborers worked only as long as necessary to get by from day to day and that alcoholism was a serious problem in the camps; see interviews with Dewey Phares, Masuria Ann McCandless Stephens, Dennis Kirkland, OMP.

18. LC, pt. 53, 19566, 19576, 19731, exhibit 8805, 19770, exhibit 8817. In November, Taber informed those who wrote inquiring about the harvest that it was too late to come for the 1937 season.

19. LC, pt. 53, 19564–65, 19723–25, exhibit 8798, 19728, exhibit 8801, 19732, exhibit 8806, pt. 72, 26588, exhibit 13336; *Daily Oklahoman*, 23 Sept. 1937, p. 15. Taber's labor scouts told their contacts to arrive by the first of November, and the last several newspaper advertisements specified a need for pickers by the latter part of the month. However, ads placed earlier in the season noted that the harvest lasted until February.

20. LC, pt. 53, 19732, exhibit 8806.

21. LC, pt. 47, 17238, exhibit 7943.

22. Ibid., 19574–75. Cassmore, like many New Dealers in the WPA and the FSA, advocated the development of a more efficiently organized labor market in which supply was more carefully matched with actual demand, so that the principle of a wage equilibrium would provide a better standard of living for agricultural workers. A good example of this type of argument is in TC, *Final Report*, 364–65.

23. LC, pt. 53, 19593, 19774, exhibit 8824, pt. 72, 26608, exhibit 13353-I; *Daily Oklahoman*, 7 Oct. 1937, p. 1; WPA, *Migratory Cotton Pickers*, 4; Brown and Ware, *Cotton*, 350. In areas of the south-central states where closed-boll varieties of cotton were grown, workers

snapped the entire boll off the branch; in Arizona, harvesters had to pick the seed cotton from open bolls. A field worker could pull bolls at about twice the rate as he or she could pick cotton. On the other hand, workers who picked cotton from open-boll varieties in Oklahoma, where the bolls were smaller and the plants less productive, found they could pick cotton somewhat faster in Arizona. Oklahomans who grew open-boll varieties paid more for picking cotton, however, from 65¢ to $1 per hundred; see the interviews with Masuria Ann McCandless Stephens, Dennis Kirkland, James Edward Gladden, OMP.

24. LC, pt. 53, 19590, exhibit 8826, 19719, exhibit 8790, 19731, exhibit 8805, pt. 72, 26608, exhibit 13353-I; WPA, *Migratory Cotton Pickers,* 59; Maricopa County Farm Bureau, Board of Directors Minutes, 12 Oct. 1937, 6 July 1938, 3 Aug. 1938, Maricopa County Farm Bureau office, Tempe; *Casa Grande Dispatch,* 27 Aug. 1937, p. 1; *Arizona Republic,* 2 Nov. 1937, sec. 2, p. 1; Bureau Census, *Cotton Production, 1937–38,* p. 15. The boom in cotton production drove the average price for Arizona lint down from about 12.43 cents per pound in 1936 to 9.2 cents per pound in 1937.

25. LC, pt. 72, 26598, exhibit 13351-A. In Arizona, as elsewhere, "Communist" was a code word for the CIO.

26. LC, pt. 53, 19731, exhibit 8805. One limited strike, led by UCAPAWA organizers, occurred early in the season at Higley, southeast of Phoenix (see WPA, *Migratory Cotton Pickers,* 59).

27. McWilliams, *Ill Fares the Land,* 81.

28. Brown and Ware, *Cotton,* 545; Bureau Census, *Cotton Production, 1937–38,* 20, 41; Arizona Agricultural Extension Service, *An Economic Survey of Pinal County Agriculture,* 22; WPA, *Migratory Cotton Pickers,* 56–57; interview with Edwards Hooper, OMP. Daniel makes this point regarding California's agribusiness in *Bitter Harvest,* 179.

29. LC, pt. 59, *California Agricultural Background: California's Migrant Problem,* 21791.

30. LC, *Violations of Free Speech and Rights of Labor,* 319–20, 533–37, *Hearings,* pt. 53, 19566, 19580–81.

31. U.S. Cong., Senate, Committee on Education and Labor, *Violations of Free Speech and Rights of Labor,* 536.

32. Ibid., 394–97.

Chapter 6

1. Agricultural Adjustment Act of 1938, 31–36; Arizona Crop and Livestock Reporting Service, *Arizona Agricultural Statistics,* 12; Ganger, "Impact of Mechanization," 298–99, 303.

2. LC, pt. 72, 26605, exhibit 13353-G.

3. Ibid., 26595, exhibit 13346.

4. LC, pt. 53, 19581, 19728–9, exhibit 8801, 19770, exhibit 8817, pt. 72, 26594, exhibit 13345, 26597–98, exhibits 13349, 13350, p. 26605, exhibit 13353-G; The quote is from the last exhibit.

5. LC, pt. 72, 26592–93, exhibits 13341, 13343, pp. 26595–96, exhibit 13348. Taber's colleague at the Arizona State Employment Service Lewis Irvine maintained that clearance orders were canceled as soon as the supply seemed adequate.

6. Earl R. Beckner, Acting Chief, Labor Relations Section, to Omer Mills, Labor Relations Representative, FSA, 5 Oct. 1939; notes on telephone conversations between Laurence Hewes, acting regional director, Region 9, FSA, and J. A. Waldron, state director, Arizona FSA, 5 Oct. 1939, and between Hewes and Spear [sic], director, Arizona Office of Government Reports, 5 Oct. 1939; Waldron to Hewes, 6 Oct. 1939; Hewes to George S. Mitchell, assistant administrator, FSA, 7 Oct. 1939, 12 Oct. 1939, all in Region 9, general file, 1936–1939, box 11, Migratory Labor Camps, Records of Region 9, Records of the Resettlement Division (RD), Records of FHA, RG 96, NA. See also LC, pt. 53, 19583–85, 19589, pt. 72, 26587, exhibit 13335; *Arizona Producer,* 1 Oct. 1938, p. 7.

Although Taber and Gilbert insisted that they had asked for only 3,000 farm workers, J. A. Waldron, state director of the FSA office in Arizona, and David Kinkead, then manager for the FSA camp in Brawley, California, maintained that Taber had specified 8,000 pickers. The truth remains unclear, but the FSA could document only the 3,000 figure with any certainty. Hewes surmised that the Associated Farmers of California was behind the inflated request. In light of rumors of an impending strike in the San Joaquin Valley by UCAPAWA and the Workers Alliance, Hewes speculated that the Associated Farmers were hoping "to bring in a large number of workers to Arizona and then flood them into California when the strike is at its peak" (Hewes to Mitchell, 7 Oct. 1939).

7. LC, pt. 53, 19585, exhibit 8821; *Arizona Republic,* 21 Oct. 1939, p. 2.

8. LC, pt. 53, 19586, exhibit 8822.

9. Ibid., 19772, exhibit 8823.

10. Hewes to C. B. Baldwin, assistant administrator, FSA, 24 Jan. 1940, Region 9, Grants file, box 11, Migratory Labor Camps, Records of Region 9, Records of RD, Records of FHA, RG 96, NA; LC, pt. 59, 21786; *Arizona Producer,* 1 Aug. 1938, p. 3, 15 Dec. 1938, p. 1, 27 May 1939, p. 3. Under the commodities program, eligible migrant families obtained fifteen

days' worth of food as soon as they filed their applications. A family received additional assistance only after a caseworker had made a home visit to verify eligibility. Families could continue to obtain commodities as long as they remained eligible, subject to confirmation visits every ninety days. In addition, the FSA continued to provide small cash grants to purchase clothing and textbooks for school children. Eligibility was limited to agricultural workers who needed aid "to maintain health and prevent human suffering" but did not meet Arizona's three-year residency requirement and thus could not obtain state relief (see FSA, *Study of 6,655 Migrant Households,* 3–4). In 1938, the five commissaries were located in Phoenix, Chandler, Buckeye, Glendale, and Casa Grande; commissaries later opened in Avondale and Gilbert.

11. *Arizona Producer,* 15 Dec. 1938, p. 1, 27 May 1939, p. 3; *Arizona Farmer-Producer,* 16 Mar. 1940, pp. 3–4; *Casa Grande Dispatch,* 22 Mar. 1940, p. 1, 19 Apr. 1940, p. 1; LC, pt. 59, 21934, exhibit 9376; Arizona State Board of Social Security and Welfare (ASSW), Minutes, 15 Mar. 1940, Records of ASSW, State Archives, ADL.

12. Interview with Murrel "Mo" Harris, 16, 51, OMP.

13. Interview with Arthur Mercer, OMP; *Casa Grande Dispatch,* 5 Apr. 1940, p. 2. The schools in Palo Verde and Avondale also offered lunch programs, and other districts may have (see interview with Thomas Cambron, OMP).

14. *Arizona Producer,* 15 Dec. 1938, p. 1; Hewes to Baldwin, 24 Jan. 1940, Arizona Grant Program attachment, Region 9, Grants file, box 11, Migratory Labor Camps, Records of Region 9, Records of RD, Records of FHA, RG 96, NA; LC, pt. 59, 21785.

15. TC, pt. 6, 2460, 2523, pt. 7, 2953. Shepard made his assessment after the FSA medical program had been in operation for nearly a year and a half.

16. 1 Aug. 1938, p. 3.

17. LC, pt. 59, 21787; TC, pt. 6, 2513–19; *Arizona Producer,* 1 Aug. 1938, p. 3, 15 Oct. 1938, p. 3; R. C. Williams, medical director, FSA, to W. W. Alexander, administrator, FSA, 31 Mar. 1939, Williams to Alexander, two memos 5 Mar. 1940, all in box 11, Correspondence Concerning Migratory Labor Camps, Region 9, Medical Care file, Records of RD, Records of FHA, RG 96, NA; "A Survey of the Program of the Agricultural Worker's Health and Medical Association," 3, folder 217, carton 6, Regional Office 9 Correspondence and Papers, FSA Collection, Bancroft Library; "Medical Care for Farm Workers in California and Arizona," *Monthly Labor Review* 55 (Nov. 1942): 957–59; *Casa Grande Dispatch,* 5 Jan. 1940,

p. 1, 19 Jan. 1940, p. 1, 17 Apr. 1942, p. 5; interview with W. D. Durant and Naomi Dixon Durant, OMP. The Agricultural Workers Health and Medical Association was incorporated in California in March 1938 and given legal authority to do business in other states, including Arizona. The clinic at Buckeye was moved to the Agua Fria camp when it opened, and the Eleven Mile Corner clinic replaced the referral service in Coolidge. Doctors also called regularly at the FSA mobile camps.

18. The FSA developed similar housing projects in California, Washington, Idaho, Texas, and Florida. For general background on the FSA and its housing programs, see Baldwin, *Poverty and Politics;* Conkin, *Tomorrow a New World,* chaps. 5–8. For specific information on the California precursors to Arizona's migrant housing programs, see Stein, *Dust Bowl Migration,* chap. 6.

19. *Arizona Producer,* 1 Jan. 1938, p. 1, 15 Mar. 1939, p. 4; *Yuma Daily Sun,* 7 Jan. 1938, p. 5, 4 Feb. 1938, p. 1; *Phoenix Gazette,* 5 Feb. 1938, sec. 2, p. 10; *Arizona Republic,* 24 Apr. 1938, sec. 2, p. 6; "Migratory Labor Camp Program as of January 1, 1940," mimeographed, Housing file, box 8, Migratory Labor Camps, Records of RD, Records of FHA, RG 96, NA. Photographs of the Agua Fria camp are available on microfiche in Library of Congress, *America, 1935–1946.*

In a typical year, temperatures in the Phoenix area climbed to 99 degrees in April and reached as high as 112 degrees in July before dropping back to 98 degrees in October (see, for example, Salt River Project, *Annual History,* 1938, p. 100).

The Agua Fria camp was the first FSA migrant-labor camp to provide these enclosed metal dwellings, constructed at a cost of $160 each. The early camps in California offered only wooden platforms, shaded by metal ramadas, on which migrant families could pitch their tents or build makeshift structures. Unfortunately for the laborers who remained in the Agua Fria camp during the summer months, the first 210 metal cabins contained a design flaw that made it impossible to raise the hinged sections fully and achieve maximum ventilation. Moreover, relatively few met the economic standards for living in the 36 labor homes, which required year-round agricultural employment, so many of those houses stood vacant or were occupied by the camp staff.

20. *Arizona Producer,* 1 Jan. 1938, p. 1; *Tulsa Tribune,* 14 Apr. 1940, sec. A, p. 15; *Yuma Daily Sun,* 4 Feb. 1938, p. 1; *Phoenix Gazette,* 5 Feb. 1938, Sec. 2, p. 10; *Desert Sentinel,* 27 Nov. 1940; ibid., 24 Feb. 1941; "Narrative Report, Region IX, Migratory Labor Camp Program," Mar. 1940, July 1941, Oct. 1941, mimeographed, folder 54, carton 2,

Regional Office 9 Correspondence and Papers, FSA Collection, Bancroft Library.

21. *Arizona Producer,* 1 Oct. 1938, p. 1; *Arizona Republic,* 17 Dec. 1939, sec. 2, p. 7; LC, pt. 59, 21922, exhibit 9374, 21927, exhibit 9376; FSA, "Migratory Labor Camps," 1 Sept. 1942, mimeographed, Migratory Labor Camps file, box 281, General Correspondence, 1934–43, Records of the Public Finance Section, Records of BAE, RG 83, NA. Fifteen of the 215 metal cabins were designated as "isolation units" for migrants with contagious diseases. In the camp's first two years, relatively few of the migrants could meet the economic qualifications for living in the Garden Home apartments; most stood vacant or housed camp staff, including girls working for the National Youth Administration.

To give an idea of the size of the steel structures, home to most of the migrants in the camp, when the Eleven Mile Corner camp was dismantled in the mid-1950s, the cabins were sold at auction to residents throughout the Casa Grande Valley, who used the "houses" as storage sheds. (See Shirley Weik, "History of the (Home Economics) Extension Service in Casa Grande—1914 to 1978," CGVHS.)

22. *Arizona Producer,* 1 Oct. 1938, p. 12; *Casa Grande Dispatch,* 5 Apr. 1940, p. 4; *Buckeye Valley News,* 4 Aug. 1938, p. 1; *Desert Sentinel,* 13 Jan. 1941; *Eleven Mile Corner News,* 22 Nov. 1940; "Narrative Report, Region IX, Migratory Labor Camp Program," Aug. 1941, folder 54, "Facts About Burton Cairns Convalescent Center," Mar. 1942, folder 61, carton 2, Regional Office 9 Correspondence and Papers, FSA Collection, Bancroft Library.

23. *Casa Grande Dispatch,* 5 Apr. 1940, p. 4.

24. Ibid. Heflin served at the Eleven Mile Corner Migratory Labor Camp until April 1941, when he was transferred to another FSA camp and replaced by William Berkenbosch; see *Eleven Mile Corner News,* 28 Apr. 1941.

25. For a discussion of the bias against the migrants' southern cultural heritage, see Stein, *Dust Bowl Migration,* 167–80, Gregory, *American Exodus,* 108–13.

26. *Casa Grande Dispatch,* 5 Apr. 1940, p. 4.

27. Activities at Eleven Mile Corner were chronicled in the "11-Mile Camp News" column (later "Eleven Mile Corner News") in the *Casa Grande Dispatch.* For the migrants' interest in movies, see especially the following issues of the *Dispatch:* 24 May 1940, p. 8; 26 June 1942, p. 7; 3 July 1942, p. 7; 10 July 1942, p. 3; 11 Sept. 1942, p. 3; 25 Sept. 1942, p. 2; 23 Oct. 1942, p. 3. Also consult issues of the camp newspaper, *Eleven Mile*

Corner News, in the government documents division of the library at the University of California, Berkeley. A wealth of information on activities at the Agua Fria Farm Workers Community is found in that camp's newspaper, *Desert Sentinel,* also in the documents collection at Berkeley, and a listing of activities at the camp in 1939 is provided in LC, pt. 59, 21931–32, exhibit 9376. The interviews with Thomas Cambron and Donel Leatherbury, OMP, confirm that people who did not live in the camps attended movies there.

28. Group activities are chronicled in the following issues of the camp column in the *Casa Grande Dispatch:* 26 Apr. 1940, p. 5; 10 May 1940, p. 3; 24 May 1940, p. 8; 7 June 1940, p. 4; 14 June 1940, p. 5; 3 Apr. 1942, p. 3; 22 May 1942, p. 3; 19 June 1942, p. 3; 26 June 1942, p. 7; 10 July 1942, p. 3. See also *Eleven Mile Corner News,* 22 May 1941; *Desert Sentinel,* 27 Nov. 1940, 4 Dec. 1940, 30 Dec. 1940, 13 Jan. 1941, 3 Mar. 1941, 17 Mar. 1941, 3 Nov. 1941.

29. An excellent examination of the development of a country-music subculture in California's migrant population is found in Gregory, *American Exodus,* chap. 8. For a discussion of the rise of country music in Oklahoma and the south-central region, see Savage, *Singing Cowboys,* especially chaps. 4, 7. Evidence of the migrants' interest in musical entertainment may be found in the following issues of the *Desert Sentinel:* 27 Nov. 1940, 13 Jan. 1941, 20 Jan. 1941, 28 Jan. 1941, 27 June 1941, 5 Jan. 1942; *Eleven Mile Corner News,* 15 Nov. 1940, 29 Nov. 1940; and the camp column, *Casa Grande Dispatch,* 26 Apr. 1940, p. 5, 10 May 1940, p. 3, 24 May 1940, p. 8, 7 June 1940, p. 4, 14 June 1940, p. 5, 19 June 1942, p. 3, 10 July 1942, p. 3, 24 July 1942, p. 5, 25 Sept. 1942, p. 2, 23 Oct. 1942, p. 3. See also the interviews with Donel Leatherbury, Thomas Cambron, Dewey Phares and Jewel Phares, Dennis Kirkland, OMP. Margaret Valiant, an amateur folklorist, collected a number of songs performed by migrant farm workers on a visit to central Arizona and California in 1938. Perhaps because she sought primarily to document "how deeply rooted in American traditions" were the uprooted citizens, many of the songs she recorded were traditional. See Margaret Valiant, Migrant Camp Recordings (especially records no. 5056, 5057), box 179, Records of WPA, RG 69, NA.

30. "Eleven-Mile Corner News" column, *Casa Grande Dispatch,* 12 June 1942, p. 3, 19 June 1942, p. 3, 26 June 1942, p. 7; the quotes are from the 12 June issue.

31. See "Eleven Mile Corner News," *Casa Grande Dispatch,* 26 Apr. 1940, p. 5, 24 May 1940, p. 8, 7 June 1940, p. 4, 3 Apr. 1942, p. 3, 17 Apr. 1942, p. 5; *Eleven Mile Corner News,* 15 Nov. 1940, 29 Nov. 1940, 20

Mar. 1941; *Desert Sentinel,* 27 Nov. 1940, 4 Dec. 1940, 16 Dec. 1940, 23 Dec. 1940, 30 Dec. 1940, 20 Jan. 1941, 28 Jan. 1941, 3 Feb. 1941, 3 Mar. 1941, 9 Mar. 1941, 17 Mar. 1941, 24 Mar., 1941, 20 June 1941, 18 Aug. 1941; *Migrant Mike,* 14 Mar. 1941, 21 Mar. 1941, 11 Apr. 1941. See also "Narrative Report, Region IX, Farm Workers Communities and Grant Offices," Mar. 1941, "[Narrative Report], Region IX, Migratory Labor Camp Program," Sept. 1941, folder 54, carton 2, Regional Office 9 Correspondence and Papers, FSA Collection, Bancroft Library. The Agua Fria baseball team may not have competed with school teams. It did play such teams as those at Abbott's camp and Rhodes's camp, both operated by growers for African American farm workers; the Hispanic team at Guadalupe Village; and the Arizona State Prison team at Florence.

32. "Eleven-Mile Corner News," *Casa Grande Dispatch,* 14 June 1940, p. 5.

33. LC, pt. 59, 21932, exhibit 9376; "Monthly Narrative Report, Migratory Labor Camp Program," Oct. 1941, folder 54, carton 2, Regional Office 9 Correspondence and Papers, FSA Collection, Bancroft Library; *Desert Sentinel,* 14 Apr. 1941, 20 Oct. 1941, 27 Oct. 1941; *Casa Grande Dispatch,* 27 Dec. 1940, p. 5; fund-raising correspondence and canceled checks in folder 6, box 222, Helen Gahagan Douglas Collection, Carl Albert Congressional Research and Studies Center, University of Oklahoma, Norman.

34. *Casa Grande Dispatch,* 26 Apr. 1940, p. 5, 10 May 1940, p. 3, 2 Aug. 1940, p. 1, 23 Oct. 1942, p. 3; *Eleven Mile Corner News,* 29 Nov. 1940, 7 Mar. 1941; *Desert Sentinel,* 4 Dec. 1940, 29 Dec. 1941; LC, pt. 59, 21925–26, 21931, exhibit 9376; "Narrative Report, Region IX, Migratory Labor Camp Program," May 1940, folder 54, carton 2, Regional Office 9 Correspondence and Papers, FSA Collection, Bancroft Library. At the Agua Fria camp, the Reverend Ludlow, a Baptist minister, held services every Thursday and Sunday. A discussion of the religious practices of the migrant population in California is in Gregory, *American Exodus,* chap. 7.

35. *Casa Grande Dispatch,* 29 Mar. 1940, p. 1, 27 Dec. 1940, p. 1, 3 Apr. 1942, p. 3, 22 May 1942, p. 3, 7 Aug. 1942, p. 2; *Eleven Mile Corner News,* 22 May 1941. Edwin Charles Pendleton visited the camp in the mid-1940s to conduct research for his dissertation in economics, prepared under the direction of Paul S. Taylor. Pendleton reported that the camp school was necessary because the Casa Grande school district "refused" to provide school facilities for the migrant children (see "History of Labor," 335). Other evidence indicates that the electorate voted to exclude the camp from Elementary School District 25 (O. O. McCracken, assistant

economist, to Hugo C. Schwartz, acting head, Land Policies Section, BAE, n.d., "Bankhead—Ariz." envelope, Region 9 file, box 281, General Correspondence, Records of the Public Finance Section, Records of BAE, RG 83, NA). It appears that the exclusion stemmed from the cost of constructing additional facilities for the migrants rather than a desire to segregate the migrant children from the rest of the school population. High school students continued to be bused to classes in Casa Grande, and migrant children who did not live in the federal camp attended public schools.

36. *Casa Grande Dispatch,* 27 Dec. 1940, p. 6. In a countywide school competition held in Florence, the Eleven Mile Corner School students won four prizes; see *Eleven Mile Corner News,* 22 May 1941.

37. The most complete overview of the New Deal community programs is provided by Conkin, *Tomorrow a New World,* chap. 8. My discussion also draws on Stein, *Dust Bowl Migration,* 172–73.

38. "Constitution for Migratory Labor Camps," mimeographed, folder 54, carton 2, Regional Office 9 Correspondence and Papers, FSA Collection, Bancroft Library; see also Stein, *Dust Bowl Migration,* 173.

39. "Constitution for Migratory Labor Camps," folder 54, carton 2, "Agua Fria Migratory Labor Camp," Feb. 1940, mimeographed, folder 213, carton 6, Regional Office 9 Correspondence and Papers, FSA Collection, Bancroft Library; *Casa Grande Dispatch,* 29 Mar. 1940, p. 1, 5 Apr. 1940, p. 4, 10 May 1940, p. 3, 3 July 1942, p. 7, 10 July 1942, p. 3; *Eleven Mile Corner News,* 28 Apr. 1941; *Desert Sentinel,* 24 Feb. 1941, 17 Mar. 1941, 14 Apr. 1941, 20 June 1941, 27 June 1941, 12 Jan. 1942. At Eleven Mile Corner, women were equally represented on the first council. By mid-1942, however, no women served. Similarly, at Agua Fria women made up half of the council until June 1941, when for reasons that are unclear the size of the council was slashed. In January 1942, however, the former size of the council was restored, and women again made up half the governing body.

40. *Casa Grande Dispatch,* 29 Mar. 1940, p. 1.

41. Stein discusses the problems with democratic camp government at length in *Dust Bowl Migration,* 173–78. Hints of the manager's "guidance" in council decision making are evident in *Eleven Mile Corner News,* 15 Nov. 1940, *Desert Sentinel,* 14 Apr. 1941.

42. *Arizona Producer,* 1 Oct. 1938, p. 12; *Arizona Republic,* 17 Dec. 1939, sec. 2, p. 7; LC, pt. 59, 21928–29, exhibit 9376; FSA, "Chandler Farms, Incorporated," mimeographed, Apr. 1939, Arizona Collection, ADL. Chandler Part-Time Farms was the first of its type in the nation. The FSA subsequently organized similar cooperatives in Glendale and Phoenix (called jointly Camelback Farms) and in California at Indio, Thornton, and

Yuba City. Although each enterprise differed somewhat from the others, the basic operation was the same.

43. LC, pt. 59, 21922, exhibit 9374, 21928–29, exhibit 9376; FSA, "Chandler Farms," Arizona Collection, ADL.

44. "Narrative Report, Region IX, Monthly Labor Camp Program," June 1940, "Narrative Report, Region IX, Farm Workers Communities and Grant Offices," Apr. 1941, folder 54, carton 2, Regional Office 9 Correspondence and Papers, FSA Collection, Bancroft Library; *Casa Grande Dispatch,* 17 Apr. 1942, p. 5, 12 June 1942, p. 3, 3 July 1942, p. 7, 7 Aug. 1942, p. 2, 16 Oct. 1942, p. 7; *Eleven Mile Corner News,* 7 Mar. 1941, 22 May 1941; interviews with Dennis Kirkland, Ewell Bennett, OMP.

45. A thorough study of the Casa Grande Valley Farms cooperative is provided by Banfield in *Government Project,* chaps. 2, 6, 15. See also LC pt. 59, 21784, 21822; Conkin, *Tomorrow a New World,* 210; FSA, "Casa Grande Valley Farms, Inc.," mimeographed, Apr. 1939, Arizona Collection, ADL; *Coolidge Examiner,* 23 Sept. 1937, p. 1. Ewell Bennett provides important insight in his interview, OMP.

46. LC, pt. 59, 21928–29, exhibit 9376; the quote is from an interview with Ewell Bennett, 28, OMP. By 1940, the cooperative showed signs of discord. According to a survey of the settlers, while 61 percent felt satisfied with the operation of the cooperative, 13 percent expressed indifference, and 12 percent were openly antagonistic.

47. Banfield, *Government Project,* 60–61, 66–69; LC, pt. 59, 21818.

48. Banfield, *Government Project,* 27, 36; LC, pt. 59, 21817; FSA, "Casa Grande Valley Farms," Arizona Collection, ADL; *Coolidge Examiner,* 23 Sept. 1937, p. 1.

49. Hewes to Baldwin, 29 Apr. 1941, Projects file, box 3, Correspondence Concerning Migratory Labor Camps, Records of RD, Records of FHA, RG 96, NA.

50. Ibid.; *Arizona Farmer-Producer,* 17 Feb. 1940, p. 13; "Camp Population," Jan. 1942, mimeographed, "Narrative Report, Region IX, Migratory Labor Camp Program," Jan., Aug., Oct. 1941, folder 54, carton 2, Region 9 Correspondence and Papers, FSA Collection, Bancroft Library. See also interview with Murrel Harris, OMP. For a brief time, a fourth unit was established in Waddell. As at the permanent camps, a community council governed each mobile unit, and a variety of group activities were available to the residents.

51. *Arizona Farmer-Producer,* 29 Apr. 1939, p. 8; *Arizona Producer,* 1 Jan. 1938, p. 1; the quote is from the former. Pendleton, "History of

Labor," 334–35, contended that the major agricultural organizations, including the Arizona Cotton Growers' Association, the state farm bureau federation, and the Associated Farmers, at first opposed the FSA camps, viewing them as an interference and as pampering. This sentiment did not surface in the *Arizona Farmer-Producer,* although one editorial did express reservations about the long-term wisdom of government paternalism (6 Jan. 1940, p. 8). No records of the Maricopa County Farm Bureau or the Arizona Cotton Growers' Association are extant for this period, and access to the records of the Arizona Farm Bureau Federation was denied.

52. Minutes, Pinal County Land Use Planning Committee, 24 Jan. 1941, p. 3; K. K. Henness, [Pinal] County Agricultural Agent, to Robert F. Black, State BAE Representative, 24 Dec. 1941, Pinal County file, box 56, Memo-Pinal County, Records of the Arizona State Representative, Records of State Offices, Records of BAE, RG 83, NA; "Narrative Report, Region IX, Migratory Labor Camp Program," July 1941, folder 54, carton 2, Regional Office 9 Correspondence and Papers, FSA Collection, Bancroft Library; my interview with K. K. Henness, 13 July 1989.

53. 29 Apr. 1939, p. 8.

54. 23 Sept. 1937, p. 4. After one year, the FSA asked for Faul's resignation, ironically because some felt his management style was dictatorial. When the disaffected Faul branded the Casa Grande experiment as "Russian Communistic," E. H. Boyd, writing for the *Casa Grande Dispatch,* 3 Feb. 1939, p. 1, expressed his faith in the FSA and stood by the cooperative, maintaining that it was a democratic venture, not a communistic one. A series of testimonials from prominent residents of Coolidge supporting the Casa Grande Valley Farms is in FSA, "Casa Grande Valley Farms," Arizona Collection, ADL.

55. *Arizona Producer,* 15 Mar. 1939, p. 4; *Casa Grande Dispatch,* 1 Jan. 1939, p. 1; LC, pt. 53, 19590–91, exhibit 8826; *Chandler Arizonan,* 8 Apr. 1938, p. 1; "Narrative Report, Region IX, Migratory Labor Camp Program," Aug. 1941, folder 54, carton 2, Regional Office 9 Correspondence and Papers, FSA Collection, Bancroft Library.

56. "[Narrative Report], Region IX, Migratory Labor Camp Program," Sept. 1941, p. 10, folder 54, carton 2, Regional Office 9 Correspondence and Papers, FSA Collection, Bancroft Library. Murrel Harris makes a similar observation in his interview, OMP.

57. 17 Aug. 1940, pp. 1, 21.

58. Arizona Agricultural Experiment Station, *Arizona's Agricultural Population,* [iv], 71.

59. LC, pt. 59, 21922, exhibit 9374; Pendleton, "History of Labor," 334; FSA, "Farm Workers Camps and Labor Homes: District Supervisors, Managers and Addresses," mimeographed, 1941, 2, Projects file, box 3, Migratory Labor Camps, Records of RD, Records of FHA, RG 96, NA; interview with Thomas Cambron, OMP. In addition to the FSA facilities for migratory labor, more permanent housing was available in the labor and garden homes, the part-time farms, and the Casa Grande cooperative. Because these housing projects were selective, they have not been included in the total number of spaces available to migrant workers at the federal camps.

60. Interview with Edwards Hooper, 27, OMP.

61. Hewes to Mason Barr, director, Management Division, FSA, 8 Apr. 1942, attachment, Projects file, box 3, Correspondence Concerning Migratory Labor Camps, Records of RD, Records of FSA, RG 96, NA; FSA, "Descriptions of Camps," by Eugene McDonough, mimeographed, 1941, Farm Labor Housing Surveys file, box 53, Correspondence—Flood Control, Records of the Arizona State Representative, Records of State Offices, Records of BAE, RG 83, NA. The "fair" camps described herein were Martin's Camp (listing no. 37), with twelve cabins and two houses, and Jack's Camp (no. 42), a medium-sized camp with twenty cabins and six tents, both in the Buckeye area. Descriptions of Miller's Camp, Abbott's Camp (a small site with only six tents), and Percy Camp, which had four tents and one cabin, are found in nos. 47, 51, 77, respectively.

62. FSA, "A Survey of Farm Labor Camps in Gilbert, Arizona Farm Security Grant Office District," n.d., "Pinal County Grant Office Housing Survey," 1942, "Survey of Housing Facilities for Migratory Farm Families in the Area Served by the Phoenix Grant Office," 1942, all mimeographed, Farm Labor Housing Surveys file, box 53, Correspondence—Flood Control, Records of the Arizona State Representative, Records of State Offices, Records of BAE, RG 83, NA; TC, pt. 7, 2954. The housing surveys included camps for farms growing crops other than cotton. For the Casa Grande area, no distinction was made between those camps that were in excellent, good, or fair condition. In the area encompassing Phoenix, Tempe, Scottsdale, and Laveen, almost all of the grower-owned camps were rated poor. The data on these camps, however, were aggregated, making the information less reliable. Few of the squatter camps were enumerated. Throughout central Arizona, many migratory workers continued to congregate in squalid ditch-bank camps near the intersections of irrigation canals with public roads. In the summer of 1940, hundreds of migrants were driven by flood waters from squatters' camps along the Santa Cruz River near Eloy.

63. Interview with Lee Faver, OMP.

64. Interview with Rosie Harlas Laird, 43, COP.

65. Interviews with Masuria Ann McCandless Stephens, Lee Faver, Murrel Harris, Dennis Kirkland, OMP.

66. Interview with Vera Ruth Woodall Criswell, 27, COP.

67. Excerpt from Dorothy Rose, "Enroute to the Promised Land: Phoenix, 1936," *Valley Grapevine* 5 (1980): 23. Reprinted with permission.

68. Interviews with Dennis Kirkland, Thomas Cambron, Donel Leatherbury, Lee Faver, OMP; Rosie Harlas Laird, COP.

69. Interviews with Samuel Cambron, Thomas Cambron, Masuria Ann McCandless Stephens, Murrel Harris, Jarrell Eugene Bowlan, OMP.

70. Interviews with Dennis Kirkland, W. D. Durant and Naomi Dixon Durant, OMP.

71. Interviews with Masuria Ann McCandless Stephens, Betty Lyon McGrath, Murrel Harris, OMP; *Casa Grande Dispatch,* 9 Oct. 1942, p. 3; Stewart, "Increasing Needs," Arizona Historical Society, Tucson; Christian, *Buckeye,* 41.

72. Bogue, Shryock, and Hoermann, *Subregional Migration,* table 2, pt. 4, table 3; Arizona Agricultural Experiment Station, *Arizona's Agricultural Population,* 58, *Volume and Characteristics of Migration to Arizona,* 303. The 3,900 figure does not include family members who were not counted as agricultural workers.

73. McWilliams, *Ill Fares the Land,* 71, referred to Arizona as the "Migrant Way Station."

74. Arizona Agricultural Experiment Station, *Volume and Characteristics of Migration to Arizona,* 298, 300, *Arizona's Agricultural Population,* 60.

75. This study, initiated by the U.S. Bureau of Agricultural Economics in cooperation with the state Agricultural Experiment Station and the Arizona Department of Education attempted to survey all school-children attending the public schools during the week of 15–20 January 1940. Questionnaires were returned by 20,881 students, representing 13,334 families. Of these, 2,204 were farm-labor families. Although useful, the study is least helpful in understanding agricultural workers, compared with those in other occupations. The study necessarily excluded couples who had no children of school age as well as single persons. Most significant when examining cotton pickers, it excluded those whose children were, for example, working in the fields rather than attending school. Also open to question is the reliability of the youthful informants.

76. Arizona Agricultural Experiment Station, *Volume and Characteristics of Migration to Arizona,* 316–17. The percentage who planned to leave the state may well be understated since those who kept their children out of school after the Christmas break in anticipation of moving would not have been enumerated.

77. Arizona Agricultural Experiment Station, *Arizona's Agricultural Population,* 58, *Statistical Supplement to Volume and Characteristics of Migration to Arizona,* 23; Tetreau, "People of Arizona," 178; Bureau Census, *Fourteenth Census of the United States Taken in the Year 1920,* Vol. 2, *Population, General Report and Analytical Tables,* table 17, *Fifteenth Census of the United States: 1930: Population,* Vol. 2, *General Report, Statistics by Subjects,* table 21, *Sixteenth Census of the United States: 1940: Population: State of Birth of the Native Population,* tables 20, 31, 32; Manuscript Census, Maricopa and Pinal Counties, Ariz., 1920, NA; Christian, *Buckeye,* 37–41.

In 1936, Tetreau conducted a survey of agricultural households in the Salt River, Casa Grande, and Yuma valleys and the Safford area. He supplemented this study with a survey of migrant labor households in March 1940, conducted principally in the Salt River Valley. Three-fourths of the migrants were from Oklahoma or Texas in roughly equal proportions and another 7 percent were from Missouri or Arkansas. The findings of these studies were published in three reports. *Arizona's Agricultural Population* reported a sample of 653 farm operators, 1,401 resident farm laborers, and 378 migrant farm laborers, studied in March 1940. The data published in the *Rural Sociology* article are based on 2,761 rural households (including those in towns of fewer than 2,500 people). The information published in *Arizona's Farm Laborers* came from interviews with 1,500 farm laborers, although in general only 1,313 interviews were utilized.

78. Arizona Agricultural Experiment Station, *Arizona's Agricultural Population,* 56, *Arizona's Farm Laborers,* 301.

79. Interviews with Dennis Kirkland and Edwards Hooper, OMP.

80. Quoted in Banfield, *Government Project,* 155.

81. WPA, *Migratory Cotton Pickers,* 7–8; Arizona Agricultural Experiment Station, *Arizona's Farm Laborers,* 321; Ellis Marshburn, "As Sheep Without a Shepherd, A Migrant Work Report on the Southside of the Salt River Valley, Arizona, October 1940–March 1941," n.p.: Home Missions Council of North America, 15 Feb. 1941, 4–9, quoted in Pendleton, "History of Labor," 343–44.

82. *Arizona Republic,* 12 Dec. 1937, sec. 3, p. 10, 19 Dec. 1937, sec. 3, p. 10, 26 Dec. 1937, sec. 3, p. 8, 31 Dec. 1937, sec. 2, p. 1.

5. Ibid., 1069–75; *Casa Grande Dispatch,* 28 Aug. 1942, p. 1, 4 , p. 3; Baldwin, *Poverty and Politics,* 223–34; J. O. Walker, dministrator, FSA, to A. E. Taber, secretary, Arizona Farmers Committee, 27 Aug. 1942, Arizona Farmers Production Com- box 7, General Correspondence, Records of FHA, RG 96, NA.

6. Earl Maharg to Congressman John R. Murdock, 21 Aug. ona Farm Bureau Federation file, box 7, General Correspon- ords of FHA, RG 96, NA.

7. *Casa Grande Dispatch,* 28 Aug. 1942, p. 2, 11 Sept. 1942, p. 1.

3. Ibid., 2 Oct. 1942, p. 1.

9. 9 Oct. 1942, p. 1.

). *Arizona Republic,* 14 Nov. 1942, p. 4; *Casa Grande Dispatch,* 2, p. 1, 16 Oct. 1942, p. 2, 30 Oct. 1942, p. 1; Taber to H. W. ector in charge, Yuma Inspection Station, 29 Oct. 1942, Letters file, Records of the Commission on Agriculture and Horticul- Archives, ADL; FSA, "Recruitment and Transportation of gricultural Workers," reel 21, "Cooperative Employment Agree- 23, STFU.

1. *Casa Grande Dispatch,* 20 Nov. 1942, p. 1.

2. Ibid., 30 Oct. 1942, p. 1; also consult the issues for 6 Nov. 0 Nov. 1942, p. 1; C. Edgar Goyette, secretary, Tucson Chamber ce, to Senator Carl Hayden, 19 Aug. 1943, folder 37–40, Misc.—1939–48, box 651, Hayden Collection, Arizona Collec- lthough the cotton industry blamed the FSA, Laurence Hewes, ector for the agency, maintained that the stipulations to the gram had been made by the Republic of Mexico and agreed to Department, the War Manpower Commission, the Department ure, and the U.S. Employment Service. Hewes's agency had n assigned the duty of administering the program.

3. *Casa Grande Dispatch,* 23 Oct. 1942, p. 1.

4. Ibid., 30 Oct. 1942, p. 1, 20 Nov. 1942, p. 1; *Arizona Republic,* 2, p. 4; Pendleton, "History of Labor," 373, 396. Arizona growers raceros the following year; see interview with Lee Faver, OMP. . The STFU also led a successful campaign to raise the icking rate in the South to equal that paid the braceros.

. A wealth of documents about the program to recruit cotton he Arizona fields, including correspondence between various ters from cotton pickers, and official documents, is contained 22, 23, STFU. See especially "Recruitment and Transportation Agricultural Workers," reel 21; FSA, "Work Agreement," reel

83. Both quotes are from Draft WPA Report, 38, 39, Records of FHA, RG 96, NA. See also the interviews with Edwards Hooper, Samuel Cambron, Thomas Cambron, OMP. Even E. D. Tetreau, often sympathetic with the harvest workers, revealed a similar attitude toward at least some of the migrants in his criticism of out-of-state advertising for cotton pickers: "Why should there not be as much concern about the kind of people drawn into a given farming area by advertisement for additional workers as there now is about plant diseases and pests?" he asked rhetorically. "Whether we like it or not, one factor in the selection of immigrants into your state and mine is the demand for seasonal workers" (see Tetreau, "Seasonal Labor on Arizona Irrigated Farms," paper presented at the annual meeting of the Western Farm Economics Association, June 1937, typescript, p. 7, Special Collections, University of Arizona, Tucson).

84. Interview with Edwards Hooper, 21, OMP.

85. Quoted in WPA, *Migratory Cotton Pickers,* 8.

86. TC, pt. 7, 2952.

87. WPA, *Migratory Cotton Pickers,* 8.

88. Draft WPA Report, 38, Records of FHA, RG 96, NA. See also the interviews with Lee Faver and Flora Davis Faver, Samuel Cambron, OMP.

89. 5 Apr. 1940, p. 5.

90. *Arizona Republic,* 19 Nov. 1939, sec. 9, p. 7. Consult Ban- field, *Government Project,* chap. 9, for a discussion of attitudes in Pinal County.

91. Tetreau and Fuller, "School Achievement," 425, 427; Okla- homa Agricultural Experiment Station, *A Descriptive Study of the Rural and Small City Relief Population in Oklahoma,* 21; interviews with Samuel Cambron, Thomas Cambron, Flora Faver Davis, OMP. By the time they reached tenth grade, most migrant students had caught up with their age group. This may simply reflect the perseverance of the brightest students rather than any accelerated progress at a later age.

92. Interview with Dennis Kirkland, OMP, 33.

93. Marshburn, "Sheep Without a Shepherd," quoted in Pen- dleton, "History of Labor," 343–44. See also interviews with Donel Leath- erbury, OMP; Vera Ruth Woodall Criswell, COP.

94. "[Narrative Report], Agua Fria Migratory Labor Camp," Feb. 1940, 3, folder 213, carton 6, Regional Office 9 Correspondence and Papers, FSA Collection, Bancroft Library.

95. McWilliams, "California Pastoral," 116. The most perceptive discussion of the Okie stereotype in California is Gregory, *American*

Exodus, chap. 3, especially 100–13, and chap. 4. See also Stein, *Dust Bowl Migration,* chaps. 2, 3; Stein provides a cogent explanation of the hysteria against the migrants that arose in California's Central Valley.

96. Interview with Lee Faver and Flora Faver Davis, 31, OMP.

97. By contrast, in 1939 the editor of the *Casa Grade Dispatch,* 3 Feb. 1939, p. 4, proposed residential segregation of African Americans, after several alleged incidents in which black men affronted Hispanic or white girls, and called upon respectable blacks to eliminate "the undesirable, trouble-making, vagrant type among their people." The Japanese fared worse. In 1934 Japanese farmers accused of violating the alien land law were ordered by other farmers "to get out of the valley and stay out" (*Arizona Republic,* 18 Aug. 1934, p. 1).

98. Arizona Agricultural Experiment Station, *Volume and Characteristics of Migration to Arizona,* 315, 317, *Statistical Supplement to Volume and Characteristics of Migration to Arizona,* 16, *Arizona's Agricultural Population,* 58, 60–61; interviews with Donel Leatherbury and James Edward Gladden, OMP. The vast majority of farm-labor families who expected to leave had lived in the state for one year or less. This reflected the seasonal migration cycle; each year a large number of cotton pickers entered the state only to leave at the end of the harvest. Those who remained through the last weeks of the harvest would have been included in the survey if they had children attending school. Significantly, only a handful of those who had lived in the state for more than one year planned to move away. Of those who had moved to Arizona between 1936 and 1938 and were still living there in January 1940, only 8 percent had made plans to leave the state.

99. Bureau Census, *Fourteenth Census,* vol. 2, table 17, *Fifteenth Census: Population,* vol. 2, table 21, *Sixteenth Census: Population: State of Birth,* tables 20, 31, 32; Seymour J. Janow, "Volume and Characteristics of Recent Migration to the Far West," in TC, pt. 6, 2280. In 1920, 57 percent of Arizona's population had been born elsewhere (including citizens born in U.S. possessions, at sea, and abroad). By 1940, this percentage had decreased somewhat to 52 percent (including those born in U.S. possessions), reflecting a lower rate of inmigration during the 1930s. Most of those born outside the state hailed from Texas, birthplace to about 16 percent of the nonnatives in 1920 and 17 percent in 1940, but the percentage of Oklahomans rose most dramatically. In 1920, only 4,573 of Arizona's residents had been born in Oklahoma; by 1930, the Oklahoma-born population more than tripled to 13,955, accounting for 7 percent of those born outside the state. This figure nearly doubled again in 1940, with

27,852 Oklahoma natives resi
include those who had lived in (
but were born elsewhere.) The B
schoolchildren who had moved i
from Oklahoma.

100. Gregory, *America*
120, 196; interviews with Samuel
McCandless Stephens, James E
Bennett, W. D. Durant and Naom

C

1. Minutes, Arizon
U.S. Department of Agriculture
Prospective Cotton Harvest Lal
Holley and L. J. Ducoff, mimeog
Arizona, 1941–42 file, box 242
Correspondence, 1941–46, Rec
cotton, a variety of the Americar
War II.

2. John Fischer, ch
vermaster, Labor Division, FSA
of FHA, RG 96, NA; Robert F. Bla
Arizona Farm Labor Situation
Labor Situation in Arizona, Per
Rushrod W. Allin, head, Divis
Sept. 1941; "Report of Arizona
1941"; Minutes, Arizona Farm
1941, 6 Jan. 1942, 19 Jan. 1942
242, Farm Labor—Southeast-(
Records of BAE, RG 83, NA;
Wanted—Man Power for Arizon
8 May 1942, p. 1, 15 May 1942,
July 1942, p. 1, 4 Sept. 1942, p.
Oct. 1942, p. 3, 20 Nov. 1942
Dennis Kirkland, OMP.

3. *Casa Grande Di*

4. U.S. Departmer
ers," Mexico, *Treaties and Otl*
States of America, 1776–1949,

Sept. 194
assistant
Productio
mittee file

1942, Ari
dence, Re

9 Oct. 19
Smith, ins
1940–194
ture, Stat
Domestic
ment," ree

1942, p. 1,
of Comm
Corresp.—
tion, ASU.
regional c
bracero pr
by the Stat
of Agricul
merely bee

14 Nov. 19
did accept

prevailing

pickers fo
officials, le
on reels 21
of Domest

22; FSA, "Cooperative Employment Agreement," reel 23. See also Mitchell, *Mean Things,* 189–91. The STFU also contacted Oklahoma union organizer Odis Sweeden to recruit pickers in his state, but the Oklahoma office of the USES refused to cooperate by certifying the availability of surplus workers. Consequently, Sweeden made independent arrangements with a labor contractor in Eloy, Arizona, to bus his 150 recruits to Arizona.

17. FSA, "Work Agreement," reel 22, STFU.

18. The quote is from C. Y. Freemyer to Mitchell, n.d. [probably Feb. 1943], reel 23, STFU. Freemyer was picking cotton for B. C. Rhodes in Glendale. Meese's response is dated 9 Feb. 1943 (ibid.).

19. Zachary to H. L. Mitchell, 10 Feb. 1943, reel 23, STFU.

20. Zachary to Mitchell, 19 Feb. 1943, ibid.

21. Ibid.

22. *Casa Grande Dispatch,* 18 Sept. 1942, p. 1, 25 Sept. 1942, p. 1; Pendleton, "History of Labor," 377, 379, 384.

23. *Casa Grande Dispatch,* 23 Oct. 1942, p. 3.

24. Ibid.

25. Ibid., 23 Oct. 1942, p. 1, 30 Oct. 1942, p. 1; the quote is from the former.

26. Pendleton, "History of Labor," 383, 405–6. Although Arizona growers began participating in the bracero program the next year, importing nearly 2,700 Mexican nationals, labor shortages continued throughout the war years, forcing growers to turn to Italian and German prisoners of war for help. The latter became highly favored by some growers, who reported that the Germans picked remarkably clean cotton. Growers also employed a group of Jamaicans, who recoiled at performing work they viewed as slave labor and resented racial bans from taverns, restaurants, and churches in Eloy. Their brief stint in the cotton fields was described by the *Arizona Farmer* as a "dismal failure" (see E. D. Tetreau, "Farm Labor Picture, Dec. 1," repr. from *Arizona Farmer,* 4 Dec. 1943, Arizona Collection, ADL; Arizona Agricultural Experiment Station, *Arizona Farm Labor Situation and Outlook for 1944,* 4; "War Prisoners to Pick Cotton," Agriculture—Cotton file, Ephemera Collection, Arizona Historical Society, Tucson; *Casa Grande Dispatch,* 24 Nov. 1944, p. 1; "Jamaicans Total Failure as Farm Help in Arizona," *Arizona Farmer,* 21. Oct. 1944, clipping in file 13, carton 1, FSA Collection, Bancroft Library).

27. See, for example, Barrera, *Race and Class,* 211–12; Deutsch, *No Separate Refuge,* 36–37; Montejano, *Anglos and Mexicans,* 199. Montejano, however, provides a provocative analysis of the complex dynamics between race and class.

28. Arizona Agricultural Experiment Station, *Wanted—Man Power for Arizona Farms*, 16.

29. Salt River Project, *Annual History*, 1933–34, 1936, 1937, 1938, temperature and precipitation tables, Research Archives, SRP; *Casa Grande Dispatch*, 23 Oct. 1942, p. 1. Although they were called volunteers, Victory Laborers received the prevailing wage of $4 per hundred pounds for their labor.

30. WPA studies of agricultural workers included the Mexican American laborers of Crystal City, Texas, and the La Follette committee hearings in California focused on union busting against primarily Mexican American farm workers. Much of the President's Commission on Farm Tenancy focused on black tenants and sharecroppers in the South. Nonetheless, those who succeeded in convincing La Follette to hold hearings in California used the predominance of white workers from the south-central states in the fields as their lure, and the Southern Tenant Farmers Union proved unsuccessful in convincing La Follette to investigate the exploitation of southern tenants.

31. The phrase is borrowed from Limerick, *Legacy of Conquest.*

32. *Washington Post,* 27 Oct. 1977, sec. A, p. 3.

Bibliography

Books and Articles

Appel, Benjamin. *The People Talk: American Voices from the Great Depression* (1940). New York: Simon and Schuster, Touchstone, 1982.

Arizona Statistical Review, 1948. Phoenix: Valley National Bank, 1948.

Auerbach, Jerold S. *Labor and Liberty: The La Follette Committee and the New Deal.* Indianapolis: Bobbs-Merrill, 1966.

Baldwin, Sidney. *Poverty and Politics: The Rise and Decline of the Farm Security Administration.* Chapel Hill: University of North Carolina Press, 1968.

Banfield, Edward C. *Government Project.* Glencoe, Ill.: Free Press, 1951.

Barrera, Mario. *Race and Class in the Southwest: A Theory of Racial Inequality.* Notre Dame, Ind.: University of Notre Dame, 1979.

Benson, Jackson J. *The True Adventures of John Steinbeck, Writer.* New York: Viking Press, 1984.

Bogue, Donald J., Henry S. Shryock, Jr., and Siegfried A. Hoermann. *Subregional Migration in the United States, 1935–40.* Vol 1. *Streams of Migration Between Subregions: A Pilot Study of Migration Flows Between Environments.* Miami, Ohio: Scripps Foundation, 1953.

Bonnifield, Paul. *The Dust Bowl: Men, Dirt, and Depression.* Albuquerque: University of New Mexico Press, 1979.

Brown, Clayton D. "Hard Times for Children: Disease and Sickness During the Great Depression." In *Hard Times in Oklahoma: The Depression Years,* edited by Kenneth D. Hendrickson, Jr. Oklahoma City: Oklahoma Historical Society, 1983.

Brown, Harry Bates, and Jacob Osborn Ware. *Cotton.* 3d ed. New York: McGraw-Hill, 1958.

Brown, Malcolm, and Orin Cassmore. "Earnings of Migratory Cotton Pickers in Arizona." *Labor Information Bulletin* (U.S. Department of Labor) 6 (November 1939): 10–12.

Christian, Edith Mae Sandell. *Buckeye: The First 100 Years, 1888–1988.* Buckeye, Ariz.: Buckeye Valley Centennial Commission, 1988.

Conkin, Paul K. *Tomorrow a New World: The New Deal Community Program.* 2d ed. New York: De Capo Press, 1976.

Cox, Christopher, ed. *Dorothea Lange.* New York: Aperture Foundation, 1981.

Daniel, Cletus E. *Bitter Harvest: A History of California Farmworkers, 1870–1941.* Ithaca, N.Y.: Cornell University Press, 1981.

Deutsch, Sarah. *No Separate Refuge: Culture, Class, and Gender on an Anglo-Hispanic Frontier in the American Southwest, 1880–1940.* New York: Oxford University Press, 1987.

Dunbier, Roger. *The Sonoran Desert: Its Geography, Economy, and People.* Tucson: University of Arizona Press, 1968.

Duncan, Otis Durant. "Social Aspects of Rural Shifts of Farm Population in Oklahoma." *Current Farm Economics* (Oklahoma Agricultural Experiment Station) 9 (August 1936): 88–93.

Dyson, Lowell K. *Red Harvest: The Communist Party and American Farmers.* Lincoln: University of Nebraska Press, 1982.

Engineering News Record 102 (February 1929): 239.

Evans, Mercer G. "Housing for Migratory Agricultural Workers." *Public Welfare News* 7 (June 1939): 2–4.

Fite, Gilbert C. "Development of the Cotton Industry by the Five Civilized Tribes in Indian Territory." *Journal of Southern History* 15 (August 1949): 342–53.

Fleischhauer, Carl, and Beverly W. Brannan. *Documenting America, 1935–1943.* Berkeley: University of California Press, 1988.

Fossey, W. Richard. "'Talkin' Dust Bowl Blues': A Study of Oklahoman's Cultural Identity During the Great Depression." *Chronicles of Oklahoma* 55 (Spring 1977): 12–33.

Ganzel, Bill. *Dust Bowl Descent.* Lincoln: University of Nebraska Press, 1984.

Goke, A. W., and Charles A. Hollopeter. "Some of the Influences of Soils upon Farming in Southwestern Oklahoma." *Report of the Fourteenth Annual Meeting of the American Soil Survey Association,* Bulletin 15. Houma, La., May 1934.

Graves, Gregory R. "Exodus from Indian Territory: The Evolution of Cotton Culture in Eastern Oklahoma." *Chronicles of Oklahoma* 60 (Summer 1982): 186–209.

Gregory, James N. *American Exodus: The Dust Bowl Migration and Okie Culture in California.* New York: Oxford University Press, 1989.

Grossman, James R. *Land of Hope: Chicago, Black Southerners, and the Great Migration.* Chicago: University of Chicago Press, 1989.

Grubbs, Donald H. *Cry from the Cotton: The Southern Tenant Farmers' Union and the New Deal.* Chapel Hill: University of North Carolina Press, 1971.

Hale, Douglas. "The People of Oklahoma: Economics and Social Change." In *Oklahoma: New Views of the Forty-Sixth State,* edited by Anne Hodges Morgan and H. Wayne Morgan. Norman: University of Oklahoma Press, 1982.

Hecht, Melvin E., and Richard W. Reeves. *The Arizona Atlas.* Tucson: University of Arizona, Office of Arid Lands Studies, 1981.

Hurt, Douglas. "Cotton Pickers and Strippers." *Journal of the West* 30 (April 1991): 30–42.

Hurt, R. Douglas. *The Dust Bowl: An Agricultural and Social History.* Chicago: Nelson-Hall, 1981.

Janow, Seymour J., and William Gilmartin. "Labor and Agricultural Migration to California, 1935–40." *Monthly Labor Review* (U.S. Department of Labor) 53 (July 1941): 18–34.

Lange, Dorothea, and Paul Schuster Taylor. *An American Exodus: A Record of Human Erosion in the Thirties* (1939). Rev. ed. New Haven: Yale University Press, 1969.

Lewis, Christine. "The Early History of the Tempe Canal Company." *Arizona and the West* 7 (Autumn 1965): 227–38.

Limerick, Patricia Nelson. *The Legacy of Conquest: The Unbroken Past of the American West.* New York: Norton, 1987.

Lowitt, Richard. *The New Deal and the West.* Bloomington: Indiana University Press, 1984.

Lowitt, Richard, and Maurine Beasley. *One-Third of a Nation: Lorena Hickok Reports on the Great Depression.* Urbana: University of Illinois Press, 1981.

Luckingham, Bradford. *Phoenix: The History of a Southwestern Metropolis.* Tucson: University of Arizona Press, 1989.

McDean, Harry C. "The 'Okie' Migration as a Socioeconomic Necessity in Oklahoma." *Red River Valley Historical Review* 3 (1) (Winter 1978): 77–91.

McElvaine, Robert S. *The Great Depression: America, 1929–1941.* New York: Times Books, 1984.

McGowan, Joseph C. *History of Extra-Long Staple Cottons.* El Paso, Tex.: Hill, 1961.

Maciel, David R. "Mexican Migrant Workers in the United States." In *American Labor in the Southwest,* edited by James C. Foster. Tucson: University of Arizona Press, 1982.

McMillan, Robert T. "Some Observations on Oklahoma Population Movements." *Rural Sociology* 1 (September 1936): 332–43.

McWilliams, Carey. "California Pastoral." *Antioch Review* 2 (March 1942): 103–21.

———. *Factories in the Field: The Story of Migratory Farm Labor in California.* Boston: Little, Brown, 1939.

———. *Ill Fares the Land: Migrants and Migratory Labor in the United States.* Boston: Little, Brown, 1942.

Mitchell, H. L. *Mean Things Happening in This Land: The Life and Times of H. L. Mitchell, Co-Founder of the Southern Tenant Farmers' Union.* Montclair, N.J.: Allanheld, Osmun, 1979.

Montejano, David. *Anglos and Mexicans in the Making of Texas, 1936–1986.* Austin: University of Texas Press, 1987.

Morris, John W., Charles R. Goins, and Edwin C. McReynolds. *Historical Atlas of Oklahoma.* 2d ed. Norman: University of Oklahoma Press, 1976.

Nall, Garry L. "King Cotton in Oklahoma, 1825–1939." In *Rural Oklahoma,* edited by Donald E. Green. Oklahoma City: Oklahoma Historical Society, 1977.

Patterson, James T. *The New Deal and the States: Federalism in Transition.* Princeton, N.J.: Princeton University Press, 1969.

Replogle, Fred A., and F. Lyman Tibbitts, eds. *Survey of Welfare Activities in Oklahoma City.* Oklahoma City: Oklahoma City University Press, 1936.

Robinson, Harrison S. *Migrants: A National Problem and Its Impact on*

California. California State Chamber of Commerce, 1940.

Rose, Dorothy. "Enroute to the Promised Land: Phoenix, 1936." *Valley Grapevine* 5 (1980): 23.

Saloutos, Theodore. *The American Farmer and the New Deal.* Ames: Iowa State University Press, 1982.

Savage, William W., Jr. *Singing Cowboys and All That Jazz: A Short History of Popular Music in Oklahoma.* Norman: University of Oklahoma Press, 1983.

Scales, James R., and Danney Goble. *Oklahoma Politics: A History.* Norman: University of Oklahoma Press, 1982.

Schetter, Clyde E. *Story of a Town: Litchfield Park.* Litchfield Park, Ariz.: Litchfield Park Library Association, 1976.

Schlesinger, Arthur M., Jr. *The Coming of the New Deal.* Boston: Houghton Mifflin, 1958.

Scruggs, Otey M. "The First Mexican Farm Labor Program." *Arizona and the West* 2 (Winter 1960): 319–26.

Smith, Karen L. *The Magnificent Experiment: Building the Salt River Reclamation Project, 1890–1917.* Tucson: University of Arizona Press, 1986.

Stein, Walter J. *California and the Dust Bowl Migration.* Westport, Conn.: Greenwood Press, 1973.

Steinbeck, John. *The Grapes of Wrath.* New York: Viking Press, 1939.

Taylor, Paul S. "Again the Covered Wagon." *Survey Graphic* 24 (July 1935): 348–51.

Taylor, Paul S., and Edward J. Rowell. "Refugee Labor Migration to California, 1937." *Monthly Labor Review* (U.S. Department of Labor) 47 (August 1938): 240–50.

Tetreau, E. D. "The People of Arizona Irrigated Areas." *Rural Sociology* 3 (June 1938): 177–87.

Tetreau, E. D., and Varden Fuller. "Some Factors Associated with the School Achievement of Children in Migrant Families." *Elementary School Journal* 42 (February 1942): 423–31.

Thompson, John. *Closing the Frontier: Radical Response in Oklahoma, 1889–1923.* Norman: University of Oklahoma Press, 1986.

U.S. Works Progress Administration, Federal Writers' Program. *Arizona: A State Guide.* American Guide Series. New York: Hastings House, 1940.

Walker, Henry P., and Don Bufkin. *Historical Atlas of Arizona.* 2d ed. Norman: University of Oklahoma Press, 1986.

Worster, Donald. *Dust Bowl: The Southern Plains in the 1930s.* New York: Oxford University Press, 1979.

———. *Rivers of Empire: Water, Aridity, and the Growth of the American West.* New York: Pantheon, 1985.

Wright, Gavin. *Old South, New South: Revolutions in the Southern Economy Since the Civil War.* New York: Basic Books, 1986.

Government Publications

Agricultural Adjustment Act. P.L. 73-10, 12 May 1933. *United States Statutes at Large* 48, ch. 25, 31–41.

Agricultural Adjustment Act of 1938. P.L. 75-430, 16 February 1938. *United States Statutes at Large* 52, ch. 30, 31–77.

Arizona. Agricultural Experiment Station. *Agricultural Land Ownership and Operating Tenure in the Casa Grande Valley,* by Philip Greisinger and George W. Barr. Bulletin 175. Tucson: University of Arizona, November 1941.

———. *Arizona Farm Labor Situation and Outlook for 1944,* by E. D. Tetreau. Mimeographed Report 58. Tucson: University of Arizona, 1944.

———. *Arizona's Agricultural Population,* by E. D. Tetreau. Technical Bulletin 88. Tucson: University of Arizona, December 1940.

———. *Arizona's Farm Laborers,* by E. D. Tetreau. Bulletin 163. Tucson: University of Arizona, May 1939.

———. *Growing Upland Cotton in Arizona,* by G. E. Thompson and E. H. Pressley. Timely Hint 148. Tucson: University of Arizona, April 1924.

———. *Hired Labor Requirements on Arizona Irrigated Farms,* by E. D. Tetreau. Bulletin 160. Tucson: University of Arizona, May 1938.

———. *Statistical Supplement to Volume and Characteristics of Migration to Arizona, 1930–39,* by Varden Fuller and E. D. Tetreau. General Bulletin 176, Supplement. Tucson: University of Arizona, November 1941.

———. *Upland Cotton Production in Arizona,* by W. I. Thomas. Bulletin 214. Tucson: University of Arizona, March 1948.

———. *Volume and Characteristics of Migration to Arizona, 1930–39,* by Varden Fuller and E. D. Tetreau. Bulletin 176. Tucson: University of Arizona, November 1941.

———. *Wanted—Man Power for Arizona Farms: Seasonal and Year-Round Farm Labor Requirements, Arizona, 1935–42,* by E. D. Tetreau. Bulletin 186. Tucson: University of Arizona, November 1942.

Arizona. Agricultural Extension Service. *An Economic Survey of Pinal*

County Agriculture. Extension Circular 64. Tucson: University of Arizona, April 1931.

Arizona. Board of Public Health. *Public Health in Arizona.* Phoenix, 1938.

Arizona. Department of Agriculture. Crop and Livestock Reporting Service. *Arizona Agricultural Statistics, 1867–1965.* Phoenix, 1966.

Bankhead Act of 1934. P.L. 73-169, 21 April 1934. *United States Statutes at Large* 48, ch. 157, 598–607.

"Cooperation of United States Employment Service and State Employment Agencies." *Code of Federal Regulations,* title 29, pt. 21, 1938 ed.

"Cotton! Cotton!" *Arizona Public Health News* (Arizona State Board of Public Health) 145 (March 1938): 1–2.

"Getting at the Bottom of Oklahoma's Landlord-Tenant Problem." *Extension Service Review* (U.S. Department of Agriculture) 9 (November 1938): 162.

Laws of Arizona, 1933.

Laws of Arizona, 1937.

"Medical Care for Farm Workers in California and Arizona." *Monthly Labor Review* (U.S. Department of Labor) 55 (November 1942): 957–59.

Oklahoma. Agricultural Experiment Station. *Cotton Experiments at the Lawton (Oklahoma) Field Station, 1916–1931,* by W. M. Osborn. Bulletin 209. Stillwater: Oklahoma Agricultural and Mechanical College, March 1933.

———. *Cotton Growing in Eastern Oklahoma,* by William F. LaGrone. Bulletin B-345. Stillwater: Oklahoma Agricultural and Mechanical College, February 1950.

———. *Cotton Growing in Southwestern Oklahoma,* by William F. LaGrone. Bulletin B-350. Stillwater: Oklahoma Agricultural and Mechanical College, June 1950.

———. *A Descriptive Study of the Rural and Small City Relief Population in Oklahoma,* by T. G. Standing. Bulletin B-251. Stillwater: Oklahoma Agricultural and Mechanical College, November 1941.

———. *The Economic and Social Aspects of Mobility of Oklahoma Farmers,* by J. T. Sanders. Bulletin 195. Stillwater: Oklahoma Agricultural and Mechanical College, August 1929.

———. *Farm Housing in Southern Oklahoma,* by Robert T. McMillan. Bulletin B-290. Stillwater: Oklahoma Agricultural and Mechanical College, November 1945.

———. *Farm Tenancy in Oklahoma,* by John H. Southern. Bulletin 239. Stillwater: Oklahoma Agricultural and Mechanical College, December 1939.

————. *Legal Aspects of Landlord-Tenant Relationships in Oklahoma,* by William J. Coleman and H. Alfred Hockley. Bulletin 241. Stillwater: Oklahoma Agricultural and Mechanical College, August 1940.

————. *Population Trends in Oklahoma,* by Otis Durant Duncan. Bulletin 224. Stillwater: Oklahoma Agricultural and Mechanical College, March 1935.

————. *Recent Population Trends in Oklahoma,* by Otis Durant Duncan. Bulletin B-269. Stillwater: Oklahoma Agricultural and Mechanical College, August 1943.

————. *Social Aspects of Farm Mechanization in Oklahoma,* by Robert T. McMillan. Bulletin B-339. Stillwater: Oklahoma Agricultural and Mechanical College, November 1949.

————. *A Socio-Economic Atlas of Oklahoma,* by Meredith F. Burrill. Miscellaneous Paper. Stillwater: Oklahoma Agricultural and Mechanical College, June 1936.

Oklahoma Session Laws of 1936–1937. Oklahoma City: Harlow Publishing Corp., 1937.

Oklahoma Session Laws of 1939. Guthrie: Co-operative Publishing Co., 1939.

Soil Conservation and Domestic Allotment Act. P.L. 74-461, 29 February 1936. *United States Statutes at Large* 49, ch. 104, 1148–52.

U.S. Congress. House. Committee on Immigration and Naturalization. *Seasonal Agricultural Laborers from Mexico.* Hearings, 69th Cong., 1st sess., 1926.

————. National Resources Committee. *Farm Tenancy: Report of the President's Committee.* Washington, D.C.: Government Printing Office, 1937.

————. Select Committee to Investigate the Interstate Migration of Destitute Citizens. *Interstate Migration.* Hearings of the Select Committee, pt. 5, *Oklahoma City Hearings,* 76th Cong., 3d sess., 1940.

————. *Interstate Migration.* Hearings of the Select Committee, pt. 6, *San Francisco Hearings,* 76th Cong., 3d sess., 1940.

————. *Interstate Migration.* Hearings of the Select Committee, pt. 7, *Los Angeles Hearings,* 76th Cong., 3d sess., 1940.

————. *Interstate Migration.* Report of the Select Committee, H. Rept. 369, 77th Cong., 1st sess., 1941, serial set 10559.

U.S. Congress. Senate. Committee on Education and Labor. *Violations of Free Speech and Rights of Labor.* Hearings Before a Subcommittee, pt. 47, *California Agricultural Background,* 76th Cong., 2d sess., 1940.

———. *Violations of Free Speech and Rights of Labor*. Hearings Before a Subcommittee, pt. 53, *Open-Shop Activities,* 76th Cong., 3d sess., 1940.

———. *Violations of Free Speech and Rights of Labor*. Hearings Before a Subcommittee, pt. 58, *Open-Shop Activities,* 76th Cong., 3d sess., 1940.

———. *Violations of Free Speech and Rights of Labor*. Hearings Before a Subcommittee, pt. 59, *California Agricultural Background: California's Migrant Problem,* 76th Cong., 3d sess., 1940.

———. *Violations of Free Speech and Rights of Labor*. Hearings Before a Subcommittee, pt. 71, *Supplementary Exhibits,* 76th Cong., 3d sess., 1940.

———. *Violations of Free Speech and Rights of Labor*. Hearings Before a Subcommittee, pt. 72, *Supplementary Exhibits,* 76th Cong., 3d sess., 1940.

———. *Violations of Free Speech and Rights of Labor*. Report of the Committee, S. Rept. 1150, 77th Cong., 2d sess., 1942, serial set 10660.

U.S. Department of Agriculture. Bureau of Agricultural Economics. *County Variation in Net Migration from the Rural-Farm Population, 1930–1940,* by Eleanor H. Bernert. Washington, D.C., 1944.

———. *Farm Wage Rates, Farm Employment, and Related Data*. Washington, D.C., 1943.

———. *Oklahoma Cotton: Estimated Acreage, Yield, and Production, 1928–1937, by Counties*. Oklahoma City: Office of the Agricultural Statistician, 1934.

U.S. Department of Agriculture. Bureau of Chemistry and Soils. *Soil Survey of Carter County, Oklahoma,* by E. G. Fitzpatrick and W. C. Boatright. Ser. 1933, no. 18. Washington, D.C.: Government Printing Office, 1938.

———. *Soil Survey of Greer County, Oklahoma,* by A. W. Goke and R. E. Penn. Ser. 1932, no. 21. Washington, D.C.: Government Printing Office, 1937.

———. *Soil Survey of Kiowa County, Oklahoma,* by A. W. Goke and C. A. Hollopeter. Ser. 1931, no. 14. Washington, D.C.: Government Printing Office, 1935.

———. *Soil Survey of Le Flore County, Oklahoma,* by E. W. Knobel, C. B. Boatright, and W. C. Boatright. Ser. 131, no. 15. Washington, D.C.: Government Printing Office, 1936.

———. *Soil Survey of McIntosh County, Oklahoma,* by E. W. Knobel and

O. H. Brensing. Ser. 1933, no. 11. Washington, D.C.: Government
Printing Office, 1938.

———. *Soil Survey of Pittsburg County, Oklahoma,* by M. H. Layton, M. E.
Carr, and C. B. Boatright. Ser. 1931, no. [29]. Washington, D.C.:
Government Printing Office, 1937.

———. *Soil Survey of Tillman County, Oklahoma,* by A. W. Goke, E. G.
Fitzpatrick, and W. C. Boatright. Ser. 1930, no. 24. Washington,
D.C.: Government Printing Office, 1934.

U.S. Department of Agriculture. Bureau of Plant Industry. *Soil Survey of
Pontotoc County, Oklahoma,* by E. G. Fitzpatrick, et al. Ser. 1936, no.
4. Washington, D.C.: Government Printing Office, 1941.

———. *Soil Survey of Washita County, Oklahoma,* by A. W. Goke, C. A.
Hollopeter, and C. F. Fisher. Ser. 1935, no. 17. Washington, D.C.:
Government Printing Office, 1941.

U.S. Department of Agriculture. Farm Security Administration. *A Study of
6,655 Migrant Households Receiving Emergency Grants, Farm Security Administration, California, 1938,* by Alma Holzschuh. San
Francisco: Works Progress Administration, 1939.

U.S. Department of Agriculture. Office of Markets and Rural Organizations. *The Handling and Marketing of the Arizona-Egyptian Cotton of
the Salt River Valley.* Bulletin 311. Washington, D.C., 1915.

U.S. Department of Commerce. Bureau of the Census. *Cotton Production
and Distribution, Season of 1937–38.* Bulletin 175. Washington, D.C.:
Government Printing Office, 1938.

———. *Fifteenth Census of the United States, 1930: Agriculture,* Vol. 2, pt.
2, *The Southern States.* Washington, D.C.: Government Printing
Office, 1932.

———. *Fifteenth Census of the United States, 1930: Agriculture,* Vol. 3, pt.
2, *The Southern States.* Washington, D.C.: Government Printing
Office, 1932.

———. *Fifteenth Census of the United States, 1930: Agriculture,* Vol. 3, pt.
3, *The Western States.* Washington, D.C.: Government Printing
Office, 1932.

———. *Fifteenth Census of the United States: 1930: Population,* Vol. 2,
General Report, Statistics by Subjects. Washington, D.C.: Government Printing Office, 1933.

———. *Fifteenth Census of the United States: 1930: Population,* Vol. 3, pt.
2, *Reports by States . . . Montana-Wyoming.* Washington, D.C.: Government Printing Office, 1932.

———. *Fourteenth Census of the United States: 1920.* Bulletin, *Agriculture:*

Oklahoma: Statistics for the State and Its Counties. Washington, D.C.: Government Printing Office, 1921.

_____. *Fourteenth Census of the United States Taken in the Year 1920,* Vol. 2, *Population, General Report and Analytical Tables.* Washington, D.C.: Government Printing Office, 1922.

_____. *Sixteenth Census of the United States, 1940: Agriculture,* Vol. 1, pt. 6, *Statistics for Counties.* Washington, D.C.: Government Printing Office, 1942.

_____. *Sixteenth Census of the United States: 1940: Population, First Series: Oklahoma.* Washington, D.C.: Government Printing Office, 1941.

_____. *Sixteenth Census of the United States: 1940: Population, State of Birth of the Native Population.* Washington, D.C.: Government Printing Office, 1944.

_____. *United States Census of Agriculture, 1925: Reports for States with Statistics for Counties,* pt. 2, *The Southern States.* Washington, D.C.: Government Printing Office, 1927.

_____. *United States Census of Agriculture, 1935: Oklahoma, Statistics by Counties, Second Series.* Washington, D.C.: Government Printing Office, 1936.

_____. *United States Census of Agriculture, 1935: Reports for States with Statistics for Counties,* Vol. 1, pt. 2, *The Southern States.* Washington, D.C.: Government Printing Office, 1936.

_____. *United States Census of Agriculture, 1945,* Vol. 1, pt. 25, *Oklahoma, Statistics for Counties.* Washington, D.C.: Government Printing Office, 1946.

U.S. Department of the Interior. *Annual Report of the Commissioner of Indian Affairs to the Secretary of the Interior for the Fiscal Year Ending June 30, 1930.* Washington, D.C.: Government Printing Office, 1930.

U.S. Department of Labor. Bureau of Labor Statistics. *Labor Unionism in American Agriculture,* by Stuart Jamieson. Bulletin 836. Washington, D.C.: Government Printing Office, 1945.

U.S. Department of State. "Agreement on Migratory Workers." Mexico, *Treaties and Other International Agreements of the United States of America, 1776–1949.* Vol. 9, 1069–75. Executive Agreement Series 278. (Entered into force 4 Aug. 1942.)

U.S. Works Progress Administration. Division of Research. *Migratory Cotton Pickers in Arizona,* by Malcolm Brown and Orin Cassmore. Special Report. Washington, D.C.: Government Printing Office, 1939.

_____. Division of Social Research. *The People of the Drought States,* by Conrad Taeuber and Carl C. Taylor. Division of Social Research ser. 5, no. 2. Washington, D.C.: Government Printing Office, 1937.

United States v. Butler et al. 297 U.S. 1 (6 January 1936).

Wagner-Peyser Act. P.L. 73-30, 6 June 1933. *United States Statutes at Large* 48, ch. 49, 113–17.

Manuscript Collections

Bakersfield. California State University. California Odyssey Project. 1981.

Berkeley. University of California. Bancroft Library. Farm Security Administration Collection.

Casa Grande. Casa Grande Valley Historical Society. K. K. Henness, "A History of Agriculture in Pinal County." Typescript. 1979.

_____. James M. Smithwick, "Casa Grande: From Mining to Agriculture: Population Growth and Economic Expansion." Typescript. 1986.

_____. Shirley Weik, "History of the (Home Economics) Extension Service in Casa Grande—1914 to 1978." Typescript. [1979].

Chapel Hill. University of North Carolina Library. Southern Historical Collection. *Southern Tenant Farmers Union Papers.* Microfilm. Glen Rock, N.J.: Microfilming Corporation of America, 1971.

Coolidge. Coolidge Historical Society. Newsletter. October 1988.

Norman. University of Oklahoma. Carl Albert Congressional Research and Studies Center. Helen Gahagan Douglas Collection.

Oklahoma City. Oklahoma Department of Libraries. State Archives. Oklahoma Industrial Development and Parks Department Collection. Box 1, Oklahoma State Planning Board, "A Compendium of Graphic Studies Relating to Farm Tenancy." 1936.

Phoenix. Arizona Cotton Growers' Association. Minutes, 1930–1933, 1942–1947.

Phoenix. Arizona Department of Library, Archives, and Public Records. Arizona Collection. Anderson, Clayton and Co. *This Is Anderson, Clayton.* Pamphlet. Houston, Tex.: Anderson, Clayton, n.d.

_____. Arizona Collection. Mexico. Consulate, Phoenix. "Partial Report . . . Regarding the Conditions of the Mexican Cotton Pickers Brought to the Salt River Valley by the Arizona Cotton Growers' Association." Mimeographed. February 1921.

_____. Arizona Collection. National Association of Travelers Aid Societies. *Transient Families in Arizona.* Mimeographed. New York: President's Organization on Unemployment Relief, 1931.

————. Arizona Collection. U.S. Works Progress Administration. *Transient Camps: Emergency Relief Administration of Arizona.* Mimeographed. [1935].

————. Arizona Collection. U.S. Department of Agriculture, Farm Security Administration. *Casa Grande Valley Farms, Inc.* Mimeographed. April 1939.

————. Arizona Collection. U.S. Department of Agriculture, Farm Security Administration. *Chandler Farms, Incorporated.* Mimeographed. April 1939.

————. State Archives. Arizona State Board of Social Security and Welfare. Minutes, 1938–1940.

————. State Archives. Governor B. B. Moeur Papers.

————. State Archives. Governor R. C. Stanford Papers.

————. State Archives. Records of the Commission on Agriculture and Horticulture.

Phoenix. Maricopa County Courthouse. Maricopa County Superior Court. *Arizona v. Bill Walker, Bill Walker v. Arizona,* Criminal Record 14538. Microfilm. 1938.

Tempe. Arizona Historical Society. Oklahoma-Arizona Migration Project. 1992.

Tempe. Arizona State University. Hayden Library. Arizona Collection. Carl Trumbull Hayden Collection.

Tempe. Maricopa County Farm Bureau. Board of Directors Minutes, 1933–1938.

Tempe. Salt River Project. Research Archives. *Annual History,* 1933–1940.

Tempe. Tempe City Hall. Office of the City Clerk. Council Minutes, 1921, 1938.

Tempe. Tempe Historical Society. Index to *Tempe News.*

Tucson. Arizona Historical Society. A. C. Stewart, "Increasing Needs Among the Cotton Camps." *Sunday-School Missionary.* n.d.

Tucson. Arizona Historical Society. Ephemera collection. Agriculture, Cotton file.

Tucson. University of Arizona. Special Collections. E. D. Tetreau, "Seasonal Labor on Arizona Irrigated Farms," paper presented at the annual meeting of the Western Farm Economics Association, June 1937. Typescript.

Washington, D.C. Library of Congress. Manuscript Division. La Follette Family Collection. Container C403: Civil Liberties Committee, 1932–42 files.

————. Prints and Photographs Division. *America, 1935–1946,* photographs of U.S. Department of Agriculture, Farm Security Administration, U.S. Office of War Information, Southwest Region. Microfiche. Cambridge: Chadwyck-Healey, 1980.

Washington, D.C. National Archives. Manuscript Census. Maricopa and Pinal Counties, Arizona. 1920. Microfilm.

Washington, D.C. National Archives. Central Reference Branch. Records of the Works Progress Administration. Record Group 69.

————. Records of the Bureau of Agricultural Economics. Record Group 83.

————. Records of the Farmers Home Administration. Record Group 96.

Phonograph Record

Guthrie, Woody. *Dust Bowl Ballads*. RCA Victor, Vintage Series, LPV-502.

Newspapers

Anadarko (Oklahoma) *Daily News*
Arizona Daily Star (Tucson)
Arizona Farmer-Producer (Phoenix)
Arizona Labor Journal (Phoenix)
Arizona Producer (Phoenix)
Arizona Republic (Phoenix)
Arizona Republican (Phoenix)
Associated Arizona Producer (Phoenix)
Buckeye (Arizona) *Valley News*
Casa Grande (Arizona) *Dispatch*
Chandler Arizonan
CIO News (Washington, D.C., Harrisburg, Pa.)
Coolidge (Arizona) *Examiner*
Daily Oklahoman (Oklahoma City)
Desert Sentinel (Agua Fria Farm Workers Community, Coldwater)
Eleven Mile Corner News (Eleven Mile Corner Migratory Labor Camp, Coolidge)
Lawton (Oklahoma) *Constitution*
Los Angeles (California) *Times*
Migrant Mike (Yuma Migratory Labor Camp, Somerton)
New York Times
Oklahoma Farmer-Stockman (Oklahoma City)
Phoenix (Arizona) *Gazette*
Tucson (Arizona) *Citizen*

Tulsa (Oklahoma) *Tribune*
UCAPAWA News (New York City, Chicago)
Washington Post
Wewoka (Oklahoma) *Times-Democrat*
Yuma Daily Sun and Yuma Arizona Sentinel

Theses and Dissertations

Dean, Claud Leslie. "A Study of Some of the Social Forces Contributing to Poverty in the Community Camp of Oklahoma City." Master's thesis, University of Oklahoma, 1936.

Duchemin, Michael. "Introducing the Urban Form: The Arizona Improvement Company in Phoenix, 1887–1890." Master's thesis, Arizona State University, 1992.

Gibson, Mattie Cal. "The Dependent Family in the Oklahoma City Community Camp." Master's thesis, University of Oklahoma, 1934.

Gilbert, Judith Anne. "Migrations of the Oklahoma Farm Population, 1930 to 1940." Master's thesis, University of Oklahoma, 1965.

Ganger, David Wayne. "The Impact of Mechanization and the New Deal's Acreage Reduction Programs on Cotton Farmers During the 1930s." Ph.D. diss., University of California, Los Angeles, 1973.

Kotlanger, Michael J. "Phoenix, Arizona: 1920–1940." Ph.D. diss., Arizona State University, 1983.

Manes, Sheila Goldring. "Depression Pioneers: The Conclusion of an American Odyssey, Oklahoma to California, 1930–1950: A Reinterpretation." Ph.D. diss., University of California, Los Angeles, 1982.

Mawn, Geoffry. "Phoenix, Arizona: Central City of the Southwest, 1870–1920." Ph.D. diss., Arizona State University, 1979.

Moore, Tom. "Farm Tenancy in Oklahoma, 1925–1935." Master's thesis, Oklahoma Agricultural and Mechanical College, 1938.

Pendleton, Edwin Charles. "History of Labor in Arizona Irrigated Agriculture." Ph.D. diss., University of California, Berkeley, 1950.

Peterson, Herbert B. "A Twentieth Century Journey to Cibola: Tragedy of the *Bracero* in Maricopa County, Arizona, 1917–21." Master's thesis, Arizona State University, 1975.

Sherman, Jacqueline Gordon. "The Oklahomans in California During the Depression Decade, 1931–1941." Ph.D. diss., University of California, Los Angeles, 1970.

Smith, Susan M. "Litchfield Park and Vicinity." Master's thesis, University of Arizona, 1948.

Index

229

Tolan Committee on Interstate
Migration, 87
Tolleson, Ariz., 106
Tovrea Company, 134
Tulsa, Okla., 26

Union organizing: in Ariz., 80–
83; discouraging, 5, 42, 47–
48, 83, 94–95, 100; strikes,
45, 47, 82, 161, 177n.21,
178n.25, 194n.26; in Okla.,
27, 30
United Cannery, Agricultural,
Packing and Allied Workers
of America, 30, 80–83, 94,
153, 171n.34
U.S. Department of Agriculture,
147, 152; food stamps, 104.
See also Farm Security Administration, commodities
program
U.S. Employment Service, 3,
152–53; Farm Placement
Service, 55, 88–90, 96–97,
99–101
U.S. Farm Placement Service.
See U.S. Employment
Service

Valiant, Margaret, 199n.29
Vernon, Guy, 177n.19
Victory Laborers, 157, 159–60
Vosburgh, Clarence O., 38, 82–
83, 145, 186n.35

Waddell, Ariz., 71, 202n.50
Waddell, R. W., 79
Wagner-Peyser Act of 1933, 89
Wagoner County, Okla., 27
Waldron, James A., 84–85, 130,
195n.6
Ward, A. M., 152
War Manpower Commission,
152–53
Washita County, Okla., 25
Weatherford Family String Band,
116
Welfare. See Farm Security Ad-
ministration; Relief
West Avondale Ranch, 43
Western Cotton Products Com-
pany, 39, 46–47
Wilson, William B., 44
Woody, Cleo, 80
Woody, June, 80
Works Progress Administration,
12, 26, 54, 70, 128; study of
cotton pickers in Ariz., 60–
61, 64–65, 90–91, 160,
183n.20
World War II, effects on cotton
industry, 147–50, 156–58

Yochum, Charlie, 143
Yuma, Ariz., 49–51, 82
Yuma Farm Workers Commu-
nity, 118

Zachary, B. V., 155–56